THE SENSE OF SPACE

SUNY series in
Contemporary Continental Philosophy

Dennis J. Schmidt, editor

THE SENSE

OF SPACE

DAVID MORRIS

STATE UNIVERSITY OF NEW YORK PRESS

Published by
STATE UNIVERSITY OF NEW YORK PRESS, ALBANY

© 2004 State University of New York

For information, contact the State University of New York Press, Albany, NY
www.sunypress.edu

Production, Laurie Searl
Marketing, Anne M. Valentine

Library of Congress Cataloging-in-Publication Data

Morris, David, 1967–
    The sense of space / by David Morris.
        p. cm. — (SUNY series in contemporary continental philosophy)
    Includes bibliographical references and index.
    ISBN 0-7914-6183-1 (hc : alk. paper); 978-0-7914-6184-6 (pb : alk. paper)
        1. Merleau-Ponty, Maurice, 1908–1961. Phénoménologie de la perception. 2. Body,
Human (Philosophy) 3. Movement (Philosophy) 4. Space perception. I. Title.
II. Series.

B2430.M3763P476 2004
121'.34—dc22   2004045291

10 9 8 7 6 5 4 3 2 1

CONTENTS

PREFACE

THE SENSE OF SPACE is the basis of all social experience and of perceptual experience in general. Without it we would have no sense of a world beyond us. But what is the basis of spatial experience, and what does our sense of space tell us about us and our social being?

The concern here is not the space that would be measured by the surveyor, geometer, or scientist, but perceived space as we experience it before objectifying it, what I shall call lived space. The answer demands a study of perception in terms of the moving body.

Merleau-Ponty's *Phenomenology of Perception* placed the body at the center of philosophy. Contemporary and previous thinkers had discussed the body: one can think of Sartre, de Beauvoir, Marcel, Bergson, the body as haunting Husserl's *Nachlass*, the curious peripheral glimpses of the body in Heidegger, the current of bodily discussion that runs through Nietzsche, the discussion in Dewey and James, even the focus on the body that we find in Spinoza and Aristotle—and there are others to be mentioned as well. But no one had put as deep an emphasis on beginning philosophy with the lived body—the body of experience; no one had taken the study of the lived body into such great depth.

Since the *Phenomenology*, the philosophy of the body has been transformed. Post-structuralism enjoins suspicion of a body that would be granted positive primacy, and detects in what we call "body" the shaping or constitutive forces of outside powers. Feminist philosophy draws attention to the body as the site of sexual difference neglected by phenomenology. Critics of phenomenological method urge that the phenomenology of the body repeats the prejudices of the philosophy of consciousness that it aims to avoid, merely cloaking the Cartesian ego in corporeal disguise. All of these movements question and complicate the concept of the body to be found in Merleau-Ponty. When it comes to the *Phenomenology*, however, the most important critic is Merleau-Ponty himself: his posthumous *The Visible and the Invisible* appears to throw the earlier work into question, as being caught up in phenomenological presuppositions insufficient to the ontology of the body. A survey would show that the literature and discussion of Merleau-Ponty after the publication of *The Visible and the Invisible* increasingly focuses on that work rather than the earlier *Phenomenology* or *The Structure of Behaviour*. Merleau-Ponty, though, repeatedly urges that a book is never something complete and that the thinker never quite fully grasps his or her work. In short, a thinker can never close the book on her or his work.

This book tries to reopen the *Phenomenology*, to rethink its concept of the body in a way that critically engages dominant traditions and current results of philosophy and science. Specifically, it rethinks what Merleau-Ponty calls the body schema—rethinks it in terms of movement in a way that draws on the philosophy of Bergson (an underplayed thread in the weave of Merleau-Ponty's philosophy) and the contemporary scientific program called dynamic systems theory (an offshoot of J. J. Gibson's ecological psychology). The book shows how the moving body is inherently open to the world, how the schema and meaning of perception are not possessions of a closed body-subject, but are rooted in an inherently developmental body, a body that contracts perceptual meaning through learning that is both social and constrained by the body's own topology and relation to place. Securing this point about perception and the topology of the moving body is the task of part one, "The Moving Sense of the Body." Part two, "The Spatial Sense of the Moving Body," shows how our sense of depth and orientation emerge from such a topology in relation to place, and how this sense is rooted in movement and development in a social place.

Previous works by Elisabeth Ströker (1987), Sue Cataldi (1993), Patrick Heelan (1983), and Edward Casey (1993, 1997) present studies of spatial perception in relation to phenomenology, Merleau-Ponty's philosophy, and place. (Also see Hatfield 1990; Plomer 1991.) Part one of this book adds to this literature by approaching perception through the expressive topology of the moving, developmental body. Part two adds to the literature by giving a detailed study of the way that our sense of space points back to a moving body that envelops and is enveloped by things, that resides on earth and that develops.

Parts one and two, though, are inherently joined, for a moving developmental body is a body in place, and a body developing in place is a spatial body. Our sense of space arises in the intersection of movement and place, specifically developmental movement and social place. The intersection will have an ethical aspect, since a social, developmental body is a body placed in an ethical situation. The conclusion unpacks some implications by showing how our responsibility in face of others and in face of place inheres in our sense of space, and how our sense of space thus entwines with our sense of the ethical and of place.

This book has been a long time coming, and many thanks are due. I would especially like to thank Graeme Nicholson, for his unfailing support of the earlier explorations and writing that led to this book; John Russon for his teaching, observations, and advice that made this book possible; Edward S. Casey for his work on place, which inspired my investigations, and for his careful comments and enthusiasm. Thanks are also due to Peter Simpson, Maria Talero, Kym Maclaren, David Ciavatta, and Gregory Recco for ongoing philosophical conversation on concepts central to the book; to my colleagues in the Department of Philosophy at Trent University for their support and interest, and especially to Constantin V. Boundas for his guidance on Deleuze-Bergson. The critical comments of anonymous referees were indispensable in improving the book. I would also like to acknowledge the Social Sciences and Humanities Research Council of Canada and Trent University for supporting various stages of this work, and Andrew Robinson, Karen Hicks and Michael Bruder for their proofing of and comments on drafts. Most of all, thanks are due to Emilia Angelova for her immense support, confidence, and deeply critical and insightful engagement with this work.

This book is dedicated to the memory of Ida Jupiter, my grandmother, who died on the day the first version of the book was completed; and to Mr. Haller, a survivor of the concentration camps who lived across the street when I was a child, and who could not walk down the street without turning around to check behind his back.

LIST OF ABBREVIATIONS

Abbrev.	Title	Citation Form
OE	Merleau-Ponty, *L'Oeil et l'esprit* / "Eye and Mind" (In *The Primacy of Perception*)	OE [page # in the French] [page # in English]
PP	Merleau-Ponty, *Phénoménologie de la perception* / *Phenomenology of Perception*	PP [page # in the French] / [page # in the English]
SdC	Merleau-Ponty, *La Structure du comportment* / *The Structure of Behaviour*	SdC [page # in the French] [page # in the English]
MM	Bergson, Henri, *Matter and Memory*	MM [page # in the English]

INTRODUCTION

THE PROBLEM OF DEPTH

IMAGINE SITTING IN an outdoor plaza, watching things go on around you. I am thinking in particular of City Hall in Toronto. I am sitting on a bench near the fountains, whose pool is used as a skating rink in winter; to my right, paraboloid ribbons of concrete arch over the pool, connecting its near and far sides. In front, in the distance, are the two buildings of City Hall, which curve toward me in a semicircle around the lenticular council chamber nestled in between. Large squares of concrete tile the floor of the plaza, sponging up the sun and hurling it back through air that shimmers with heat. The tiles incise a grid that sometimes tinges the plaza's visual expanse with the aura of a perspective study, an effect reinforced by the overhead walkway which marks the perimeter of the square, running above the sides and back of the plaza, along Queen Street behind me. Within this gridwork, people move back and forth buying ice cream cones from pedal-carts, vanishing into City Hall on errands, chatting with clothing aflutter in the wind; children splash their feet in the pool.

The sense of this situation, or any other situation, depends on people and things appearing and moving around in depth. Depth is what gives bodies volume in the first place, it is what makes situations possible. As Edward Casey puts it, following Merleau-Ponty, depth should really be called the "first dimension" rather than the "third"; that is, depth is the most primordial dimension, not a 'bonus' dimension added to the other two.[1] All our studies and all our inquiries begin in depth: without depth, there would be no things and no people, nothing to study, and there would be nobody who could perceive or study things. This is one reason for beginning a study of spatial perception with a study of depth.

In what follows, "depth" designates the "first dimension," in which one experiences the distance between oneself and other things, in which one

1

experiences things as having volume. Depth is to be distinguished from height and width, in which one experiences the spread of already voluminous things and the distance between things that stand side by side.[2] Once we have a way of modeling our environment geometrically, and techniques for measuring it, we can treat depth as an objective dimension interchangeable with height and width. But before that we must have a more basic perceptual experience of voluminous things, and that is our focus: how do we first of all perceive things and ourselves as standing out in depth? That is to say, our focus is lived depth, depth as we experience it, before we objectify it through geometry and measurement.

Given the primordiality of depth, accounts of depth perception inevitably couple with basic claims about the being of the perceiver and the perceived world. Consider Berkeley's infamous problem about visual depth perception. Crudely put, images on the retina are wide like things are wide, but they are not deep like things are deep. Retinal images are flat, so how can they give us a sense of depth? Berkeley's solution reconfigures the problem: depth perception is not a leap from flat images to a mind-independent depth, it is the perceiver's transition from one ordering of ideas to another. The solution is inseparable from Berkeley's radical metaphysical claim that to be is to be perceived, that matter and depth are orderings of ideas, not mind-independent realities. Merleau-Ponty shows that analysis of perception always amounts to analysis of the perceiver's existence, but this sketch of Berkeley's solution suggests that the coupling of perception and existence is especially deep in the case of depth perception, which is not surprising if depth manifests our most primordial contact with the world. This is another reason for beginning in depth: it opens a connection between spatial perception and our existence.

This introductory exploration of depth perception will press us into basic points and problems of spatial perception. A full account of depth perception must wait for subsequent chapters.

DEPTH AND THE CROSSING OF THE BODY AND THE WORLD

To map a central point about the being of the body in depth, I return to the bench at City Hall, describing my experience. But the description would equally apply to anyone reporting on their experience of any situation.

First, I am on a bench in the very world I am perceiving. So I would seem to be part of the depths that I perceive. There is a problem, though. I perceive things in depth as here or there, near or far, in front or behind, and so on. But I do not perceive myself in this way. I am neither in front of nor behind myself, neither near nor far from myself; I am not over there and I am not even here in the way that the bench is here. I am not a point within a coordinate system already fixed outside me. My body is the original 'here,' the origin from which here and there, near and far, exfoliate; my body appears to escape the depth orderings that apply to things around me, to belong to a different order.[3]

I am on a bench, perceiving the depths of the world, but I appear to be at odds with those depths. The depth of my body appears to be extra-ordinary. Ordinary depth is a matter of ordered relations and distances between things, whereas my body, while having depth, does not fit into this ordered framework; it is extra-ordinary. What is at stake in the contrast between these two sorts of depth, ordinary and extra-ordinary depth, is *ordinality*. The hyphenated construction *extra-ordinary* is a reminder of this usage. As opposed to *one, two,* and *three,* which are cardinal numbers, *first, second, third,* are *ordinals,* numbers that denote order rather than quantity. The ordinary depths of the perceived world are ordered by 'here-there,' 'near-far,' and so on, while my body usually has an extra-ordinary depth that is not subject to that ordering.[4] As Heidegger observes, I am not in the plaza in the way that water is in the pool, and I touch the bench in a different way than the bench touches the ground (Heidegger 1962, §12). My being and the being of the bench are different, and this difference is reflected in the experienced difference between different sorts of depth.

Yet if I experience myself as the extra-ordinary origin of the order of 'here' and 'there', I must also belong to that ordinary order. I must be distant from things as things are distant from me, and although my body appears to escape ordinary depth, my body also has a thickness and depth within the world. The extra-ordinary depth of the body joins with the ordinary depth of the world. How is this join, a join of different orders of depth and being, to be conceived? At stake in this question is the concept of the body. Our reflex is to think of the body as a self-contained sensing system positioned within a spatial container, to join the depths of body and world in terms of a larger, already established order of depth. In fact, there is no fixed threshold between ordinary and extra-ordinary depth, and we must revise our concept of the body.

In ordinary experience the body is not spread out in the way that people and things are spread out in a plaza. It would be odd for me to say "I am here, but my leg is there, in a different spot." This is another sense in which the depth of the body is extra-ordinary. The entire spread of the body counts as 'here'; unlike other things, the body appears as having little or no interior ordinality. (Again, in my car the turn signal is to the left of the steering wheel, but it would be strange to say that my writing hand is to the left of my head; my left hand is not *on* my left, it defines or *is* my left.) But now my foot is hurting, and I reach down to find out if my shoe is too tight or if there is a stone in it. In reaching down I am in part treating my body as a thing in ordinary depth, as having an interior ordinality of 'heres' and 'theres.' And there would be no perception at all if my body did not spread out amidst things in ordinary depth. The extra-ordinary depth of the body and the ordinary depth of the world are in exchange.

But the exchange between ordinary and extra-ordinary depth is not described by a fixed threshold. When I am just going about doing things, my watch, shoes, coat, and so on, are neither here nor there in ordinary depth, they are incorporated into the extra-ordinary depth of my body. But I can doff my coat, slough the outer coating of my body's extra-ordinary depth into ordinary depth. Things are incorporated into the extra-ordinary depth of the body, or the extra-ordinary depth of the body seeps outward into things; either way you put it, there is no fixed threshold between ordinary and extra-ordinary depth. It is tempting to draw a fixed threshold, but in doing so *we* are imposing fixity on something fundamentally flowing.[5]

The fluctuating threshold of ordinary and extra-ordinary depth manifests a living tension between body and world. It is rather like the threshold in Rilke's ninth *Duino Elegy*. Rilke suggests that an angel who looks on the world from above might define the word *threshold* in terms of a material construction such as a doorsill. But angels cannot say things with the intensity of those who toil a mortal life. For mortals "threshold [*Schwelle*]" is "what it means to two lovers that they too should be wearing down an old doorsill [*Schwelle der Tür*] a bit more" (Rilke 1978, 80). Place a doorsill anywhere you like. If nobody crosses it, it will not be a threshold. On the other hand, a tree trunk or rivulet in the forest is a threshold when people cross it in moving from one region to another. Before there are thresholds, there is region-crossing that wears down things, which things then manifest thresholds. Similarly, skirmishes do not begin over already fixed borders, borders are first of all drawn in the midst of skirmishes. What is primary is not the material of thresholds, but the need for region-crossing, which need inheres in the life of moving yet place-dwelling mortals.[6]

The most primordial region-crossing is the crossing of body and world. In "Eye and Mind" Merleau-Ponty writes that "There is a human body when, between the seeing and the seen, between touching and the touched, between one eye and the other, between hand and hand, a blending of some sort takes place—when the spark is lit between sensing and sensible, lighting the fire that will not stop burning until some accident of the body will undo what no accident would have sufficed to do . . ." (OE 21/163, ellipsis Merleau-Ponty's). Life is a spark of desire that crosses body and world in the very moment that it constitutes a living difference between them. This crossing of body and world marks the first threshold, the root of all other thresholds and the root of our sense of depth and space.

The usage of "crossing" here and below draws on multiple resonances of the term and is meant to resonate with the concepts of "chiasm" and "reversibility" that haunt Merleau-Ponty's later philosophy.[7] A child's play-chant is cross between speech and song, a spontaneous sing-song that marks a difference between speech and song even while showing how the two cross in a common origin; a person living between cultures crosses those cultures in a way that reciprocally marks new differences and new commonalities;

crossed messages are mixed up, yet the mix-up plays on and therefore plays up distinctive meanings of the messages; two things that are mixed up yield a cross between them. Crossing differentiates by mixing, mixes by differentiating, marks differences through reciprocating mixes and overlaps. Whereas the phrase *interaction of body and world* suggests that body and world are two already independent things that subsequently interact, speaking of their crossing suggests that the two are inherently interdependent, differentiated only in being mixed. "Crossing" captures Merleau-Ponty's point, in his early and late philosophy, that body and world are in a living tension.

And the experience of a difference between ordinary and extra-ordinary depth, and of their flowing threshold, shows that body and world cross one another. The body is not simply contained on its side of things as a sensory machine within which signs of depth are decoded, the body is in the depths of the world, yet is in those depths through a flowing threshold that overlaps body and world. At a deeper level, a body of this sort is neither the cladding of pure subjectivity nor an object in the world; the crossing of body and world turns any simple division of subject and object into a problem. Accordingly, this book's study of depth and spatial perception moves beyond the division of subject and object to focus on the perceiving body; but the perceiving body is not self-contained and the perceived world is not a self-contained system. The focus is the crossing of body and world, and the aim is to show how the sense of space is rooted in that crossing.

This calls for a reversal of traditional approaches to depth and spatial perception. In traditional approaches, the primary datum is an already given space, characterized apart from the living activity of the body. The problem is how a self-contained body within that space, which therefore cannot directly contact space as a whole, retrieves measures of space via sensory signals received by the body. For thinkers such as Merleau-Ponty, William James, and John Dewey, this is a grand version of what is often called the "experience error": a result of perceptual experience—the concept of space as a container that appears as independently possessing its own well defined structure—is taken to be the basis and object of spatial perception.[8] The tradition begins with a space already understood in terms of a geometrical or objective model and looks into it to see how the body interacts with it: from space to the body via geometry or another objective model. This book works in the reverse direction, beginning within the crossing of body and world, and seeing how our sense of space emerges from it: from the crossing of body and world to space via living perception. To put it in Bergsonian terms, the proper beginning is a difference in kind, not degree: the beginning is not degrees of measurement within an already defined geometrical system, but the living difference in kind that emerges in the crossing of body and world (MM; Deleuze 1988).

Kant and William James, each in his own way, claim that our sense of space is not the result of synthesizing nonspatial data to yield a spatial result.

Spatiality is a primitive, so primitive that a sense of space must already be given, must already be constituted by us, on our side of things; we are not merely passive receptors of spatial information, we actively constitute the sense of space. This claim is an important thread in the tradition, and vital to what follows. But Kant's transcendental argument claims that spatial experience is constituted by an a priori cognitive structure; and James's empirical argument claims that what might now be called the neurobiology of the body is constitutive of spatial experience, as if experience were rooted in fixed structures of a body-machine (here I am pushing things to an extreme that is likely foreign to James, but not simply so).[9] In contrast to Kant, lived space is constituted within bodily life, not in cognition merely; in contrast to James, lived space is not a primitive of neurobiological structures. Our sense of depth and space is rooted in living dynamics that inherently cross body and world; and our sense of depth and space expresses the sense of the crossing of body and world. Our sense of space is not constituted by cognitive or neurobiological structures that are merely on our side of things; our sense of space is enfolded in an outside, in a world that crosses our body.

To secure this point and approach to the body and space, I first turn to an analysis of traditional accounts of depth perception.

THE CONCEPTUAL DIALECTIC OF TRADITIONAL ACCOUNTS

Traditional philosophical and scientific accounts of depth perception begin by presuming an already established space, and ask how depth perception reconstitutes measures of that space. This presumption is counterpart to the presumption that meaningful perception is built out of meaningless sensations.[10] Bits of sensation are interchangeable, determinate independent of their context, atomic. Single atoms of sensation cannot carry perceptual meaning: they can specify red or orange, but not "flower" and "far." "Flower" and "far" are reconstructed from an array of sensations, and since sensations are neutral to their combination and cannot carry perceptual meaning, the object of the reconstruction is an underlying order of the world, say the flower which causes the array in the perceiver. Spatial perception and perception in general refer to an underlying order that is fixed in advance of perception. Contra this presumption, the meaningful order of perceived depth reflects the dynamic crossing of body and world.[11]

Consider the infamous problem that the images projected on our retinas are flat, or, at least, since they really are projected on a curved surface, specify only a two-dimensional array of data. This poses the problem of depth in terms of a difference between two- and three-dimensional orders. But isn't there something wrongheaded about this? Can the perceiver really be flattened into a passive, two-dimensional sensory surface, as if the body and eyes did not already have depth, as if their volume had nothing to do with perception? Can the problem really be reduced to a gap between two and three

dimensions, a gap crossed with a projective geometry, as if the crucial difference were one of dimensional degree? Is depth perception an exercise in
geometry, or in living? The initial point about the crossing of body and world
suggests the traditional problem is badly put, but the objection cannot simply
be hurled at the tradition from the outside. I want to step into the tradition
and show that problems that arise within it demand a turn toward the crossing of body and world.[12]

Descartes's solution to the problem of the flat images hinges on the fact
that there are two eyes. An object at a distance may project "only one point
in the fund of the eye" as Berkeley famously put it—hence the problem.[13]
But the lines of sight formed by two eyes directed at one object specify a
triangle. For Descartes, depth perception amounts to a geometrical inference
of the height of this triangle, an inference based on the angles at the eyes
and the distance between them.[14] Descartes's account, together with the
Cartesian geometry and coordinate system that facilitate his analysis, inspires
a class of accounts that bridge two and three dimensions by means of an
inferential process. I call them inferential accounts. Inferential accounts are,
perhaps, falling out of favor, but still influence current research programs. For
example, roboticists might try to construct a robot that infers depth based on
the disparity between two images given to the robot's visual sensors. Some
would claim that this is the way our vision works. On my left retina, the
image of this sheet of paper is a trapezoid in which the projection of the left
edge is longer than the right, whereas on the right retina the projection of
the right edge is longer; given that these are images of one rectangular thing,
the thing must be so many units distance away from my eye. So I can infer
depth from binocular disparity.[15]

Central to Descartes's account is the hypothesis that the contents of
perceptual experience, namely ideas, are nothing like that which is perceived. Descartes insists on this at numerous points; he has to, since in the
Cartesian philosophy experience belongs to an unextended mind, whereas it
refers to extended matter.[16] The mind's inferences therefore cross a gap between ideas and things, between two very different sorts of beings. A similar
gap between perceptual content and things is crucial to inferential accounts
in general. Why? If the content of perceptual experience is nothing like that
which is perceived, then the content is neither two- nor three-dimensional.
So the transition between two and three dimensions is freed from the being
of actual two- and three-dimensional things; tying the transition to actual
two- and three-dimensional things would repeat the problem of the flat
images. In the Cartesian account, the transition takes place in the unextended
Cartesian mind. In fact, a Cartesian mind can infer an *imagined* three-dimensional space from an array of *imagined* two-dimensional data. In more recent
accounts, the transition takes place in a computational process that qua com-
putation is unextended, even if carried out by a materially extended computer:
a computer program can navigate a simulated, nonexistent three-dimensional

space, reconstructing that space from two-dimensional arrays of data constructed by the experimenter. (Such programs exist, and are an easy way of
testing out robot algorithms without actually building robots.) The ideas in
the Cartesian mind, the data in the computer, are neither two-dimensional
nor three-dimensional, and the transitions between the two are transitions
between signs.

In being freed of the relation between actual two- and three-dimensional things, the problem is in one sense solved. The Cartesian perceiver
and the inferential robot in the real world are making exactly the same sort
of transition between signs when detecting depth: they are just inferring one
array of data from another. Inferential accounts work by abstracting the
problem of depth from the actual depths of the world, converting a problem
about bodies with depth into a problem of signs and geometry.

This abstraction, though, skips over the initial problem of three-
dimensional things and two-dimensional receptive surfaces; the solution con-
ceals a deeper problem. The inferences of the unextended mind, the calculations of the robotic eye, do refer to the depths of the world. How is this
reference possible? By hypothesis of the inferential account, depth needs to
be inferred, because the perceiver has no direct contact with the world in
depth, just ideas or signs. The two-dimensional grist of the inferential mill
is nothing like depth itself. But grounding the inference from two-dimensional data to a world in depth requires knowledge of the world in depth,
knowledge of how projection works. Somewhere along the way the perceiver
must have something more than an inference about a world in depth, must
already have a veridical encounter with a world in depth, some premises and
principles to bootstrap and ground inferences.

There is a circle at the core of inferential accounts. If depth can only
be inferred, then the ground of this inference cannot itself be inferred. Any
attempt to infer the ground would already require this ground and get stuck
in a circle. There must be some already established framework that grounds
and is prior to the inference of depth, what I call an inferential framework.

On first glance, the circle is not completely vicious. Descartes, for
example, establishes an inferential framework by proving that the world of
matter can be known and is susceptible of geometrical analysis. But this
precisely means claiming an inferential framework established *prior* to perception. In the example of inferring the distance of a sheet of paper via
binocular disparity, my perceptual process in effect assumes that there is one
sheet of paper and that the sheet is actually rectangular, not trapezoidal. But
how could the given justify this assumption? By an inference from the very
same images. One and the same set of images must justify the inferences (a)
that the sheet is so many units distance away from me, and (b) that there
is just one sheet of paper and that it is rectangular. But conclusion (a)
depends on conclusion (b) as a premise, and vice versa. The assumption
must remain an assumption, because it must be in place prior to any infer-

ence. The case of the sheet of paper is unduly simplistic, but recent work on vision supports the claims that assumptions would have to be built into visual processes.[17]

Basing perception in assumptions leads to vicious consequences. In machines that take two-dimensional visual inputs as premises for inferences about a three-dimensional world, it turns out that the input radically underdetermines what there is in the world. The machine needs to assume quite an elaborate model of the world. Putting aside the question of where all those assumptions come from (could the machine *learn* them?), and whether we, as opposed to machines, really need an elaborate model of the world to see it in depth, building machines upon assumptions makes them extremely limited and inflexible. Put them in a different sort of environment and they fail. In contrast, our living vision, as we shall see, is quite plastic and resilient.

Inferential accounts begin by supposing a gap between two-dimensional givens and the three-dimensional world. If the gap is not filled in, then perception falls to circularities or equivocations that underdetermine the perceived world. But filling the gap entails assumptions that overdetermine the world and reduplicate it in an internal model. Such assumptions are an instance of what Merleau-Ponty calls a ready-made world, that is, a world specified prior to, and independent of, the dynamics of perceptual life.[18] Not only does the ready-made world neglect the crossing of body and world detected above, not only does it render perception frail in face of a changing world, it fails to account for the meaningful dynamics of lived depth, of which more below.

The inferential approach to perception is also a fine example of the experience error. It is true that a human being with proper tools can, as Descartes claims, infer distance by means of geometrical triangulation. But that is no ground for presuming that depth perception works by triangulation. The presumption is sound only if triangulation is the sole means for gaining a sense of depth. That is certainly not true: as J. J. Gibson (1979) points out, horses and chickens have a fine sense of depth, but their eyes are on opposite sides of their heads, so their visual fields do not overlap and they cannot triangulate on things in the Cartesian manner. We should not presume that our geometry, which results from perception, is the appropriate framework in which to analyze depth perception. (A more expansive form of the error is rampant in Descartes: artificial phenomenon X works by mechanism Y; so a natural phenomenon that resembles X also works by mechanism Y. Tennis balls blasted through a fabric sheet would refract in the manner of light, so light refraction works in this way; heated fluids push their way through vessels, so the heart is a heat pump.[19] The problem with Descartes is not so much that he is an idealist, it is that his idealism is brought short by a bad empiricism, or the other way around, if you like.)

In brief, in inferential accounts, the problem of depth is badly put, obscured by the presumptions of the ready-made world and the reduction of experience to its terms.

The objection is in harmony with Berkeley. Against the Cartesians, Berkeley notes that we do not know the angles made by our eyes, that we are not aware of making inferences about depth, that geometrical relations do not hold sway when it comes to our sense of distance, and so on.[20] Berkeley turns from geometry to experience. His turn depends upon (and supports) his claim that there is nothing, not depth, not even matter, outside of the mind. The word *depth* simply refers to certain ordered, anticipatory relations between sensations within the mind. I learn that if the image of the pool at City Hall gets bigger, and keeps getting bigger as I feel my feet thumping the ground, then eventually I will feel cold wetness as my feet splash into the pool. To perceive the pool as distant is just to grasp that certain sensations intrinsically anticipate another series of sensations. Since all the ingredients of depth are given directly to the mind, there is no need to pose the problem in terms of a geometry of an extra-mental world.

For Berkeley the object of depth perception is an order detected within the given. Where Descartes appeals to a geometrical inference from the given to an order beyond the given, Berkeley appeals to a comparison between perceptual givens and language.[21] To learn to perceive the pool in depth is to learn the order in which sensations anticipate one another, and this is much like learning the meaning of words. Crucially, the linguistic order is not like a geometrical system, it is conventional, not axiomatic and deductive, and it cannot be specified once and for all as a systematic whole; meanings circle back on themselves in an ever expanding web. We learn language by tuning into shifts in the linguistic web we weave, from within. And for Berkeley, we learn to perceive depth by tuning into shifts within the web of experience, which web is woven by the author of nature, God.

The Cartesian body is like a web that catches sensation, and the Cartesian mind a spider sitting on the web, inferring flies from sensations; to justify its inferential leap, the skeptical spider must prove that material flies could exist and could be inferred from the geometry of their impact. In contrast, Berkeley trumps skepticism by urging that flies are nothing other than vibrations within the web of ideas.

In this way Berkeley turns from an inferential framework that enables a leap to an extra-experiential order, toward the intrinsic ordering of the web of experience. We can take him as the inspiration or forerunner of accounts in which depth and space perception depend on an intrinsic ordering. I call these intrinsic accounts. The questions that immediately arise when we turn to intrinsic accounts are where does the intrinsic ordering of experience come from and what does it refers to—that is, how does an intrinsic account really work?

According to Berkeley, the ordering of experience is akin to the grammar of a language authored by God, and the meaning of a given ordering refers to nothing other than relations between words of God's visual language. This is nicely consistent. But if the order of ideas is fixed by God, we have no part in constituting it. In truth Berkeley's order is a new variant of the ready-made world. As in an inferential framework, a fixed order of this sort neglects the crossing of body and world and fails to account for the meaningful dynamics of lived depth.

The Kantian philosophy is an advance upon Berkeley, for at least the ordering of depth is rooted on the side of the subject. The *Critique of Pure Reason* replaces the authority of God, the author of nature, with the authority of the transcendental ego: for experience to be possible, it must already be ordered by the manifold of space, a pure intuition. But the pure intuition of space is a new version of the ready-made world: it is fixed in advance of perception, and would likely fail to account for the dynamic experience of depth that impresses itself upon us.[22] Even Kant suggests that there is something empirical or dynamic at the bottom of our experience of space. In his metaphysical exposition of the concept of space, he refers to the place [Ort] in space "in which I find myself" (Kant 1929, A23/B38); but it would be odd to think that the transcendental ego has a place in space, and in general we can suspect that there is a complex and difficult mix of the transcendental and the empirical in Kant. And something empirical and dynamic surely enters judgments of the sublime, which surely also have a spatial aspect, as when the enormousness of a distant storm occasions an experience of the sublime. More, as Edward S. Casey notes in *The Fate of Place* (1997), Kant is quite taken by the difference between left- and right-handedness; this difference is tied to the body, rather than transcendental structures. In any case, if the intrinsic order of experience is to account for the dynamics of experience, it cannot be fixed in advance by the Kantian transcendental ego or the Berkeleian language of the author of nature.

We can find a dynamic order in J. J. Gibson's (1950, 1966, 1979) ecological psychology. His investigations were inspired by his criticism of inferential accounts and by the conviction that most experiments misconceive the perceiver. In the worst case, experimenters treat the perceiver as a cyclopean creature with one immobilized eye who sees only impoverished, artificial optical displays. But we are not like that at all. We are moving beings who probe the world with two glancing eyes, and our natural and built environments are richly textured. Gibson therefore went out of the laboratory and into the field, or constructed experiments to test features that would be native to the field.[23]

Gibson's central insight is that perception is the pick-up of invariants in the flow of information that is generated when the perceiver moves in an environment. In a bit more detail: the information flow generated by movement has intrinsic properties; the properties have an environmental significance that remains invariant through movement; so invariants directly specify certain aspects of the perceived environment. For example, natural outdoor environments are covered by textured material like grass or stone, and man-made environments have texture too. As I look at things further and further away, the grain of this texture becomes finer and finer, since there is more texture squeezed into the same visual expanse. To see fine-grained texture (a smooth wash of concrete-colored gray) between me and the doors of City Hall is to see those doors as far in the distance; to see coarse-grained texture between me and the next bench (bubble-pits and pebbles nubbed into a concrete background) is to see that bench as close by. No appeal to an inferential framework is required; texture intrinsically signifies distance.

Gibson, like Berkeley, gives an intrinsic account of perception.[24] But for Gibson the intrinsic ordering of sensation is constituted by the body's moving interaction with the world, rather than being fixed by divine grammar.[25] Consider the problem of sensing one's motion in an environment. In inferential accounts, the problem comes down to this: having what amounts to a model of the environment in one's mind, and updating one's position in it by way of inferences. For example, at City Hall, the retinal images of the surrounding walkway, the grid of tiles, and so on, form a matrix that distorts in different ways as I move around; inferring backward from the distortion to the motion that causes it lets me infer my position in the plaza (assuming that the plaza and its tiles in fact form an orthogonal grid). Gibson points out that such complexity is unnecessary. There is no need to infer a three-dimensional environment from two-dimensional retinal images, because *retinas are not really two-dimensional*, they are the curved backs of two eyes in a voluminous body moving in the environment. I do not need to infer my position from distortions of the matrix of the plaza, because, given the constraints inherent in my moving, ocular body, information in the visual field will, for example, stream outward as I move forward. As I move closer to the statue in front of me, its edge moves from the center of my visual field toward the periphery, and the rate of this outward flow invariantly and directly specifies a rate of motion. Against Descartes, bodily movement amounts to an inference in the flesh: by inherently streaming visual information outward, movement accomplishes what inference does in inferential accounts. And against Berkeley, perception is not the reading of a fixed, divine grammar: the moving order of perception is authored by bodily movement and reflects it. Consider the different sorts of 'grammars' of moving depth perception that one quickly learns when moving at different speeds in different environments, for example, in cities with broad streets, cities with skyscraper canyons like New York or Chicago, cities with enclosing tunnel streets like Italian hill towns; at highway versus city speeds; in indoor shopping centers bombarded with mirrors, in libraries, in monotonous splayed-out airport terminals. Each movement-environment authorizes its own patterns, which become habitual guides of movement and depth perception.

The roboticist Rodney Brooks, who leans in Gibson's ecological direction, makes a related point. The inferential tradition builds robots by first of all programming them with a model of the environment, an explicit instance of what Merleau-Ponty calls a ready-made world. When an inferential robot navigates the environment, in effect it navigates its own internal model. Brooks thinks this a useless duplication of the environment and demonstrates that a model is not necessary.[26] The actual environment 'models' itself. Brooks builds little insectoid robots that have no central brain or model yet successfully walk over all manner of terrain. Each leg interacts locally with a spot of ground, sending signals up to a higher unit, which modifies the rhythm of "push" signals sent down to the legs. Leg-ground interactions and interactions of up and down signals combine, resulting in a quasi-coordination of the legs. The environment, with its various bumps and frictions, helps coordinate the overall rhythm of walking. Inferential robots need a model of the environment, a model that makes assumptions about types of leg movement appropriate to types of terrain; and they need a further system that identifies different types of terrain and switches models accordingly (another example of the convolutions of inferential accounts). Brooks's robots have no need for either of these devices. Insectoid robot and terrain co-authorize movement that is generally appropriate to the terrain (Brooks 1991; cf. Clark 1997).

Merleau-Ponty makes a related point by way of observation of animal behavior: when the leg of an insect is severed, it simply substitutes another leg and uses a different pattern of leg movements to continue walking. This leads Merleau-Ponty to argue that walking and other movements are not governed by a central program, since we would not imagine that an insect stores a special program for each type of terrain or damage to the body (PP 92–93/77–78). Brooks's robots suggest much the same thing. When damaged they would do something similar to the insect: undamaged legs will keep pushing, but coordinate in a new way. Walking is not ordered by a grammar of movement fixed in advance, the interaction between the organism and the environment intrinsically orders itself.

These points address the origin of the ordering intrinsic to experience. According to Gibson, the ordering emerges within movement. But what does this ordering refer to? How are we to understand the object of perception?

Gibson is committed to the principle that perception gives us a veridical encounter with a real environment. The ordering of experience is informed by the body's interaction with the physical layout of the environment, and the perceptual meaning of this ordering thus refers to the environment *as it figures for the body that interacts with it*. We do not, according to Gibson, perceive naked properties of the environment, rather we perceive what the environment affords to our bodies, what we can do with, or in, the environment. And what we can do depends on us. Gibson calls these perceived features of the environment, that are there for our acting bodies, "affordances."[27]

In Berkeley's account flies are nothing other than vibrations in an already ordered web, but in Gibson's account perception affords no flies apart from the web cast by the moving perceiver. The object of perception, an affordance, emerges within and reflects perceptual activity. In this way Gibson aims to overcome dualistic divisions between subject and object, body and environment. Behind Gibson's concept of affordances is an attack on the doctrine of atomic sensation and the doctrine of primary versus secondary qualities: there are no sensations or qualities independent of the perceiver; the distinction between primary and secondary qualities is not the starting point of perception, but a result of it, something that we introject by analysis of experience. In this attack, Gibson joins thinkers such as Merleau-Ponty and Dewey in dismantling the traditional framework noted at the beginning of this section. Altogether, his account reconfigures the problem we have been pursuing and takes us one step closer to the crossing of the body and the world.

But it is controversial whether Gibson's ecological psychology succeeds in overcoming the dualism of body and environment, and if it does not, it stops short of the crossing of the body and the world.[28] We can approach the issue by noting a tension within ecological psychology. Ecological psychology roots the ordering of perception in the moving body in the environment, but it ultimately tries to conceive that moving relation in terms of physics. In the words of M. T. Turvey and Robert E. Shaw, two of the most important theoreticians of ecological psychology following Gibson, they are looking for a "physical psychology" (Turvey and Shaw 1995). At the same time, ecological psychology discovers that the body is social. This is particularly evident in ecological accounts of developmental psychology, which show how individual history and culture are crucial in shaping perception. The perceiving body is social and cultural, not a merely biophysical entity, so how can it be grasped in terms of a physical psychology?[29] But could not ecological psychology overcome this problem by showing how individual life histories and the social can be conceived in terms of biophysical and ecological aspects of life?

Suppose we follow this strategy and try to explain the intrinsic ordering of perception by appealing to basic and universal biophysical laws, to what amounts to a ready-made world fixed outside the flow of perceptual activity. This strategy in effect claims that the ordering of perception is *not* intrinsic to living perception, that it is the result of more basic laws that can be specified independent of the body's interaction with its environment. This would also suggest a dualism of body and environment, since it would allow us to conceive body and environment independent of their interaction with one another, in terms of an overarching physics, rather than their interrelation. Given the aim of ecological psychology, this is a conceptually contradictory strategy. We are not in a position to judge whether current versions of ecological psychology simplistically fall to this contradiction, but we can extract an important dialectical point. If ecological psychology aims for an intrinsic account that consistently and coherently responds to the problems of inferential accounts, if it aims to locate the significance of perception directly within the body's ecological interaction with its environment, then it must appeal to intrinsic structures at every level, instead of bottoming out in a ready-made world.

This is why, perhaps, ecological psychology turns to dynamic systems theory, which conceives perception as a *self-organizing* phenomenon, as a system whose ordering spontaneously 'assembles' through its own dynamic changes.[30] (The chapters below give more details on dynamic systems theory.) An account of self-organization would show how self-ordering is intrinsic at every level of description, and would capture something like the crossing of body and world. But dynamic systems theory also tends to bottom out in universal biophysical laws, and this leads to a problem. In *The Structure of Behaviour* Merleau-Ponty studies living phenomena that we would now call self-organizing. He conceives them as constituting an order of being different from that of physical-mechanical phenomena; he calls this the vital order. He is not advocating vitalism, but arguing that living self-organization ought not to be understood merely in terms of physical law, for the very thing that characterizes the vital order is that it establishes its own norms, its own laws of organization (*SdC*, especially chapter 3). Both Merleau-Ponty and dynamic systems theory in effect argue that self-organization is fundamental. But Merleau-Ponty conceives living, self-organizing beings as constituting a new order of organization that must be understood in its own terms, whereas dynamic systems theory conceives living self-organization in terms of lower-level laws of organization. But if self-organization is to be reduced to physical organization, if it does not constitute a new order that is to be understood in its own terms, through reference to itself, then is it really *self*-organization? If the organization of a system is to be explained in terms of laws fixed independently of that system, isn't its organization the product of something else? (The difference is rather like the difference between a cosmos ordered by an external designer, and a cosmos that orders itself from within through its own development.) On the other hand, if we answer this problem by saying that self-organization is fundamental to the physical cosmos itself, that local self-organization is a facet of universal self-organization, then don't we have to revise our concept of physics and reduction?

In any case, the conceptual tension we have been tracing reflects an explanatory problem. To return to inferential accounts for a moment: these have a structural problem accounting for the dynamic aspect of perception, because this requires a baroque profusion of inferential frameworks that (a) specify perceptual inferences that would apply in new situations, and (b) specify when new frameworks are to be switched in, and so on. For example, an inferential robot in a changing environment would need to know when to switch to a different set of assumptions about its environment. The inferential Hydra keeps growing new heads.

Intrinsic accounts, especially in dynamic systems theory, are much better at grappling with the problem of dynamics. Dynamics are simply shifts in

self-organization; the intrinsic ordering of perception always reflects the interaction of body and environment, and changes to either will, as a matter
of course, produce changes in self-organization. But this appeal works only if
perceptual shifts are truly intrinsic within a self-organizing body-environ-
ment dynamic. The minute an appeal is made to a ready-made world fixed
in advance of these dynamics, the Hydra springs new heads, for it is necessary to explain why a specific ready-made world comes into play. The whole
account begins unraveling.

The moral of both the conceptual and explanatory problems is this: for
an intrinsic account to be rigorous, for it to escape the Hydra of explanatory
heads that bloom in the face of the dynamics of perception as we learn, grow,
become diseased, and so on, it must appeal to intrinsic structures at every
level. Tackling the Hydra is indeed a Herculean task, since there can be no
terms in the account that are isolated from perceptual life, and all terms must
therefore unfold within one living dynamic that crosses body and world.
Moreover, structures that emerge in the dynamic crossing of the body and
the world are inherently situational and therefore might not be repeatable,
or might be repeatable only in a very specific situation. So the demand for
intrinsic structures at every level, for dynamism all the way down, may be at
odds with the scientific demand for objective structures that can be tested
through experimental repetition. In brief, the program of ecological psychology and its sequel, dynamic systems theory, is empirically sensitive to the
dynamic crossing of the body and the world, and analysis of this program
shows why such a turn to this crossing is empirically warranted; but analysis
also shows that the conceptual and experimental demands of such programs,
namely demands for objective terms that are fixed in advance of perception,
are at odds with empirical results. There is a conflict within ecological psychology, a conflict between empirical results and ontology.[31]

At any rate, ecological psychology helps dislodge the Cartesian mind
from its perch above the web of experience, hoping to infer flies. It turns us
to a body whose very movement in the environment casts the web of perception. But if body and world cross one another, then we cannot understand
their interaction in terms of a physical psychology that would precede them,
we have to understand the two as having a sense, a meaning, that is constituted within their reciprocal relation. Heidegger is support here: we are not
Cartesian spiders shuffling data from the web of sensation into the "'cabinet'
of consciousness," an interior compartment in which alone sensation is synthesized into perceptual experience; Dasein as knowing and perceiving "remains outside" in the world.[32] We are "being-in-the-world." Heidegger's
hyphenated phrase is meant to remind us that spider and web, Dasein and
world, are not two things, but one existence; this existence is woven out of
meaning, and cannot be reduced to the being-in-itself of things. David Michael
Levin draws an even stronger connection for us when he hints at a connection between what Gibson would call the layout of the environment and

what the Heideggerian would call the *Legein* of the *Logos*: the layout of the environment is not a merely physical order, but a meaningful one involving a *Logos* that unfolds in relation to our moving existence.[33] The next section directs us toward meaning by showing how our perceptual life and experience of depth is more than environmental and physical. It is what Merleau-Ponty calls being in the world.

The point of the dialectical analysis given above is not to arrange traditional accounts in a sequence, or claim that they must develop in such a sequence, but to tie the different accounts together around the central problem they are meant to solve, and to show that the problem turns us to an ordering of perception that emerges within the dynamic crossing of body and world. Study of the labile and meaningful character of lived depth only deepens this turn.

FROM THE LABILITY TO THE *SENS* OF LIVED DEPTH

These meditations on depth have occupied me through the afternoon, and I now realize that it is getting late, that I must hurry if I am to make it to the library before its early summer close. I look north toward my destination, as if City Hall were not there. In the film *The Thin Red Line*, there is a very long sequence in which the camera dwells on a sea of grass cloaking a hill the soldiers are to occupy; the camera moves as if an eye transfixed by every swaying movement of the grass. This moving absorption conveys a sense of an immense distance up the hill; the distance would appear much smaller if the camera approached the hill as someone looking at its top or over it, as someone not possessed by what might be hidden in the cloak of grass. My being late and far from my destination provokes a similar but converse effect: in my haste I do not linger over details spread within the plaza, the spread of the plaza slips into the background of my perception, and correlatively the plaza seems to contract. Again, a city block usually appears longer if one is dawdling and window-shopping, absorbed in detail, as opposed to driving through the block, treating it as a thoroughfare.

On another occasion I am extremely sick, lying in bed. The thermostat marks the house as being at its normal temperature, but I feel cold. Not my usual feeling of cold, in which I experience my body as having a warmth and integrity protected by clothing, with the cold being something outside me in ordinary depth. The cold infiltrates me, it has no distance from me, it has seeped into the extra-ordinary depth of my body. Likewise, smells and sounds in the house are unavoidable infestations, they hurt within, although I *know* they are outside me. The sun breaking through the curtains pains my eyes, and again there is a strange transformation: I *know* the sun is distant, but its spreading light is within, curdling my eyes into aches. This is not the feeling of the sun painfully lighting on the backs of healthy eyes. Sickness puts in question my everyday experience of a division between ordinary and extra-ordinary depth, it suggests that the meaningfulness of experienced depth is rooted in a living tension that crosses body and the world, a tension that swings in the balance when I am sick.

Tiredness swings my experience in a related direction. When I am drowsy in a movie theater, I sometimes experience rustlings and noises in the world around me as oddly hallucinatory jostlings and disturbances in my body, as if things outside echo within. My sense of depth is not rooted in a ready-made world independent of the disturbances and diseases of life.[34]

Disturbances of emotional life reveal this connection too, for example, moods such as despair.[35] In despair, things, circumstances, and events around me can make a claim on me as being inevitable. They weigh in and obliterate the realm of possibilities in which I carry out my life. This mood is reflected in perception: there is nothing to do, there is nowhere to go, the sky closes in, actions seem pointless, and so on. The ordinary depths of the world are transformed, this time, it seems, by the mood of my relation to the world. When the buoyant dimensions of life are collapsed in a mood of despair, despair worms outward into the ordinary depths of the world, collapsing them too.

A young child is playing happily, although tired to the verge of crankiness. Somebody drops a book, making a loud, sharp noise. This shatters her play. She cannot stand any relation to things outside her, she pushes everything and everyone away. Even a mere look sets off a reaction in which she yells at everybody not to look at her. We can imagine that in these cases the child experiences an invasion of herself by a social world that had, when she was in possession of it as a place for play, given her some moment of separation, a place from which she could deal with things. Social gestures in the ordinary depths of the world can collapse the living depths of bodily activity that usually buoy us with a sense of our own place in the world, and this can lead to a shift in the meaning of ordinary depth. Probably we have all snapped at a closing-in social world when worn out or under pressure; sometimes others "get in our face."[36]

Ishmael remarks in Moby-Dick:

Now, in calm weather, to swim in the open ocean is as easy to the practiced swimmer as to ride in a spring-carriage ashore. But the awful lonesomeness is intolerable. The intense concentration of self in the middle of such a heartless immensity, my God! who can tell it? Mark, how when sailors in a dead calm bathe in the open sea— mark how closely they hug their ship and only coast along her sides. (Chapter 93)

And Hamlet exclaims:

O God, I could be bounded in a nutshell and count myself a king of infinite space, were it not that I have bad dreams.[37]

Some of these examples concern unusual or extreme situations, but the phenomenon of changing senses of depth is not all that strange. We have probably all experienced shifts in our sense of depth that correlate with shifts in mood, attitude, health, situation.[38] Not only Melville and Shakespeare, but countless authors use descriptions of depth to capture points about characters and their moods; and in film, sculpture and painting it is quite conventional to convey mood, emotion and psychological focus by playing with the sense of depth. None of this would make any sense if experienced depth were a fixed dimension independent of our activity and our relation to the world. On the contrary, the examples suggest that experienced depth changes in relation to our living situation. As we shall see, our usual sense of fixed depth rests upon changing, living depths, not the other way around. Lived depth is labile.

When I say that lived depth is labile, I mean that it is open to alterations that propagate from within our experience of it, where the kinds of alterations are themselves open to alteration. In this usage a piece of clay is malleable but not labile (since it does not alter itself from within), and the caterpillar's metamorphosis into a butterfly is not a case of lability, since the change is biologically fixed, it cannot alter its way of altering; our sexual being, on the other hand, is labile, since it alters itself and develops new ways of self-altering (this is the sense in which we find the term in psychoanalytic literature).

How are we to account for the lability of lived depth? Everyday accounts of the examples would suggest that the world objectively stays the same whilst the subjective sense of depth changes: the sun and room remain the same, but I get sick and my sense of depth changes. Traditional accounts would follow suit, urging that our labile sense of depth starts from an objective encounter with a world. Beneath our labile experience there is a fixed depth that remains the same; we veridically reconstruct that fixed depth, but subjectively assign it different values in different situations. The hypothesis returns us to the conceptual dialectic discussed above, since it ultimately supposes something like an ordering of sensations fixed in advance of perceptual activity. But it also raises new problems.

The traditional hypothesis implies two stages in labile depth experience. The first stage gives us an objective encounter with a fixed depth, the second stage assigns a subjective, changing value to the first stage. (Note how this echoes the traditional distinction between stages of raw sensation and perceptual synthesis.) But then in the first stage the perceiver has some sort of access to a fixed, objective depth. We would have to ask, along with Merleau-Ponty, who raises the like question in his analyses of perception, why the perceiver has so much difficulty encountering objective depth. If objective depth is accessible, why is it so difficult to perceive it? Why do we instead experience a labile, changing sense of depth?

More than that, if in the first stage depth remains fixed and objective, what prompts changing subjective valuations? We could appeal to changing factors within the perceiving subject, but we would still need to say precisely why particular fixed givens prompt particular changes; we would need a mechanism that maps from fixed inputs to changing outputs. We would need, for example, to talk about modifications to depth-processing modules. But why should a modification in a module, the task of which is to veridically reconstruct objective depth, result in the specific meaningful shifts observed above, rather than reports that could be cashed out in terms of objective dimensions of the world? Why is the dropping of the book an invasion, rather than an event at a certain distance? We could answer by speaking of links between modules responsible for veridical processing of depth cues, and modules involving emotion, planning, meaning, etc. But why should there be links between such modules? Why would the experience of depth and emotion ever become linked in a living being if depth and emotion were not somehow already implied in one another, if their linkage did not already specify an important issue for that living being? To pursue this question with an ecological voice: what benefit is there in first reconstructing an objective depth, and then giving it an emotional valuation? Why not just respond to depth-as-emotionally-significant? Do I first perceive how close the tiger is coming to me and then experience this as a danger, or do I experience something frightful closing in? The study of the phenomenon of "looming" in ecological psychology suggests the latter, rather than the former: what perceivers, even infants, pick up is a threat in the sudden increase in the size of things, rather than a decrease of distance as such. If you have ever, when watching a horror movie or in real life, cringed away from a shadow that expands in size, you are familiar with this phenomenon; objectively, the shadow is not getting any closer to you, nonetheless it is a threat closing in. We do not first perceive something moving objectively closer, and therefore subjectively value it as a threat; from the start the looming figure is an encroaching threat, and in light of this we sense it moving closer.

For ecological psychology the point is that the organism does not first reconstruct the objective space that the scientist measures, and then give it an organismic (subjective) valuation. The ecological relation between the organism and its environment constitutes the environment as having dimensions that are inherently significant. The organism never deals in inches or meters or anything like objective measures; it deals, if we could speak for it, with strides, striking distances, safe removes. The lion does not first take the measure of its cage in objective units, and then, finding it small, pace its confines; its elliptical, perpetual stride *already is* the 'measure' of its environment, the 'measure' of an environment in which there is no striking distance, no safe remove; correlatively, the caged lion's stride is the 'measure' of an animal warped by confinement.

A consideration of illusions opens a different approach to the issue. We asked how fixed inputs could map onto changing outputs, and why it is so difficult to experience objective depth as the scientist would measure it.

Illusions pose the same sort of question: Why does the Nekker figure, which is objectively fixed, first look like a cube popping out of the page, and then like a cube digging into the page? Why do we have no control over the way we see it? And why is it so hard to see the figure as a flat set of lines? The phenomena described at the beginning of this section could be considered illusions, and are like the Nekker cube in being dynamic. After all, City Hall does not stretch or distort, the sun does not all of a sudden leap into my body, it is just my perception that changes. Why not conceive these phenomena as errors of perception, illusions? Merleau-Ponty in his phenomenology, and more recently Turvey and Carello in their psychology, urge that in cases of illusion the perceiver is not in error. The one who is in error is the scientist who claims that illusions should be understood as errors of perception.

Merleau-Ponty makes his case by analysis of the Müller-Lyer's illusion, in which a line segment bounded by outward-pointing arrowheads is seen as different in length from a line segment bounded by inward-pointing arrow-heads, even though the line segments are, according to a ruler, the same length. Merleau-Ponty's point is simple but deep. The line segments are welded into arrow structures the visual expanse of which bulges outward or pinches inward. In the visual field, the line segments are therefore of neither equal nor unequal size, since the eye is neither abstracting line segments nor comparing their size, it is seeing and comparing arrows that each constitute their own standard of expanse. It is as if, Merleau-Ponty writes, the one line "did not belong to the same universe as the other." Since the figure gives no basis for comparing objective size, it is misguided to call the phenomenon an error of size perception, an illusion (PP 12/6). On the moon, with its weaker gravitational field, an apple will feel lighter than the same apple on earth; does this mean you are in error about the apple, since its mass remains the same? No, your perception is correct. With respect to perceived weight, the apple on the moon and the apple on the earth are not quite the same apple. It is as if they belong to different 'universes' of weight. Comparison across these 'universes' does not really give a basis for comparing objective weights, rather (granted other knowledge that the apple's mass remains the same) the comparison indicates differences between the lunar and terrestrial perceptual fields: things feel lighter on the moon. Similarly with the Müller-Lyer's figure. The unaided (or untrained) eye can no more escape the visual 'weight' of arrows that each constitute their own 'gravitational field,' leaping to a measure of the optical 'mass' of line segments, than the unaided body can escape the gravitational field in which it weighs the apple, leaping to a measure of the apple's mass. Indeed, these fields with their 'distorting' influence are the condition for perceiving the things in question (arrows with a visual expanse, an apple with a weight) and are thus intrinsic to perception. The Müller-Lyer figure provides no basis for objective comparison of line segments, rather (granted other knowledge that the line segments are objectively the same) comparison of the arrows tells us about the influence of shapes on the visual field: arrows bulge things inward or outward.[39] In the Müller-Lyer figure we are seeing our own vision almost as much as we are seeing things, and it is no illusion that our vision sees arrows differently from other things.

Turvey and Carello make their case by studying the way we feel the lengths of things wielded in hand, for example, canes and tennis rackets. When wielding something that is not visible to us, our feeling of its length can diverge from its measured geometrical length. Most scientists would conceive this as an error, an illusion. But Turvey and Carello show that when we wield things we do not really perceive their geometrical length. What we perceive is, in effect, what we can do with the thing in hand, its "wieldiness" (very roughly, if it is easier to wield, to move about, it is shorter; if it is harder to move about, it is longer). Misperception of geometrical length is not an error, since the object of perception is "wieldiness," not geometrical length. Again, the point is that we cannot escape the influence of the field in which we perceive things; in this case, Turvey and Carello show us that we cannot escape the fact that the felt length of things is perceived within a field constituted by wielding them, and so gives us no direct perception of their geometrical length as such.[40]

With respect to the dynamics of illusions, Scott Kelso suggests that our changing perception of phenomena like the Nekker cube stems from dynamic patterns inherent in our neurology (Kelso 1999). We could grant this, but it does not follow that the perceiver first of all encounters a fixed figure on the page and then overwrites it with changing values. Supposing Kelso is right, you cannot escape the fact that you see with a body that has a dynamic neurology (as if it were a perceptual error to see with such a body!). Your body is dynamic, the cube sets those dynamics in play, so within your perceptual field the cube is intrinsically dynamic. You can no more see the Nekker cube as flat and unchanging than you can stare at the sun without going blind: perceiving the cube as flipping in and out is a condition of seeing with your dynamic body, as going blind is a condition of staring at the sun with a body whose fleshy eyes are vulnerable to the heat of concentrated sunlight.[41] The flipping of the Nekker cube is no illusion, no error; it is a condition of perceiving. (Of course, in comparison to other things that stay put, or in comparison to the figure that appears when we dissect the cube geometrically, the Nekker cube is strange, and that is why we see it as an illusion. But it is not because the scientist tells us it is an illusion that we see it as an illusion; it is because it really flips in and out that we become scientific about it.)

This analysis of illusions shows that perception cannot escape the field of perception, leaping to an encounter with objects as they would be in and of themselves. Contrary to traditional accounts, the lability of perception is not a two-stage process in which the perceiver throws a dynamic coat of subjective meaning over a fixed, underlying object. Perception is inherently situational and active, perceiver and perceived cross and infiltrate each other, and this crossing already constitutes a field of perception in which the perceived already has a meaning for the perceiver.

But this meaning is more than the environmental significance remarked by the ecological psychologists in phenomena such as looming. We do not just live in an environment fixed by imperatives of our species, we live in a world with multiple and fluid imperatives of meaning.[42] When a tiger looms toward me, I move away from the tiger by moving away from the looming image; but when a car looms in the rear-view mirror, I move away from the car by moving toward the looming image. Looming is not a self-contained imperative. When I am driving, I am geared to the imperatives of the driving world, crossed with a situation that constitutes its own field of meanings, meanings acquired by habit and rooted in technology and culture. (Compare driving in Peterborough to driving in Toronto, driving in Toronto to driving in Rome or New York.) And we are social beings from the start, and it is through the social that we acquire our habitual yet changing ways of inhabiting and moving in our world. The lability of perception will then have, as shown in chapters below, a social and habitual aspect.

The dynamics of perception, then, are not anchored in a fixed, objective framework, they are intrinsic to the situation of perception, and can differ across individuals, habits, and social settings. The way my sickness relates to my experience of depth may be different from your experience of the like relation; the way the social sphere relates to the experience of depth will likely vary across cultural and individual histories. (Sue Cataldi elucidates relations of this sort in *Emotion, Depth, and Flesh*.) And the dynamic contours of these changing relations can themselves alter. Hence the use of the word *labile*, to specify an alterability that can itself alter.

Clearly this sort of lability poses a challenge to the shared assumptions of both inferential and intrinsic accounts. Both assume an already specified framework, an inferential framework or an intrinsic ordering, that founds the link between perceptual input and perceptual output. Accounting for the lability of perception thus leads to a Hydra of explanation, a tangle of mechanisms that regulate alterations, switching new circuits into place. Dynamic systems theory is much better on this head, as noted above, but as we have seen and will see in more detail, this theory still runs into problems.

The lability of depth is not just emotional or subjective color splashed over the crystalline geometry of an underlying objective space. It refers us to the tensed crossing of body and world in which perception inheres, it refers us to what Merleau-Ponty would call motivating relations, in which antecedent activities gain their acting identity only through the significance that they acquire (PP 299–300/258–9). Given that experienced depth arises in the crossing of the body and world, is labile, and is meaningful, it is appropriate to speak from now on of our *sense* of depth, drawing on linked connotations of the word *sense*. We sense depth, which is to say: we have a sensory-perceptual experience of it; but depth is constitutively differentiated as having a sense, a meaning for us, and it is *we* who make sense of that meaning; sensing is not a passive activity, it is an active, transitive activity that depends upon sustaining a difference and sameness that crosses body and world. Body and world are thus sensed to one another, their relation is constituted such that the two appear as having a directed fit, the sort of fit belonging to a glove that fits on one hand, but not the other. The sense of depth emerges within this directed fit.

In fact it would be better to speak here of the *sens* of depth. In French, "*sens*" not only connotes meaning and the senses, but direction. A sign indicating a one way street reads "*sens unique*"; "*dans le sens des aiguilles d'une montre*" means "clockwise"; "*être dans le mauvais sens*" means "to be the wrong way round." Cars, clock hands or things going the wrong way round don't quite make sense, they are out of place. The everyday connotations of the French word "*sens*" thus suggest a link between meaning and direction, a link that can be detected only in very specialized English usages. For example, the geometer may speak of the difference between mirror shapes or clockwise and anti-clockwise rotations as a difference in sense. And many of the connectors on your computer are sensed, designed so that they fit together only one way. A shape or connector with the wrong sense doesn't fit into its context and thus doesn't make sense—in the way that an out of place word or thing doesn't make sense. In his discussion of *sens* in the *Phenomenology of Perception*, Merleau-Ponty plays on this link between direction, fit and meaning. Roughly put, Merleau-Ponty's crucial discovery is that there is *sens* within the body's moving directedness toward the world. *Sens*, as will be shown below, is neither a meaning in the head nor is it interior to subjectivity, it is a meaning within a movement that crosses body and world. The concept of *sens* is so central to this book that it almost should be titled *The* Sens *of Space*. Because this book depends on developing the philosophical meaning of Merleau-Ponty's term *sens*, and because aspects of that philosophical meaning better resound in the French, I shall leave it in the French whenever I refer to meaning as arising within directed movement that crosses body and world. Since the term is close to the English, it will be left in italics, to remind the reader of the multiple connotations of the French term. (The italics also prevent the term from being taken for a typographical error.)

What we need is an account of how a labile *sens* arises in the crossing of the body and the world. We will find this by studying perception in relation to movement.

FROM DEPTH TO THE ETHICAL

The movement that crosses body and world is not simply muscular and kinetic, it is the movement of a social body, and that takes our study of depth into the ethical. We can delve into the connection between depth and the ethical by glancing at Sartre's analysis of the existence of others in *Being and Nothingness*, which very much depends upon observations about spatial experience.

I am on the benches at City Hall. "A man passes by those benches. I see this man; I apprehend him as an object and at the same time as a man. What does this signify?" To perceive the other as a man is, according to Sartre, to "register an organization *without distance* of the things in my universe around that privileged object," to perceive "a total space which is grouped around the Other, and this space is made *with my space*" (Sartre 1956, 341). The other is perceived as a constitutive alteration of my ordering of space: I am not the only one with extra-ordinary depth; the other introduces his own order, which escapes the ordinary depths of the world, into those very depths. I encounter the other in the experience of an alien order that commands my space.

And yet:

> . . . *the Other* is still an object *for me*. He belongs to *my distances* . . . it appears that the world has a kind of drain hole in the middle of its being and that it is perpetually flowing off through this hole. The universe, the flow, and the drain hole are all once again recovered, reapprehended, and fixed as an object. (Sartre 1956, 343)

There is something paradoxical here. My space is not entirely disordered by the other, since the hole in being through which I experience disorder nonetheless appears within my spatial order. The hole alters my spatial order only by appearing within it. This provokes a series of problems. Where am I to place this hole? Can it be ordered within the depths of my world if it constitutively disrupts that order? How am I related to it? But these are problems only if we try to reduce my spatial order and the hole in it to one underlying, objective order. Sartre does not do this. His solution to the problem of the existence of others hinges on the point that the encounter does not occur *within* an already established spatial order, for then we would have an endless regress on the problem of how an object in space is encountered as another subject. Rather, the encounter is constitutively a clash *between* conflicting spatial orders, a clash between spaces, not a clash within space. Perceived space is not a container whose depths serve as an arena in which we first encounter others as objects, and then infer their subjectivity; if we are ever to encounter others as others, we must have a relation to others that is prior to a relation in an objective space. The look is one such relation, and it is experienced not as an optical occurrence within space, but as a contestation, a warping of our own space. The look thus shapes our sense of depth and space. One's sense of depth and space is not simply rooted in the crossing of one's body and the world, but in the crossing of one's existence and an other's existence.

We can arrive at a similar but different point through a glance in a differ-ent direction, at Hegel's account of recognition and self-consciousness, which is surely an influence on Sartre's account, even if Sartre is critical of Hegel.

According to Hegel, the condition of the possibility of knowledge is not merely constitutive structures of transcendental consciousness, for ex-ample, the categories and pure intuitions of space and time, as Kant claims. Consciousness entails self-consciousness, and the truth of self-consciousness is that it is inherently doubled. To be self-conscious is to be conscious of oneself through an other who stands as a model of the self-consciousness to which one aspires, who reflects and recognizes one's own consciousness. In the first instance, and in the simplest sense possible, mutual recognition of this sort clearly entails that self-conscious beings exist in depth: to recognize and be recognized by other self-conscious beings is to face others, and facing others requires depth. Hegel's account of recognition calls for an account of how recognition takes place in depth. In fact, this point about Hegel prompted this investigation of spatial perception.

Consider, briefly, the struggle to the death. The discussion of Sartre gives us license to explicate the struggle in spatial terms. To struggle is first of all to share a space in which the struggle takes place. In the struggle to the death, what is being staked is the living body through which alone one is in the world. But what is at stake is not simply the body as an object in a container. The struggle arises because self-conscious beings are ready to give up their place in the world, rather than submit to the ordering com-mand of an other. Why? Because to be self-conscious is to have one's own consciousness be central to the interpretative ordering of one's world. Absent other forms of recognition (such as language and culture), staking one's life is a way of showing that one is not simply an object in a container, but the center of a space of interpretation. Hegel's analysis essentially points out that on one's own, one cannot claim to be the center of a space of interpretation. One can claim this only in face of an other who recognizes one's centrality. Paradoxically, the other must then equally be a center of interpretation, since only interpreters can recognize one another as interpreters.[43]

Whereas Sartre focuses on our experience of others as a disruption of our spatial ordering of the world, Hegel's point is that to be self-conscious is to already have meshed and clashed with others as having their own space of interpretation. To illustrate by way of an astronomical simile, for Sartre the other is like a black hole that punctures the fabric of space. For Hegel the other is like a worm-hole that opens a tunnel between one's space and that of an other; these tunnels mark self-consciousness as a phenomenon already constitutively riddled with institutions that knit one's own space into a more encompassing space of community, into a common ground of lan-guage, culture, history, and so on.

The above is both a simplification and an elaboration of Sartre and Hegel, but warranted by the goal of foreshadowing the ethical dimension of our study and situating it in relation to established discussions of the intersubjective. In what follows, though, we do not begin with existing discussions of the ethical; rather a close analysis of spatial perception will lead back to the ethical. When we turn from the ready-made world to the crossing of body and world, we inevitably plunge into the ethical, for the body in question is a moving and developing body, and the world in question is a social world. Others appear in the world that crosses the body, and the habits of a moving, developmental body are supported and shaped by the habits and movements of others. If our sense of space is rooted in the crossing of the body and the world, then our sense of space will be shaped by and reflect our ethical relations with others. So our study of the sense of space leads back to the ethical. But we learn something by being led back to the ethical through our sense of space.

The importance of the ethical to the phenomenology of perception has recently been demonstrated by Shaun Gallagher and Anthony Marcel. Like Merleau-Ponty, they point out that perceptual action is highly contextualized. A woman who has difficulty with "motor fluency" is proficient in serving mugs of tea to guests in her home, is a bit less proficient at drinking from glasses during a meal, but has difficulty when asked to grasp and lift a cylinder of the weight and size of a glass of liquid. Someone who can move glasses about when acting as a host has difficulty executing the same type of action when it is contextualized in abstract terms. To gain scientific or philosophical comprehension of perception, movement, or the sense of self, we must study such phenomena as contextually embedded, rather than composed of abstract elements. As Gallagher and Marcel (1999) argue, this ultimately means studying perception, movement, and the self as social and ethical. John Russon (1994, 2003) gives a similar argument about the ethical dimension of perception in his studies of habit and perception. Related points about perception are to be found in the work of developmental psychologists who attend to the social dimensions of development and its impact on perception. We will return to some of this work below.

But a methodological observation follows. Gallagher, Marcel, and Russon nicely show how philosophy and science go astray when they pursue abstract questions. Leaving the ethical out of our accounts of perception, pretending that the body tested in the lab is simply a sensory processor, rather than a social body, is one such abstraction. Kurt Goldstein, Merleau-Ponty, and others long ago pointed out that the organism in the laboratory is not like the organism in the wild; claims made about it are to some degree artifacts of the laboratory; nowadays we would speak of the construction of the organism (see Geison and Laublicher 2001). Gibson and ecological psychology move out of the laboratory, back into the wild. But we live in something more than the wilds, we live through a social development, and we are ethical. The nonethical perceiver, the human being as sensory processor, would seem to be just as much an artifact of the laboratory as Pavlov's dogs.

On the other hand, ethics is also guilty of abstracting us from our living ground. To drastically simplify, a great deal of ethical theorizing in the last century or so has deduced ethical principles from the idea of an abstract, atomic, individual self—the liberal individual. The procedure is constantly challenged by a stream of thinking that roots the ethical in the living existence of an inherently social, situated being, a stream manifest, for example, in the philosophy of Levinas, de Beauvoir, Merleau-Ponty, Heidegger, Hegel, going back to the roots of the ethical in the Western tradition, to Plato's and Aristotle's studies of how the good arises in the life of the *polis*, the city.

The ethical should be rooted in its living ground. But spatial perception is part of this living ground, since the ethical emerges from and first of all depends upon our encounter with one another as bodily beings in depth. Spatial perception is a condition of living ethicality. Approaching the ethical through spatial perception will contribute to dismantling an abstract ethics that does not attend to the grounds of our encounter with one another. It must be noted, however, that the following is not meant to lay out an ethical system or specific claims about the content of ethics, rather it is meant to explore the spatial aspects of ethics. It is not a grounding of a metaphysics of morals, it is an exploration of the ground of morals in lived space.

CONCLUSION: TOWARD THE MOVING, DEVELOPING BODY

Traditional accounts analyze depth perception almost as if it took place wholly inside the perceiver, in the inferences of the perceiving subject, or wholly outside the perceiver in the world, in the intrinsic ordering of the given. But of course depth perception takes place between the perceiver and the world, for depth perception is perception of the perceiver's relation to the place that she or he is in, and that relation involves life and movement; it is neither on the side of the perceiver nor on the side of the world, it is cross between them. The problem of depth that drives traditional accounts arises in this crossing of the body and world, and so traditional accounts on the one hand think about this crossing, but at the same time, as we have seen, the analytical frameworks of traditional accounts sever this crossing. But even if traditional accounts end up putting the problem badly, their explorations expose problems, as shown above, that call for a study of depth and spatial perception as rooted in the crossing of the body and the world. And this will have to be a study of the body as moving, social, and developmental, a study that will lead us to a sense of the ethical within our sense of space.

The study is conducted in two parts. Part one, "The Moving Sense of the Body," gives an account of the body, pursuing *sens* by expanding Merleau-Ponty's concept of the body schema, to show how it is in fact a moving schema that organizes itself within body-world movement. A body that manifests such a moving schema expresses the *sens* of body and world in habitual and gestural movement. The *sens* of expression ultimately stems from what I call a topology of expression, a 'topological' constraint inherent in the moving-growing body's relation to place. Part two, "The Spatial Sense of the Moving Body," draws on this account to show how our sense of depth and up-down orientation depends on aspects of this topology. It then discusses the role of development and the social in our moving sense of space. The conclusion takes up ethical implications.

PART I

THE MOVING SENSE OF THE BODY

CHAPTER 1

THE MOVING SCHEMA OF PERCEPTION

I AM TRYING TO WRITE the opening sentences of this chapter. I reach for my pen, which is sitting to the left of my coffee-filled cup, move the pen toward the paper, twiddle it, attempt a drawing of the cup, realize I am no artist, put the pen down on the right side of my cup, take up the cup and drink the coffee just to have something to actually do, as if emptying the cup will somehow repair the emptiness of the page.

Some of the classic questions of perception are implied in this simple experience. How do I see one cup with two eyes? How do I reconstruct a cup in depth from arrays of two-dimensional sensory data? How do I feel one pen with many fingers? How, in general, do I put together a multiplicity of sensations into one unified picture of the world? For traditional accounts these are questions about the association or synthesis of an array of sensations. But the introduction calls for a different sort of account, one that roots a labile *sens* of perception in the crossing of the body and the world. This chapter begins building that account by showing how perceptual *sens* arises in a moving schema that crosses the body and the world.

The chapter starts with a discussion of schemata and what Merleau-Ponty calls the body schema.[1] But a body schema that gives rise to *sens* must be conceived as arising within movement that crosses body and world. This is a subtle but perhaps vast shift in conception: the relevant schema is not, as some would suggest, to be located in an already constituted physiological or cognitive system of the body, which then serves as a standard for organizing and making sense of perception. The schema comes from movement and belongs to movement; it is dynamic through and through. More, this sort of schema is based in habit, and is thus inherently developmental and labile; and this sort of schema crosses over into the places in which we form habits, the places we inhabit. The account developed in this and the following chapters thus foreshadows two ecstatic dimensions at the heart of spatial perception: the habitual dimension in which we are outside ourselves in our temporal being and development; and the placial dimension in which we are outside ourselves in the places, social and natural, in which we move and dwell.[2]

Habitual and placial dimensions pulse within a moving schema of perception, pointing us to a labile *sens* that leads us back to the social and the ethical. These points will be secured over the next chapters, which make a conceptual addition to existing discussions of perception and the body schema precisely by emphasizing that the schema of perception is a dynamic phenomenon that appears in the intersection of movement, habit, development, and place.

SCHEMATA AND THE BODY SCHEMA

In general a schema is a form or standard that fits changing content to an already specified framework.[3] There are many different conceptual variants of schema. Computer scientists who build knowledge bases for artificial intelligence systems come up with schemata for representing various bits of knowledge. These amount to data structures with 'slots' in them: changing content is bundled into a prespecified slot-structure that the system can always manipulate. Henry Head, who first proposed the concept of the body schema, turns to the word *schema* to capture the concept of "the combined standard, against which all subsequent changes of posture are measured before they enter consciousness" (Head 1920, 605). Kant invokes transcendental schemata in order to explain how it is possible to subsume intuitions under pure concepts, how categories that are fixed a priori can be applied to changing a posteriori appearances (Kant 1929, A138/B177–A142/B181).

In each of these conceptual variants, schemata have the role of giving order to open-ended content, of fitting changing content into already specified forms. A schema fits the contingent to the necessary, or the labile to the stable, or the a posteriori to the a priori. A schema could therefore be a crucial ingredient in giving an account of the labile *sens* of perception, since it crosses changing content with a stable organization that serves as a nucleus of meaning. But a schema that is itself entirely a priori or a posteriori, entirely contingent or entirely necessary, entirely fluid or entirely stable, would return us to the problems discussed in the introduction of the book. A many-headed Hydra of explanation springs up when we ask how changing content calls a new schema into play, since this would require a schema for applying schema, an endless regress on the very task that a schema is meant to accomplish. What is required is a schema that is not severed from what it schematizes, but itself emerges in what it schematizes.

Merleau-Ponty's concept of the body schema (which transforms the psychological concept) is philosophically important and innovative in this respect, since for Merleau-Ponty the body schema emerges in the activity of the body, in the crossing of the body and the world. As I have argued elsewhere and as Dillon demonstrates, the body schema is neither a priori nor a posteriori. [4] If we had to locate the body schema within this conceptual division, we would have to say that it is a peculiar sort of a priori that keeps changing in light of the very a posteriori that it shapes, and we would have to add that this crossing of the a priori and a posteriori is from the start central to Merleau-Ponty's philosophy.

Merleau-Ponty, however, never quite spells out his conception of the body schema, nor does he put it at the focus of extended discussion; it is a concept that figures through its persistent background role in the *Phenomenology of Perception* and in his later philosophy as well. But if we had to pick one passage that captures Merleau-Ponty's concept of the body-schema in relation to perception, it would be this one, which is found in the bridge between parts one and two of the *Phenomenology of Perception*, in the bridge between Merleau-Ponty's study of the body and his study of the world as perceived (and even here it is only at the end of the passage that we are explicitly told that the body schema is the topic of discussion):

> Every external perception is immediately synonymous with a certain perception of my body, just as every perception of my body is made explicit in the language of external perception. If, then, as we have seen to be the case, the body is not a transparent object, and is not presented to us in virtue of the law of its constitution, as the circle is to the geometer, if it is an expressive unity which we can learn to know only by actively taking it up, this structure will communicate itself to the sensible world. The theory of the body schema is, implicitly, a theory of perception. (PP 239/206)

The passage implies several things. The body schema is the bridge between the body and the perceived world—the theory of the body schema is already a theory of perception. But the body schema is to be found nowhere else than in living activity that bridges body and world: the bridge cannot be built in advance, it emerges only in actively taking up the expressive unity of the body; on the other hand, this sort of bridging activity already expresses its schema. Schema and living activity are aspects of one and the same phenomenon. And within this phenomenon the schema can be said to communicate a *sens* to body and world. Notably this *sens* crosses body and world, since perception of the external world and perception of the body are reflections of one another.

It follows from this passage, from the role that Merleau-Ponty assigns to the body schema, that the body schema is inseparable from movement that crosses body and world. That is what he means when he links the schema with an expressive unity and when he elsewhere speaks of the schema as an attitude, or links it to habit.[5] Unfortunately, it is all too easy to reify the body schema, to conceive it as an independent thing, a bridge built in advance, that is to be abstracted from the movement in which it emerges, for example, to turn it into a cognitive or neurophysiological structure that would be specified in advance of movement. Once we have an "it," a schema, to talk about, our tendency is to turn it into a thing, because our minds and language—and the body schema itself—dispose us to lending a thingly, solid *sens* to the content of the world; Merleau-Ponty himself does not escape this tendency, and sometimes even invites misconception of the body schema as some sort of thing.[6] We are, as Bergson (1998) puts it, inclined to a "logic of solids," and of course a logic of solids would be at odds with thinking about a labile crossing of body and world or a schema that is itself in movement.

Behind these claims is a difficult ontological question: just what is the body schema? What sort of entity is it? We will return to this question in the next chapter. The aim of this chapter is to begin showing how the *sens* of perception is rooted in a schema that emerges in movement itself, and to draw a connection between this moving schema and habit. This is partly as a corrective to the mistaken view that the body schema is simply a new-fangled, corporeal version of an a priori, partly in aid of arriving at an account of labile *sens* through revitalizing the concept of the body schema. This revitalizing requires a shift in the language through which we conceive the phenomenon labeled "the body schema": a shift from discussion of the body schema to discussion of the moving schema of perception. So I am going to begin not from Merleau-Ponty and the language of the body schema, but from observations prompted by thinking about the body schema in Merleau-Ponty's phenomenology.

PERCEPTION AND MOVING SCHEMAS

PERCEPTION AND MOVEMENT

A simple phenomenological experiment will show that perception involves a schema of body-world movement. By *body-world movement* I simply mean movement of body and world together, as a duo, movement that crosses body and world.

Obtain a wine cork. Lay the cork on a table so that it can roll on its long axis across the table. Rest your hand beside the cork so that your finger and thumb drape down, just grazing its circular ends. Close your eyes and relax, bracketing any assumptions or claims about the cork and what it should feel like. Hold your hand very still for a minute or two, exerting as little pressure as possible on the cork, yet touching it. Then lift your hand off the table, keeping your wrist and hand relaxed so that the cork just hangs between your fingers. Now wiggle the cork.

A classic question about perception is how it fits independent sensations together into something meaningful. What the experiment shows is that body-world movement already fits perception together. When your hand just touches the ends of the cork, and you bracket anticipations about it, you may feel two independent circular surfaces. But when you let the cork hang between your fingers, the slight squeeze inherent in this body-world configuration makes this feeling of independent surfaces less convincing. And when you wiggle the cork, you feel one unified thing between your fingers, and you will probably have a feel for the dry, stiff springiness of the middle of the cork. Within the framework of traditional questions about perceptual synthesis, this appears to be a problem, since two separate surfaces, touched by two different fingers, are perceived as belonging to one thing, and the fingers provide a sense of tangible material that is not in fact touched by the fingers.

The insight prompted by the experiment is that the unity of cork does not rest in some sort of abstract synthesis of sensations. The unity is in the wiggle. To really feel the cork as a unified thing, you need to wiggle it, and wiggling it gives a compelling feeling of its unity and its springy middle. The cork participates in this wiggling: without the cork you could not quite move your fingers in the same way. The anticipatory motions of your body also participate in this wiggle: if you did not reach for the cork so as to anticipate wiggling it between finger and thumb, you might not be able to wiggle it, you might, for example, be restricted to rolling it. The perceived *sens* of the cork's unity is neither in the world nor in the body, but in their crossing, in a specific form of moving interplay. Different movements give different sorts of *sens*: if you wiggle the cork, you feel its unity as manifest in stiff springiness; if you roll it back and forth, you feel its unity as manifest in solid lightweight cylindricality. Further, to feel separate tactile sensations you have to immobilize your fingers and touch the cork as lightly as possible; in experience itself independent sensations are derivative of perception, not the other way around. This holds of sensations of your body as well: it is only when you immobilize your fingers that you can feel fingers as independent feelers; as soon as you wiggle the cork it is very hard to attend to disjoint sensations in the body. The cork-body wiggle—living body-world movement—compels a *sens* of the unity of the cork and of your hand, a unity that moreover crosses cork and hand in the movement that gives rise to this compelling *sens*.

Psychological studies by Katz and Klatzky and Lederman confirm that tactile properties of objects are correlative to ways of exploring them, and they also show that our explorations anticipate the tactile properties we expect or wish to feel. We reach out in different ways to feel sponginess, smoothness, etc. Developmental psychologists Bushnell and Boudreau have shown that these anticipatory explorations are present in young infants (Katz 1989; Klatzky and Lederman 1985, 1987, 1999; Lederman and Klatzky 1987; Bushnell and Boudreau 1993).

This observation approaches Merleau-Ponty's point, discussed above, that external perception and perception of the body reflect one another, and that in perception the body is not a transparent object given in advance, an already specified matrix that organizes perception, but an existence whose unity is expressed only through living engagement with the world. But here we approach Merleau-Ponty's point through a focus on movement. Body and world discover one another's *sens* through movement that crosses the one over into the other.

MOVEMENT AND STYLES

A wiggle is a style of movement: it has a definite dynamic contour, it is different from a poke, a shake, a joggle, a swing, and so on. None of the movements I have named specifies a fixed sequence of component movements derivable from a recipe, anymore than the term *jazz* or the name of a jazz standard names a derivable sequence of musical notes. All sorts of actual movement sequences count as a wiggle. While there is no recipe, there is nonetheless something definitive of a wiggle. More, what is definitive of a wiggle is not just in the wiggler, but in the wiggled: wiggling is not really appropriate to a wine bottle, the wiggle of a glass would have a different amplitude and frequency than the wiggle of a cork, and you just cannot wiggle a house.

The vague identity of the wiggle is central to the concept of *style*. How do I know that this music, this painting, this movement is in a given style, or that so and so has a particular style of walking? The usual answer is: I know it when I see it; the style is distinctive when I experience it, even if I cannot spell out a complete recipe. A style is an open-ended yet coherent and perceptually compelling pattern of something. But the pattern of wiggling is only compellingly apparent when it crosses bodies and things in particular instances of wiggling; here too the wiggle style is like style in painting or in jazz, where the style, the compelling pattern, is only manifest in crossing over into things patterned. Styles do not exist in abstraction from stylized activities.

We are here concerned with styles of movement, and these involve a sort of resonance in the crossing of body and world. One style of resonance is suited to exploring corks, another to exploring glasses; one style of resonance is suited to feeling the springiness of a cork, another to feeling its cylindricality. These styles are necessary to perceiving the world. Rather than synthesizing an array of sensations, perception is a matter of resonant styles of movement that first bring to light phenomena that compellingly fall together: the cork falls together in hand as a compelling unified and springy thing when we resonate with it in wiggling it.

But styles of resonance weave into an ensemble of styles. Wiggling a cork is not a movement that happens independent of other movements, it goes together with walking, reaching, moving about, and so on, with an overall way of movingly perceiving the world.

I contend that the term *body schema* refers to the ensemble of the body's styles of movement. We should thus 'locate' the body schema within movement itself, not in the body itself, nor in its neurology, nor in the world, but in movement that crosses the two—movement that is habitual, that styles itself.

The Double Marble, Habit, and Anticipation

Style depends on habit and anticipation. This can be shown through a discussion of the double marble phenomenon, which also ties us back to Merleau-Ponty's own discussion of the body schema and perception.

Aristotle had long ago noted that when touching a marble with crossed fingers, one might feel two marbles. As the psychologist Fabrizio Benedetti insightfully remarks, it is just as puzzling why we normally feel one marble through two fingers, given that the fingers touch two different surfaces. Indeed, we can sometimes feel two disjoint surfaces, as the cork experiment shows. Why should separate sensations on the fingers be experienced as sensations of one thing, and why should crossing the fingers make a difference to our experience of tactile unity?[7]

In the context of inferential accounts the illusion of the double marble thus provokes the traditional question as to how we put multiple tactile sensations together. The inferential account amounts to the claim that we have a model of where finger surfaces should be relative to one another. This gives us a way of inferring from an array of finger pressures to conclusions about the world. We need such a model, otherwise we would not know where our limbs are or how to combine sensory data from them. The latter point is what led Head and Holmes to the concept of the body schema in the first place, a schema that would representationally model or measure our body, its posture, and our postural relation to the world.

When our fingers are crossed and displaced from their usual relative locations, the inference based on this representational body schema goes awry. The pressures produced when crossed fingers probe a marble are the pressures that would be produced when uncrossed fingers touch two separate marbles pressed on the outer edges of the fingers. So we experience two separate marbles. But Merleau-Ponty cites an empirical result by Tastevin, also taken up and varied by Benedetti, that shows a curious inversion of sensations when the experiment is conducted using a teardrop-shaped object: the pointy end pressing into the middle finger is felt in the index finger, and vice versa. This result leads Merleau-Ponty to conclude that the illusion is due not to a simple spatial displacement of fingers, but to a disturbance of the exploratory possibilities of the fingers.

Like the cork-wiggle, when we roll a marble between two fingers, it is movement that gives an experience of a single marble. When the fingers are crossed, they lose their grip on the world and correlatively lose their marbles. But our bodily approach to things still anticipates this grip, hence the curious inversion, as if ghostly habit fingers that can still grip are at work beneath actual fingers. Merleau-Ponty would also point out that we experience something fishy in the case of the double marbles, that the marbles do not quite feel real. Again, this would confirm that the unified marble is correlative to the firm grip anticipated in our habitual exploratory movements, not to an inference. "[I]t is literally one and the same thing to perceive one single marble, and to use two fingers as one single organ." (PP 237/205)

As I studied this illusion, I became adept at manipulating things with my fingers crossed, and then the illusion vanished. But after a session of crossed-finger marble manipulation, the marble would double when I touched it with *uncrossed* fingers, and the keys that I reached for on my computer keyboard seemed to twist around oddly in space, although both phenomena dissipated after a while, a process speeded up by manipulating activity. *Habit and anticipation are crucial to the phenomenon*. The linkage between anticipation, exploration, and perception is also confirmed by the results of Klatzky and Lederman, and Bushnell and Boudreau, cited above, and by other results of Benedetti.[8]

These phenomena emphasize that what matters to perception is not the mere position of body parts in movement, but the overall dynamic resonance between body and world over the course of movement—movement is not to be decomposed into component positions, but has a melodic character that stretches over time.[9] The styles that, as an ensemble, constitute a moving schema of perception are thus to be understood in terms of habit and anticipation: to give an account of the double marble in terms of movement, we cannot just be looking at what the body is doing here and now, we must think about that movement in terms of habitual ways of moving the body and engaging the world. Styles are not patterns of mere material movement in the present, but habitual patterns of anticipated body-world movements that not only cross the body with the world, but cross the body with its past and future, a point we return to below.

VISION AND MOVEMENT

Vision also depends on a moving schema of perception, a way of looking. On first glance, it is not surprising that we fail to notice this about vision, since vision is the distance sense *par excellence*, it is quite insular from its object. Whereas it is clear that the cork moves our fingers, vision seems to be a passive way of receiving light into the body, rather than a way of moving influenced by what we see. To put it another way, touch obviously involves movement that crosses back and forth across body and world; this is not so obvious in the case of vision. But Gibson shows how vision depends on movement, and Merleau-Ponty shows the way that seeing depends on looking, and draws a link between movement in the case of the double marble and the case of binocular vision. The point that vision involves body-world movement is important for subsequent chapters, and emphasizes the importance of habit.

As mentioned above, Benedetti insightfully notes that when it comes to the problem of the double marble, we might as well ask why we normally feel one marble with two fingers. That question is parallel in structure to the notorious question of how we see one thing with two eyes, and in fact Benedetti coins the term *tactile diplopia* to describe the doubling of tactile objects, on the model of *diplopia,* which is the technical term for the visual doubling of objects. How is it that I see one coffee cup, one sheet of paper, and so on, with two eyes?

Merleau-Ponty's answer returns us to some points made in the introduction to this book. If seeing a unified thing amounts to an inferential process based on matching of binocular retinal images, there is a problem. The inference would already require some assumptions about shapes of things in the world, or at the very least the premise that the two images are different images of *one* thing; but if we are already assuming that we are seeing one thing, why the need for an inference that duplicates its own premises? And even if we do not explicitly know or assume that the images are of one thing, this sort of inferential process can work only if the two visual fields overlap; for example, one and the same cup must be projected on both my left and right retinas. But as J. J. Gibson points out, horses and chickens do not have overlapping visual fields, yet we would not imagine that a horse or a chicken facing a barn sees two barns (Gibson 1979). So an inference from overlapped binocular content is not even *necessary* for the experience of a unified world.

Further, we can use bifocals, trifocals, rear-view mirrors or multiple television monitors to view a situation, thus integrating multiple views into one visual world. It is as if our habits of seeing can keep on integrating new 'functional retinas' into a view that nonetheless remains unified. Overlapping content of binocular images is not necessary and is not sufficient (in and of itself) to specify the unity of the visual world; and given the plasticity of vision, the fact that habits can integrate more and more 'windows on the world,' it seems misguided to stake an account of vision on the number of retinas or the overlap of the visual field. What is at stake in vision is not the optical reconstruction of the surround, but a way of inhabiting a world at a distance.

Points of this sort lead Merleau-Ponty to some marvelously insightful conclusions about vision. He writes that "the sight of one single object is not a simple outcome of focusing the eyes, that it is anticipated in the very act of focusing, or that as has been stated, the focusing of the gaze is a 'prospective activity'." It is necessary to look in order to see, a point that is becoming more and more apparent in recent studies of vision, for example in Churchland, Ramachandran, and Sejnowski's "Critique of Pure Vision," in which they argue that vision is inherently interactive and prospective. And this prospectivity, according to Merleau-Ponty, is a matter of bodily intentionality.[10] "We pass from double vision to the single object, not through an inspection of the mind, but when two eyes cease to function each on its own account and are used as a single organ by one single gaze."

The parallel between Merleau-Ponty's claims about vision and his claims about touch are obvious: in both cases the unity of the thing and the unity of the organ are replies to one another, embedded in the crossing of one's body and the world. (In drawing this parallel we must not, however, forget Merleau-Ponty's case against Descartes's conflation of vision and touch.) And this unity is due to the "prelogical unity of the body schema,"[11] a schema that, as I am urging, we should locate in styles of movement that cross body and world: what Merleau-Ponty calls the prelogical unity of the body schema does not rest in the body only, for things are participant in drawing the eyes together. A body raised apart from things would not know how to look at them, a claim confirmed by various experiments (for example, Held and Hein 1963).

The point that vision depends on styles of movement, and that things themselves teach us how to look at them so as to see them is easy to notice once we have twigged to the fact that the eyes are not (as traditional accounts often imply) passive receptors of the outside world. To see unified things like cups is to be drawn into a certain style of looking, and to be drawn along with things as they move about. In cases of confusing situations it may take a while before the right style of looking clicks into place. But usually one's style of looking is so pervasively defined by one's inherent patterns of eye movement, and one's eyes so strongly drawn to things, that one's style communicates an unshakable unity to the world.

THE MOVING SCHEMA OF PERCEPTION

Bodily movement inherently crosses body and world, and styles of this movement are at the core of perception. To feel one marble, to see one thing, to feel or see the properties of a thing, is to engage in a particular style of moving with things, even of looking 'with' things. The concept of the body schema, as we find it in Merleau-Ponty's philosophy, is a way of marking out the ensemble of all these styles as central to perception. But we would be better off, conceptually speaking, if we retained our focus on stylings that arise within movement, a focus that is deepened when we see how these stylings arise within habit. Hence I will speak of the moving schema of perception, a schema that arises in the crossing of body and world, rather than a schema that is of the body as such.

The claim that the *sens* of perception emerges in a moving schema has the radical implications demanded in the introduction. There is no raw data on the far side of perception; sensation in the traditional sense does not figure in perception. We *sculpt* perception from the given in the way that a sculptor sculpts a statue from the stone. To encounter what is given we must already have crossed over into a moving encounter with it, and thus we must already have shaped what it is for us. That initial shaping, which is the condition of being in the world, already vaguely outlines what we can perceive, soliciting further stylized exploratory movements that develop this anticipated outline. That perception is more like sculpting than a synthesizing reconstruction of a ready-made world is, for example, shown by the familiar phenomenon of not perceiving what is in fact there, or being unable to perceive it.[12]

Given that perception emerges in a moving schema that crosses body and world, when I look at my coffee cup, the problem is not, as the tradition would have it, why I see one thing with two eyes. The problem is noticing that I look with two eyes, prying my eyes away from their lock on things, pulling them from the lock that things have on my eyes, prying myself from being crossed over into the world so that I can be responsible to the world and to my way of seeing. When I am looking at the Müller-Lyer's illusion, the thing that I am looking at pulls apart my vision, and thus shows me something about my vision: I see my way of looking reflected in the thing. But everyday things hide this reflection of my look; I see the coffee cup, rather than seeing how I look at the coffee cup. To see how I look at things, to see things as looked at by me, to see how I thus shape their look, to see my impact on the things that I look at—this is the task of the artist and also of the philosopher. If I am to make a good drawing of my coffee cup, I cannot just see how *it* looks, but must see how it looks *to me*. I must see my looking appearing in the thing seen, so that I can draw another's look into my way of looking and seeing; and it is by trying to draw another into my looking, by trying to look with my own eyes as if with the eyes of another, that I become responsible to my own looking.

With these points about movement and perception in the crossing of body and world, we begin approaching the ethical within depth. If I am to grasp how depth looks to me, I must grasp how my looking, my way of crossing into the world, impacts upon the depths that I see. This is why it is important to note how vision and perception depend on movement: we notice the ethical in depth when we notice that our movement crosses over into what we perceive in depth, that things in depth reflect our responsibility for our perception of them. As opposed to illusions, everyday things may hide the reflection of my look—although artists, as Merleau-Ponty notes, often speak of things looking at them. "The object stares back," as James Elkins puts it in a book of that title. But other people, as Sartre shows, do not hide the reflection of my look; they hold me responsible for my look; they explicitly stare back. Other people thus expose the illusion of our neutrality, expose the illusion that depth is a neutral container upon which we are mere onlookers. They make us see our responsibility for our way of seeing them in depth.

On the other hand, if, as the next section and chapters show, our movement arises in habit and thence in our social development, then the way people look in depth reflects, to some degree, their responsibility for our way of looking at them.

HABIT, LABILITY, AND MEANING IN THE MOVING SCHEMA OF PERCEPTION

DYNAMIC SYSTEMS THEORY ON THE SCHEMA IN MOVEMENT

What has been called the body schema is inseparable from movement. This point is supported by Turvey and Carello, psychologists who have done extraordinary work giving an account of bodily movement and touch within the framework of dynamic systems theory. Critical engagement with their results (and related work) will deepen the points made so far about habit and lead us to the role of meaning in the moving schema of perception.

In a study of what Gibson called dynamic touch, cases where movement of the limbs is intrinsic to what is felt by touch, Turvey and Carello draw attention to some experiments by Lackner and Taublieb and Craske. In these experiments, tendons or muscles of the experimental subject are vibrated; this induces "errors" in perceived limb position, and in some cases the perceived position was "impossible" (Turvey and Carello 1995, 440–41). Turvey and Carello note that this result poses a problem to the traditional claim that the body schema is a representation of limb positions. We could put the problem the following way: Why would a representational schema of limb position encompass representations of *impossible* limb positions, and why would rapid vibratory movement of parts of the body encode limb positions? After all, these vibrations did not appear in nature until we invented electric massagers and the like, so why would they have any particular import in representing limb positions?

Their own investigations and experiments lead Turvey and Carello to conclude that activities such as wielding a rod determine a time-dependent tissue deformation pattern in the arm and wrist that is "(1) constrained by the rigid arm-plus-rod dynamics and (2) expressed in the intrinsic co-ordinate system defined by the muscles and tendons of the forearm." The information in this deformation pattern is available in the brain, and movement of one's own body as well as artificially induced vibrations would yield such deformation patterns (Turvey and Carello 1995, 478). Recently they have argued that perceived limb length and orientation likely refer to inertial properties of the limbs as we move them about (Carello and Turvey 2000). There is no need to conceive the body schema as a schema for representing limb positions and measurements in some sort of abstract coordinate system (for example, a Cartesian or polar coordinate system) superimposed on the body. Information about limb position is right there in an "intrinsic coordinate system" specified by the very stuff of the body. Representational-inferential accounts of the body schema run into the problem that the schema has slots for impossible values (in which case just what is it representing?), and that novel body-world interactions such as vibrations yield experiences of strange or impossible bodily positions. But there is no such problem if, as Turvey and Carello argue, the schema is embedded in body-world movement itself, in the way that limbs move and muscles and tendons deform. There is not a central encoded representation of the body. The body schema, according to Turvey and Carello, is *in body-world movement itself*.

This echoes Rodney Brooks's argument, mentioned in the introduction, that there is no need for a robot to model the environment, the environment is its own model. Turvey and Carello have a complementary insight: there is no need to model the body, we can conceive the body as its own 'model' once we realize that the body 'represents' its own position not in Cartesian co-ordinates, but in the flesh.

In showing that body-world movement itself specifies a schema, dynamic systems theory concurs with and strengthens the point that the body schema is in movement. But divergences arise when we notice how the schema depends not merely on movement of the body at this moment, but on movement of a habitual body, a body stretched over time via anticipation.

THE MOVING SCHEMA OF PERCEPTION IS A HABITUAL SCHEMA

For the purposes of this discussion, I work with the following rough definition of habit: a habit is a style of movement not fully responsive to the world at present, that is shaped by a past history of movement; in some cases we would have to conceive a habit as a movement directed toward a future world that may not even be present. People have certain ways of walking and moving about; if you live with them long enough, you can tell who has come into the house just by their style of opening the door and walking up the stairs. This way of moving is not composed in the present, it is a condensation of a long history of moving about, it is a past acting in present bodily movement, it is a habit. Misplaced habits show that this past acting in present bodily motion is directed toward a future that does not belong to the present world: on my first night in the hotel, I bump into the wall because, in my grogginess, I am walking as if I were in my house, my steps are directed toward a doorway that will be there in my house, but is not present in the hotel.

Let us return to the case of binocular vision for a moment. The traditional question about binocular vision is how we see one thing with two eyes. The claim that this unity is inferred from the binocular disparity of the images begs the question, because it assumes the unity of the thing seen. A variant of this claim is that the inference amounts to a matching of symmetrical points on the retinas. The variant claim would not have to directly assume the unity of the thing seen, because the unity is, so to speak, built into the very anatomy of the eyes. (The unity would, however, have to be assumed if we asked why this matching mechanism evolved.)

But Richard Rojcewicz, in his discussion of depth perception as a motivated phenomenon, argues that the matching could not be specified anatomically, since in cases where one eye drifts from its fixation point (a condition called strabismus), a new, *functionally* defined relation between points on the retina comes into play (Rojcewicz 1984, 41). To this we would have to add the following: Heaton observes that when double vision occurs in the case of paralysis of an eye, the seer initially sees two images that both appear unreal, but later "one [image] appears solid and articulated in the visual world while the other, which usually corresponds to the paralysed eye,
· looks 'unreal' and ghost-like" (Heaton 1968, 241). Vision of unified objects is disturbed but then resumes: (1) when the images on the retina are inverted by prisms; (2) when a detached retina is reattached ninety degrees from its original position; (3) when the optical distance between the eyes is effectively increased through the use of prisms; (4) when the visual field of each eye is left-right reversed through the use of prisms; (5) when the size and shape of objects at a given distance is distorted by the use of goggles underwater.[13] When bifocals, trifocals, mirrors, or monitors divide the visual field into multiple optical regions, we can still see one complex unified world, even though the number of "retinas" has in effect been multiplied beyond the usual two. Give one's moving eyes almost anything, and one learns to look so as to see a unified world. The unity is not in the anatomy of the eyes, but in the moving schema of looking, which is plastic and habitual.

Two interrelated conclusions follow:

(A) The unity of the seen has a *sens* reflective of one's bodily style of looking at the world. When an eye is paralyzed, one may see a real, unified thing with one's active eye and a ghostly image with the paralyzed eye. When cross-eyed, one sees two oddly doubled images of one unified thing. Through inverting lenses, as Stratton's observations show, one sees a unified world that seems oddly related to one's body (Stratton 1896, 1897). So the experienced unity is not a simple matter of fusing two flat images into a reconstruction of one physical object; it cannot be conceived on a geometrical, physical, or optical model. What room is there in the realm of geometrical or optical models, in the realm of pure subjectivity or pure objectivity, for a distinction between "real," "ghostly" or "odd" images, or for a visual unity in which two or more images are seen and yet experienced as images of one thing?

(B) One's body has a *sens* reflective of different styles of looking at things. Upon getting a new pair of glasses, I feel as though I am sinking into the steps and pavement outside the optometrist's office and feel that my body is the "wrong" size. When living with lenses that optically invert the world, Stratton feels as if his head is buried into his shoulders "almost up to [his] ears," and when eating, that his mouth is on the wrong side of his eyes (Stratton 1897, 467–468). When cross-eyed, my body feels oddly ghostly or dislocated. These disturbances of *sens* do not fit into any objective model of bodily dimensions and variations: my body has not quantitatively shrunk by N units, it is the "wrong" size, and the wrongness inseparably reflects the experience of sinking into the pavement with rubbery legs while buildings bulge around me; and it would be odd to think that the distance between the head and shoulders or between the mouth and eyes is represented by a variable that can go into negative values. The disturbances are not objective, but neither are they purely subjective: they are not in our (cognitive) control, they go away as we move about in the world and habituate to our style of engagement with the world.

Overall, this suggests that the *sens* of the unity of the visual world and the *sens* of one's body are meaningful, correlative, labile, and habitual, that this *sens* is tied to one's habitual style of looking at the world, and is irreducible to purely subjective or purely objective terms. Styles of looking lag behind changes to our body and its prostheses: it takes a while to learn how to see the world with new glasses. This is a characteristic of labile habit. The unity of things could never be inferred, yet it is clearly anticipated by our body, and we learn to look so as to see a unified world, through a range of disturbances. This too is characteristic of habit: habits reestablish themselves, and to have a habit is to have a way of moving that is not responsive to the world as it actually is at this moment; a habit precisely anticipates the world to which we are habituated. I get into the right-hand drive car and I reach the wrong way for everything, because I am not reaching for parts of a material car at present, I am engaged in the sorts of movements that anticipate a car to be driven, and the car to be driven, to which I am habituated, is a left-hand drive car.

As Merleau-Ponty puts it:

> Psychologists often say that the body schema is *dynamic*. Brought down to a precise sense, this term means that my body appears to me as an attitude directed toward a certain existing or possible task. (*PP* 116/100; note that Smith's translation mistranslates "*schéma corporel*" as "body image.")

The moving schema of perception is inherently dynamic; it involves movement and it moves, dynamically changes. What this means is that it is really a network of habitual attitudes directed toward existing or possible tasks.

The moving schema of perception is a *habitual* style of moving the body.

The Labile Meaning of the Habitual, Moving Body

The points mentioned above about lability and meaning are deepened by returning to Lackner, Taublieb, and Craske's experiments on the effect of vibrations on perception of limb position.

Recall that in general such vibration induces a feeling of the limb moving from its actual position. Lackner and Taublieb (1984) contrived an ingenious experiment in which the subject's right biceps was rapidly vibrated with a mechanical device, and in which the subject was asked to visually fixate on her/his finger when the entire arm was hidden from the subject, when only the index finger was visible, or visually fixate on the hand with only the hand visible, in rooms that were lit or dark (they used glow-in-the-dark paint to make fingers and hands visible in the dark). In lit situations, subjects reported a disparity between the felt location of their visible hand or finger and the rest of their arm (which was hidden), to the extent that they felt their arm moving downward further than their hand or finger, that is, *separating* from the hand or finger, yet being *continuous* with it nonetheless, which is a "physically impossible" dissociation of the perceived body. In the dark, subjects reported that they "literally see their finger or hand move in keeping with the apparent extension [of the forearm]. This is true even though eye movement recordings show that the subjects are actually maintaining steady fixation of their stationary hand." Subjects also reported sensations of having multiple limbs; this was also reported by Craske (1977). In another of Craske's experiments, vibrations were applied in such a way as to induce in subjects the experience of their limbs being extended beyond normal range; subjects reported that "'the arm is being broken,' 'it is being bent backwards,' 'my hand is going through my shoulder,' and 'it cannot be where it feels.'" Moreover, "Although no pain is involved in the procedure, subjects displayed the overt signs which often accompany pain, such as writhing, sweating, and gasping."

Craske and Lackner and Taublieb give a more or less inferential account of these results. They claim the experience is due to the suppression of the physical movement of limbs that *would* arise from the muscle contractions artificially induced by outside vibrations. But subjects do not experience the effects of the vibration as the mere addition of component movements and distances that represent the status of a physical system, as if a variable representing limb position were running off the end of a scale. The body experienced in this experiment has characteristics that do not belong to the physiological body: (A) the arm and hand can move apart from one another yet still remain an arm; (B) the arm seen can move without any visual movement across the retina; (C) limbs can double; (D) subjects can experience pain and react to pain when the perceived body is violated, even if pain sensors are not directly affected (one would have to question Craske's claim that "no pain is involved").

Neither is the experienced body some sort of subjective image or idea, since it is affected by vibrations, and it would be hard to figure out why such an intense feeling of pain would couple with a mere image or idea of the limb being extended beyond normal range. The experienced arm does not fit into either a physical/objective or ideal/subjective paradigm, rather subjective and objective poles of description are blended in a determinate manner. Also, it should be noted that the experience varies across individuals, so it is not predicted by any general constant relation between inputs and outputs. [14]

The phenomenological claim would be that the relation between what happens to the body and what is experienced has something to do with a *meaning* of the lived body. The arm appears as a meaningful arm, as manifesting the meaning of a corporeal organ of grasping, despite disturbances of the body, and the attributes of this meaningful organ are not identical with the attributes of the organic body, since it can do things that no organic arm could do, that is, double, stretch, move in nonvisible ways. The meaning of the body is habitual and crosses over into the world and into my past and future: I expect the wheel and controls of a car to work in a certain way in my attempts to drive, to give me a certain possibility of a moving feel for the road; similarly, I expect to get a certain possibility of grasping when I try to reach. In the phenomenon of the phantom limb, Merleau-Ponty notices that the patient is expecting the possibility afforded by the limb to still be there, and maintains that expectation, so the limb that counts as fulfilling this expectation is not governed by the rules of organic limbs, but by habitual anticipations of the patient, above all an anticipation of a meaningful way of grasping the world, anticipations the fulfilment of which is modified by what has happened to the body. [15]

An experiment by Roll, Roll, and Velay (1991) enforces the point that the experienced arm has to do with habits and anticipations that cross over into the world. Roll, Roll, and Velay's experiment seems to present a case of a very complex illusion, which was induced when muscles of the hand were vibrated. When the hand was free, it felt as if the hand were extended further then it really was. When subjects leaned against a wall with the arm at shoulder height and the hand pointing forward, the subject felt the whole body as leaning forward; when the position of the hand was reversed so that it pointed backward, the subject felt the whole body as leaning backward. In both cases the subject's body was, objectively speaking, upright, not leaning. Roll, Roll, and Velay are struck by the fact that a simple "change of the orientation of the subject's hand on the wall (from fingers forward to fingers backward) sufficed to reverse the whole-body illusion from forward to backward." But Merleau-Ponty's and Carello and Turvey's analyses of illusions, discussed in the introduction, caution us against interpreting this experiment as an illusion, an error of perception.

Merleau-Ponty dissuades us from a metrical comparison of the felt orientation of the everyday body and the felt orientation of the vibrated

body in this unusual position, just as he dissuades us from metrical comparison of the two lines in the Müller-Lyer's illusion. What, then, does felt
orientation refer to? In his analysis of an experiment by Wertheimer, in
which the subject is presented with a room that is visually tilted forty-five
degrees from the vertical, Merleau-Ponty argues that "my body is wherever
there is something to be done," and it is when the subject can take hold of
the tilted room as a "possible habitat" that the room rights itself visually;
"[t]he maximum sharpness of perception and action" that is afforded by the
righted room "points clearly to a perceptual *ground*, a basis of my life, a
general milieu for the coexistence of my body and the world" (*PP* 290/250,
emphasis Merleau-Ponty's). Merleau-Ponty suggests that felt orientation correlates with possible habitat, with habitual modes of engagement with the
world, not to some measure in a ready-made world external to the crossing
of one's body and the world, a suggestion about orientation supported by
observations of Skylab astronauts, which I discuss in chapter five.

Roll, Roll, and Velay are puzzled by the fact that a simple "change of
the orientation of the subject's hand on the wall (from fingers forward to
fingers backward) sufficed to reverse the whole-body illusion from forward to
backward," and we can see why, if we construe hand orientation and whole-
body orientation as independent measures in a system for representing the
body. Why would the two be connected? However, if we construe this as a
holistic phenomenon of a moving, habitual schema of perception that crosses
over into the world, the connection becomes apparent. We reach out in
habitual ways to steady ourselves against vertical support surfaces; when we
do so, the direction of our hand, forward or back, affords different possibilities of support; the hand-forward position affords leaning forward and prevention of falling forward, and conversely with the hand-backward position;
the hand-forward position does not keep you from slipping backward. Hand
positions anticipate habitual possibilities of movement and prevention of
movement; they are not positions of the body merely, but already anticipate
their crossing into the world in which the body moves.

What the vibration seems to do is bring those anticipations into play
in a new way. The vibrations do not directly cause the phenomenon; they
modify the crossing of the body and world, thereby modifying the way the
habitual, moving schema plays out in actual activity, thereby modifying the
sens of this perceptual situation. With respect to the feeling of limb position
and bodily orientation, the vibrated body, because of its different way of
crossing with the world, is a different body from the nonvibrated body, in the
way that one arrow in the Müller-Lyer's figure is different from the other with
respect to visual expanse, or in the way that the apple on the moon is
different from the apple on the earth with respect to felt weight.

This is the phenomenological claim. What would Carello and Turvey
say? Earlier I discussed their criticism of inferential/representational accounts
of the body schema, and their claim that the body schema amounts to

information available to us in the body. I now simplify their point and push it a bit beyond the strict confines of their own claims, but the real issue is this. When asked what the experienced arm or body in the experiments discussed above refers to, I think that dynamic systems theorists would say: information in the body, specified by the overall dynamic interaction of the vibrating body and the environment. This, I think, is not enough, for we would have to ask why this information is experienced as a tilting forward or back of the whole body, as a doubling or impossible stretching of the arm, as a pain that supposedly has no physiological basis, and so on. I can imagine dynamic systems theory giving a very powerful account of how experienced limb position refers to dynamic factors specified by body-world interactions; indeed, dynamic systems theory does this. But I cannot imagine it being able to *predict* that unusual body-world interactions would be experienced as doublings, impossible limb positions, as painful, and so on, especially when these experiences vary across individuals, and if it cannot predict, then there is a serious question as to whether it can give a scientific explanation of the phenomenon. Such explanation bears upon a relation between ourselves and the world that seems to be beyond the proper compass of scientific explanation, so far as scientific explanation begins by already having presumed a basis in a certain relation to the world.

Further, Turvey and Carello suggest that the body schema be understood in terms of time-dependent nondimensional deformations within the tissue of the body itself, a "function of stimulation occurring at that moment" (Turvey and Carello 1995, 441). But it would seem that individual and meaningful variations would depend on habit and an anticipatory temporality that is not specified in the moment.

The above amounts to yet another demonstration that the perceiving body is a lived body, a body that is neither subject nor object, but an inherently meaningful and fleshy mix of the two, a body inherently mixed up with the world in which it lives. Merleau-Ponty's conceptual framework, and all of the above analyses, keep returning us to a middle region between the subjective and the objective, the ideal and the physical, the body and the world. Dillon's terms "the phenomenal world" and "phenomenal," which he develops in his analysis of the implicit ontology of the *Phenomenology of Perception*, are helpful in designating this middle region. The phenomenal world designates the world as a domain of inherently meaningful appearances, the world in which we live.

The word *phenomenal* used on its own designates the meaning characteristic of the phenomenal world. Grammatically, to say that something is phenomenal is (in the usage that follows) much like saying it is meaningful. And just as we can speak of *"the* meaningful," we can speak of *"the* phenomenal." Our philosophical and scientific traditions would lead us to believe that meaning is in the head or mind, that it is subjective. The concept of the phenomenal challenges this claim, for the meaning of the phenomenal is not in the head, it is in what appears. But this does not mean that meaning is in the purely objective sphere. The objective sphere, as we have seen, is incommensurate with the phenomenal. In Lackner and Taublieb's experiment, the experienced arm is ontologically incommensurate with either the objective or the subjective; it is neither an artifact of the subject nor an organically defined arm. It is a meaningful appearance, it is phenomenal.

Another way to put this is to say that the experienced arm is "nonontonomic," it does not obey the laws (*nomos*) of things (*ta onta*). This coinage is so ugly and bereft of euphony that I shall use it only occasionally, to frighten us into recalling that the phenomenal body and phenomenal world are not rooted in the laws of the objective or subjective world, but in meaning and habitual anticipations.

CONCLUSION: THE PROBLEM OF *SENS*

What we have discovered so far is that perception arises in the crossing of body and world, that this crossing involves movement, that this movement is habitual and anticipatory, is thus styled and constitutes a moving schema of perception. This adds to existing accounts by emphasizing that the body schema is not some sort of system specified in advance of movement, but is constituted in movement itself: a schema in movement that gives a *sens* to perception. But so far our discovery is almost entirely descriptive in character. It leaves unanswered the question of how this schema constitutes itself, what this schema really is, and where *sens* comes from. In the next chapters I show that these questions can be answered if we take the habitual aspect of the moving schema of perception seriously, and attend to the moving schema of perception as a developmental and expressive phenomenon.

CHAPTER 2

DEVELOPING THE MOVING BODY

IMAGINE WATCHING A BABY playing on its back. It kicks its two legs, together, and swings its two arms, together, toward its midriff. Then it throws its legs and arms back straight and repeats the movement. The infant's movement is symmetrical, with a one-beat rhythm: two arms move as one and two legs move as one, and arms and legs are joined together in an overall movement of the body as a whole. Contrast this with the same child later on, when she is walking. Walking involves a continual two-phase rhythm of asymmetry, first one leg is out front, and then the other, and legs and arms move in opposite directions. More, movements do not merely repeat in a symmetrical cycle confined to one spot, but string together in a continuous thread of conduct that moves about in the world. Compared to someone who walks, the infant clearly has a very different overall style of moving, and correlatively a different perceptual relation to the world.

The shift from kicking to walking amounts to the development of the moving schema of perception, which is to say a co-development of ways of moving and of perceiving. How are we to account for this development? The fact that the moving schema develops only emphasizes its dynamic character; to account for its development we must first give an account of it as dynamic. That is the first task of this chapter, and it requires reflection on the conceptual and methodological issues that attach to studying a schema that is *in* movement and is dynamic: a schema that is itself moving, changing, and that is manifest nowhere else but in movement, that is not a possession of the subject but crosses body and world. It will turn out that such an account requires a schema that is inherently developmental. Overall, this chapter develops an account of the moving schema of perception through an account of the developmental body, and vice versa.

THE MOVING SCHEMA OF PERCEPTION:
PROBLEMS AND METHODS

STRUCTURE-IN-MOVEMENT: A RENEWAL OF THE PROBLEM OF STRUCTURE

Traditional accounts root perception in the a priori or the a posteriori, in transcendental or empirical systems or faculties established in advance of acts of perception. This leads to the problems studied in the introduction. Merleau-Ponty's concept of the body schema is quite powerful in overcoming these problems, since it roots perception in an insuperable blend of the a priori and a posteriori, a 'faculty' that arises in an act that crosses body and world. But the solution names a new problem: just what *is* the body schema, this X that so nicely solves the problems of perception? If we cannot respond, we are pulling a rabbit out of a hat.

Unfortunately, the new problem is badly put. In its very wording, the problem "What is the body schema?" suggests we are seeking a fixed entity, some already established system, formula, or faculty called the body schema. But clearly any such fixed X would rip perception from the crossing of body and world, returning us to our problems. Against this tendency, chapter one argues that the body schema is really a *moving* schema of perception. It is implausible to think of such a moving schema as an independent entity and ask what it is, in the usual sense of that question. If we were seeking a 'schema' for the eye of the hurricane, we would not abstract it from stormy movement. Nonetheless, we would want an account of how such a 'schema' arises. So too with the moving schema of perception: how does it arise in movement that storms across body and world?

Gallagher (1995, 240) cautions against turning the body schema into a neurophysiological or cognitive system, and Sheets-Johnstone (1999, especially 261) cautions against rooting experience in any entity abstracted from bodily movement; she includes the body schema as one such entity. Merleau-Ponty himself argues that the body schema really names an attitudinal relation between the body and the world (*PP* 116/100). The problem is that it is tempting and easy to turn the schema of perception, the X that makes perception be perception, into an "it," an already constituted system of the body or mind, a possession of the subject. I did something like this in chapter one, in order to facilitate discussion. Indeed, the grammatical/conceptual framework of our language and thinking compel us into talking about X's that do something via linear causality. The task at hand is to resist this. We shall do this by conceiving the moving schema as an X that expresses underlying constraints in movement.

The problem here is really a variant of Merleau-Ponty's struggle with the concept of structure. In all of his philosophy, Merleau-Ponty wanted to conceive a living meaning embedded in being in the world. In his later philosophy, he did this by finding meaning nascent in the reversibility of being itself. But his first approach, in *The Structure of Behaviour*, was through structure. As Waldenfels puts it, summarizing Merleau-Ponty's position in *The Structure of Behaviour*:

> Structure and form belong to a middle dimension, they are neither 'things,' i.e. pure existents, complexions of externally connected data, nor 'ideas,' i.e. products of an intellectual synthesis. Rather, they are the result of a process of the self-organization of experiential, actional and linguistic fields, which is not governed by pre-existing principles . . . (Waldenfels 1981, 23)

Structure is a process or movement that manifests its own organizing pattern. As Dillon (1971, 1987, 1988), Gary Madison (1981), Bernhard Waldenfels (1981) and Theodore Geraets (1971) show, the problem of structure is continuous across Merleau-Ponty's thinking (also see Embree 1981) and is really, I suggest, the problem of locating meaning in being. The concept of the body schema in the *Phenomenology of Perception* amounts to an advance in the struggle, a new conceptual variant of structure.

Our task, given the emphasis on movement so far, for example, our discovery of a schema that appears within the body-cork wiggle, is to take the struggle further, getting rid of residual temptations to turn the moving schema into a thing, thoroughly thinking it in terms of movement. This is difficult, because as Bergson observes, we are geared to thinking in terms of solid things, not movement. I introduce the concept of structure-in-movement to help us focus on the difficulty. If we had to say what the moving schema is "made of," or what it is the organization of, we would have to say that it is "made of" movement and is the self-organization of movement that crosses body and world. Consider the eye of a hurricane or a traffic jam: each is a structure that appears within movement; each is composed out of (made up of) movements (of air or cars); and each is composed by (put together by) the interaction of the movements out of which it is composed. A traffic jam or hurricane eye is a structure that appears within movement, and is composed out of and composed by movement. The moving schema is such a structure-in-movement, and we were already roughly pointing to it as such when we described it as an ensemble of styles of movement. But in this chapter we are seeking a deeper conception.

In doing so we are pursuing meaning and *sens* as inseparable from moving, bodily being in the world. So the problem of structure-in-movement will turn out to be the problem of *sens*-in-movement, of meaning-in-life, of Heidegger's being-in-the-world or Heidegger's *Existenziale* conceived as rooted in movement. At this point we can break the problem in two: 1) giving an account of the moving schema as a structure arising in movement, an account that does not turn the moving schema into a thing or a passive production; 2) giving an account of structure-in-movement as comprehending things and giving rise to *sens*, that is, as the site of experience. The next chapter turns to the problem of *sens*. This chapter confines itself to the first part of the problem.

A central methodological and conceptual problem that haunts the following study of structure-in-movement is nicely captured by Bergson when he writes that we are inclined to a "logic of solids." Our practical involvement in the world gears us to put things before processes, solids before movements, and that practice seeps into our conceptual analyses.[1] We tend to decompose structure-in-movement into solid parts and an already constituted skeleton of laws that controls parts.

For example, we tend to decompose a traffic jam into vehicles and a prespecified skeleton of vehicular laws: traffic jams result from general laws applied to vehicular units. This misses the point that traffic jams likely would not form if people drove in a lawlike manner uniform in all contexts. Driver movement does not follow from a general, fixed law; rather, different rules of driving emerge in moving contexts that drivers collectively create. Experientially, this is quite palpable: there is a different way to drive in smooth flowing highway traffic versus a highway traffic jam; there are subtle differences between traffic jams; these differences do not arise from anything general, but from interaction in a given web of moving traffic. The traffic jam does not result from abstract laws; rather a multiplicity of movements form a moving structure that is the ongoing result of the very movements that are so structured. In technical terms, the traffic jam manifests a phase transition in traffic flow, rather than a series of causes that can be isolated from the flow (Daganzo, Cassidy and Bertini 1999; Kerner and Rehborn 1997; Kerner 1998). And yet we tend to put causal units before flow, to subsume laws and terms that appear only in movement to frameworks abstracted from movement. We have seen this in the case of dynamic systems theory, which identifies self-organizing movements of the body, but then tends to root this moving self-organization in an already constituted skeleton of laws.

The problem of structure-in-movement is of avoiding the logic of solids and conceiving structure as dynamic through and through. It is an important problem. In previous chapters, phenomenological analysis pressed us into thinking of labile perceptual phenomena as movement through and through. In passing we also saw that dynamic self-organization is crucial to dynamic systems theory. A brief survey of recent books in science and philosophy would show that movement, dynamism, self-organization, action, and agency are central concerns.[2] Merleau-Ponty's later philosophy can be taken as arguing that structure-in-movement, specifically flesh as an elemental entity that divides itself into body and world through a chiasmatic tension that animates it, is ontologically fundamental. And postmodern, poststructuralist philosophy makes a similar turn from things to movement so far as it conceives subjects and things as effects of power, rather than conceiving power as the effect of already constituted subjects and things. In each case what is being sought is a kind of agency, meaning, identity, or spontaneity in movement itself. It would be too much to say, yet it would not be untrue, that the problem of avoiding a logic of solids and of what I call structure-in-movement is central for current science and philosophy.

How are we to get past the logic of solids? How are we to conceive structure-in-movement? At this point conceptual and methodological issues intersect. Conceptually, we are trying to root spatial perception not in a dualism of subject and object or body and world, but in the crossing of body and world. We are well past any sort of ready-made world; everything is in movement. To study structure-in-movement we need a method for studying body and world as open to one another and as being in movement. I address this issue through a brief methodological exploration of science and phenomenology[3], and Bergson's method of intuition.

MOVING BEYOND SCIENCE

Traditional experimental science is not methodologically suited to our conceptual task. Experimental method aims at installing objects in already specified frameworks of experimental variation, treating objects as passive to interventions. Reductive explanation aims at explaining things in terms of the most general laws, which ends up meaning laws established in advance of the particular things being studied. These aims follow from science's ideal of objectivity, and ultimately lead science to conceive things in terms of a ready-made, objective cosmos, in terms of universal laws indifferent to things. This makes it difficult to keep sight of things as actively self-differentiating, as organizing themselves through movement.

The problem is especially acute in the case of living beings. As Merleau-Ponty or Goldstein (1995) might observe, science ends up studying a "preparation" rather than the organism as organizing itself. Indeed, historiographers of science show how practices of experimental preparation and framing have concrete effects on biological concepts, for example, in embryology.[4] But it would be wrong to think that working scientists are unaware of the problem. For example, Robert Full and Claire Farley (2000), who study animal locomotion, realize that "direct experimental perturbations pushed too far in search of significant difference" disrupt the "finely integrated system[s]" they are studying. So instead of designing frameworks of experimental variation and installing animals in them, Full and Farley look to evolution as generating significant differences, as in effect designing "natural experiments." By studying variations of leg movement across different sorts of creatures (for example, humans, dogs, lizards, cockroaches, and crabs), they gain insight into the way legs work. Nikolai Bernstein, whose work on kinesiology is foundational for dynamic systems theory, thinks it misguided and ludicrous to give an account of human movement by installing the body in experimental and conceptual frameworks suited to analysis of machines. Instead he develops techniques for studying the living, moving and working body (Bernstein 1967; Morris 2002a). These scientists gain insight by curtailing experimental intervention; in effect they let the body install itself in its own framework of variation.

Nonetheless, when it comes to the body, science is riven by a tension. On the theoretical side, it is inclined to step back and install the body in prespecified frameworks. On the empirical side, working scientists gain conceptual insights by noticing natural experiments, spontaneous or evolutionary variations generated by moving, living bodies. But then the tendency is to go back and fit the natural experiment into an already established framework, a tendency already noted in previous discussions of dynamic systems theory.

The tension can be put in terms of opened and closed systems. Science is theoretically inclined to pursue a closed, completed system, namely, the universe as a totality of laws and entities that would explain everything within it. In practice, science experiments with moving systems that are in some degree open to their surround, and this is emphatically the case in biology. The theoretical and experimental imperatives of science are methodologically at odds with the open, self-organizing movement of a body crossed with the world.[5]

Moving beyond the Philosophy of the Subject: Intuition and "The Turn of Experience"

Traditional philosophy of the subject tends in a direction opposite to science. Instead of appealing to a closed universe with fixed laws, it appeals to a closed subject, for example, the Cartesian or Kantian subject. Against this, Husserl's endless effort to rethink the transcendental method of Descartes and Kant drove him to a phenomenology that opened the subject to the world, first through the noetic-noematic bond of intentionality, manifest in the "I think" and the "I can," and then in the subject's relation to the life-world (see Husserl 1991, 1970). Husserl's opening is deepened in Heidegger's pursuit of being-in-the-world, in Sartre's criticism of the transcendence of the ego, in Merleau-Ponty's discovery of intentionality in movement and the "body subject." In short, phenomenology ends up trying to reinstall the thinker in the world. It is well known, though, that phenomenologists—and anti-phenomenologists—keep detecting various closures within phenomenology, a failure to get beyond the subject to something other upon which our being depends.

Indeed, in his posthumously published *The Visible and the Invisible*, in which he tries to dismantle the philosophy of subjectivity, Merleau-Ponty detects a problematic closure of consciousness in his earlier *Phenomenology of Perception*. Famously, he writes that the problems of that work are insoluble because they presume a distinction between consciousness and its object (Merleau-Ponty 1968, working note of July 1959). This is taken as a general criticism of phenomenology. Even if phenomenology opens itself to the sway of things, even if it advances past Descartes by reinstalling the thinker in the world, it still begins from the side of the thinker, and reports on its own procedure using the reflective language of a subject established in advance of its object. In the course of trying to get back to things themselves, phenomenology, according to this criticism, ends up presupposing subjectivity, closing it to the world and begging crucial questions.

It is not straightforward, however, that Merleau-Ponty is right in his criticism of his earlier phenomenology, or that the general criticism of phenomenology is right. For example, if we look from the outside at what Merleau-Ponty is *doing* in the *Phenomenology* (as opposed to looking at what he is saying, or what he, in looking back from the inside, thought he was doing), we find a thinker who is trying to install himself in the sway of phenomena in order to return to an encounter prior to the subject-object distinction. The *Phenomenology* is remarkable for giving up on the reflective practice of Husserlian variation. Reflective consciousness hands the reigns of variation to the phenomena themselves, by studying illusions, illness, and disruptions that speak for their own unique organization (this procedure echoes the scientist's turn to natural experiments). Rather than dismissing illusions and disruptions as errors, uninformative because they do not fit an already established framework or a decisive interest in truth as a particular relation between subject and object, Merleau-Ponty takes these phenomena seriously as variant configurations of experience (see *PP* 125/107)—and clearly we must understand these variations as being prior to a fixed subject-object distinction. If Husserl first elaborates his method of variation within a fixed subject-object distinction, Merleau-Ponty pursues variations that reconfigure and rise above that distinction. As he puts it, "reflection does not grasp its full significance unless it refers to the unreflective fund of experience which it presupposes" (*PP* 280/242). For Merleau-Ponty the traditional subject-object distinction begins to appear as an *empirical result* of being in the world, a *phenomenon*, rather than a presupposed beginning of all phenomenology.

Here we find an echo of Bergson's method of intuition. Bergson is a thinker intent on *not* begging the question of subjectivity. For him this means sinking into intuitions that rise above "that decisive *turn*, where, taking a bias in the direction of our utility, [experience] becomes properly *human* experience" (*MM* 184).[6] We must rise to a point prior to the subject-object distinction, which would also be prior to the reflexive framework in which traditional phenomenology describes its own method and results. Heidegger, in his turn away from a philosophy of subjectivity, also heads in this direction, and Heidegger is very often cited as the inspiration for Merleau-Ponty's project in *The Visible and the Invisible*. But as Renaud Barbaras shows, in a careful study of the chapter "Interrogation and Intuition," Bergson is also at play—Merleau-Ponty is trying to rise above the turn of experience without yet plunging into Bergson's unique tension between pure perception and pure memory (Barbaras 1998, chapter 2). (It should be added that a Bergsonian influence is unmistakable in the *Phenomenology*.[7])

In what follows I lean in Bergson's direction, seeking to reactivate a Bergsonian thread that I detect in the background of Merleau-Ponty's phenomenological philosophy. Bergson's methodological intuitions are especially important here since they go hand in hand with his insights into bodily movement and time, and since rising above the turn of experience would, for Bergson, precisely dissolve the logic of solids, since the logic of solids stems from articulating the world through utile interests that bias experience below the turn.

The results of this exploration can now be boiled down to some methodological imperatives that let us, in a Bergsonian (or Deleuzean) manner, reformulate our problem. The study of labile spatial experience demands attention to a moving schema of perception that crosses body and world. But we undermine the moving character of this structure-in-movement if we install it in a closed universe or a closed subject. Thus: Do not install the moving schema in the closed universe of theoretical science. Do not install the moving schema in the closed consciousness of traditional phenomenology or philosophy of consciousness. If we are not to foreclose the subject-object relation, we must rise to "the turn of experience." Thus: Do not install the moving schema in the framework of the subject-object distinction; see how this schema installs itself in the world. The problem "What is the body schema?" or "What is the moving schema of perception?" is badly put, for it tacitly conceives the schema that achieves the subject-object distinction as a 'solid' to be taken for granted; but that 'solid' conception of the moving schema in fact already depends on the existence of the schema, for it is the schema that first enables the subject-object distinction and a 'solidification' of experience. The real problem is "Why do these movements, which we later articulate as movements of a body in a world, appear as schematized, as having a schema, in the first place?"

MOVEMENT AND CONSTRAINT

In taking up this problem I appeal to crucial insights from Bergson. The first insight is that the schema is *not* an already constituted X *added* to an existing system so as to control it; rather, such a schema appears in an existing system when that system *removes* some movement from itself, constrains itself. This appeal to Bergson is motivated by the central role of constraints in current scientific studies of dynamic self-organization. So I return to science for a moment, and then reinterpret the scientific concept of constraint within a Bergsonian ontology, to avoid the problems addressed above. The reinterpretation takes us into a second Bergsonian insight: the intuition of time.

Styles and Invariants of Movement

The previous chapter showed that descriptively/phenomenologically, styles of movement are crucial to perception and that the moving schema is an ensemble of styles. Styles correspond to the scientific concept of invariants of movement.

As discussed in the introduction, J. J. Gibson, the founder of ecological psychology, criticized representational theories of perception that appeal to frameworks fixed in advance of the perceiver's moving, ecological relation to the environment. Models that transcend the environment are, as we saw, highly problematic, and, according to Gibson, not necessary. Perception is the detection of invariants in the flow of information generated when the perceiver moves around. Such invariants specify reciprocal information about the body and the environment (Gibson 1966, 1979). For example, if you immobilize yourself in a room and unfocusedly gaze at a ceiling corner, you might perceive that corner as flattening out into three lines meeting at an angle, but the moment you sweep your eyes back and forth, the angles flow through transformations; the invariant pattern of these transformations specifies perceptual information about the depth of the room and your position in it. It is crucial to note that invariants are in fact patterns of change: what is invariant is a pattern of variation. An analogy with a waltz is helpful: the waltzing dancers are moving around in all sorts of cycles, but the patterns of these cycles (the basic one-two-three step, the way these steps go in a circle, and so on) remains invariant.

Like styles, invariants are patterns of movement central to the reciprocal perception of body and world.

Constraint: Collapses of Freedom as Cause

Whereas phenomenology is at first content to use styles as a descriptive term, science wants to fit invariants within a causal framework. Dynamic systems theory gives a causal account of Gibson's invariants by understanding them as rooted in constraints. But the concept of constraints leads to a shift in the concept of causality.

Classical scientific analysis tends to conceive a moving system as an assembly of parts governed by laws. The system is understood on a mechanistic model in which the parts, as Merleau-Ponty would say, are external to one another, and the law is external to the system. To return to the traffic jam, the classical approach would conceive each car as an independent particle governed by universal laws of traffic; that is, the behavior of each car is specifiable independent of the behavior of any other car, in advance of actual traffic. The possibility of a jam would therefore have to be implied in universal laws of traffic, and the universal laws of traffic would have to account for and range over all possibilities of traffic behavior. Each case of traffic behavior is an actualization of a possibility specified in advance by a universal law.

Dynamic systems theory does not seek laws that cover all possibilities, for it is first of all interested in the way that actual parts of systems, through their interrelations, *constrain* possibilities. Formally, such constraint is conceived in terms of a collapse of the degrees of freedom of a system. Cars, for example, behave as independent particles only when they are on the open plane. On the road and in traffic automobile movement is inherently limited by the road and by the moving interrelation of cars. Not all movements are possible; the degrees of freedom of movement are collapsed. The traffic jam is not the outcome of a universal law, nor is the jam the actualization of a possibility implied in such an all-encompassing law. The etiology of the jam is a constraint immanent within the actual movement of traffic itself.

This point about constraints and degrees of freedom is quite important in kinesiology. The discovery is due to Nikolai Bernstein, who, as noted above, thought that conceiving the body on a machine model betrays the integrity of the living body. What matters here is that Bernstein also showed that the machine model badly misconceives control of movement (Bernstein 1967; Thelen and Smith 1994). Consider the arm. If we dissect it, we find that it has many separable parts: bones conjoin into limb segments, and attach to one another at joints. Each of these joints defines a degree of freedom of movement: several freedoms of rotation at the shoulder, some at the elbow, and so on. We could therefore represent the arm as a mechanical system by specifying the lengths of the joints and the angles at the joints in various planes of rotation, that is, represent it as a system with a large number of degrees of freedom. The task of controlling the arm and feeling its position would then amount to controlling and feeling the arm in terms of these degrees of freedom. In the way that the cause of the traffic jam is, in the classical view, reduced (taken back) to universal possibilities covered by a law, control of the arm is reduced to a way of actualizing certain possibilities within a larger number of degrees of freedom.

But the living arm is not the arm dissected, and in the living arm parts inherently link to one another in a self-constraining moving system. The arm does not avail itself of all the degrees of freedom available at each joint, as if it is a ball-and-socket machine—that sort of ball-and-socket independence of movement is visible only in dislocated joints. In the healthy arm, the material and moving interrelation of parts is an immanent constraint on the arm's possibilities.

You can see something like this in one of those desk lamps that have springs tying parallel segments to one another. You can put the lamp in only so many positions, for example, you cannot bend it back behind itself, and it stays in some positions better than others. Why? Moving a part of the lamp about inherently pulls along other segments and joints through the springs, and this internal pull constrains the overall degrees of freedom of the lamp.

The benefit of this internal constraint is that you do not have to deal with individual joints. If you disconnect the springs or get rid of the parallel segments, then you can move the lamp into almost any position. But then the lamp begins to approximate to a system that would have to be controlled in terms of abstract degrees of freedom, and you would have to control each joint separately by tightening up each nut.

Similarly with the arm. In the machine conception of the arm, the arm would have to be controlled by specifying the position at each joint, but Bernstein shows that overall properties of the arm, such as mass distribution, the way the tendons give the arm springlike properties, and so on, collapse the degrees of freedom of arm movement, that most of the control of the arm is not in an abstract control system external to the arm, but immanent within internal dynamic constraints of the arm. Moving an arm is not like moving independent segments of a broken desk lamp and then tightening up the nuts; it is like nudging an impeccably engineered, upscale designer desk lamp in the right direction and having its segments smoothly settle into place.

These immanent constraints are not merely due to the material arrangement of components, but to movements. In the desk lamp the material properties of springs are fixed, changing slightly as the lamp is moved, stretching the springs; the arm, in contrast, moves itself, and its own muscular contractions and relaxations change its own properties. For example, dynamic systems theorists Thelen and Smith (1994) show how the overall properties of the arm (for example, its 'springiness') can themselves be controlled through patterns of muscle tension and movement, and that different constraints can be brought into play as predominating in arm control. In a fascinating study they show how different individual infants learn to reach in very different ways. To cartoon their point, consider two desk lamps, one with loose springs, one with tight ones, and the problem of nudging the lamp so that it stops in a particular spot. Some infants begin the movement of reaching by loosening up the springs of the arm; it is easy to nudge the arm into movement; the problem is getting it to stop in the right place (like a floppy lamp). Other infants begin by tightening up the arm springs; their problem is flinging the arm into movement (like a tight lamp), with the problem of stopping solved by the initial tightening. Study of Turvey and Carello's results also shows that the temporal or 'melodic' contour of wielding has an impact on control and perception of the arm, and that things outside the body have a role in constraining it (Morris 2002b).

Constraints are not static components contained inside the arm, but limitations that themselves arise in and from movement that opens into the world. The collapse of degrees of freedom of movement is itself brought about in movement that crosses body and world, in the way that the traffic jam, as manifestation of a constraint, is itself brought about in movement that crosses cars and roadways. The smooth movement of an arm that swings out and stops at its destination is, if you will, due to a sort of shifting 'jam'

of parts and tensions within the arm in relation to what it holds and contacts; and the traffic jam is, if you will, an immanent control structure that
arises when the flow of traffic reaching from one city to another tightens up
a bit too much.

In the classical analysis, the claim that X causes Y ultimately refers to
universal laws that close on the universe as a whole. The laws are a template
that specifies what in general is possible, in advance of what is actual; the
template covers all possibilities and specifies that if certain possibilities become actual, others will follow, be caused. When dynamic systems theory
understands constraints as causes, for example, constraints as causing the arm
to move in a specific way, the concept of causality shifts. The constraint that
causes the arm to move in a controlled manner is a template immanent
within the body's moving relation to the world. Such a constraint does not
refer us back to what in general is possible, to relations between abstract
actualizations of the possible. The constraint is brought into being within an
actual collapse of freedoms (of possibilities), within the actual movement of
a body open to its surround. Constraints are not relations *added* to a system
from the outside by a closed framework of possibilities in which the system
is installed; constraints appear in open systems, from the inside, and specify
relations in virtue of *limiting* actual movement. To put it another way, classical causal laws specify relations between successive times, relations that can
be specified in advance of the actual unfolding of things in time. But constraints themselves appear in time. They cannot be specified in advance or
in abstraction; we have to wait for them to actually appear. We cannot apply
a logic of solids to the control of the arm, decomposing it into mechanical
parts that are recomposed under a mechanical law; the constraint that controls the arm is dynamic, fluid; it belongs to the time of movement.

This anticipates several Bergsonian themes that we take up below.
First, a word on constraints and perception.

CONSTRAINTS AND PERCEPTION

Traffic is a perceptual system of sorts. Consider driving from Toronto to
Peterborough on the four-lane 401 on a Thursday afternoon: in the beginning the traffic is light and there is a variety of driving styles that you can
choose (involving desired speed, following distance, and lane change frequency). But then at a certain point (it's usually Oshawa) these degrees of
freedom collapse; a wave of brake lights washes back through the column of
cars ahead; you ease your foot on the accelerator to avoid a collision with the
congealing jam ahead. Like the blind man perceiving things through his
cane, you are, through the traffic jam—maybe even through the feeling of
your foot easing back—perceiving an obstruction up ahead. You might not
be able to tell what the obstruction is (accident, spectacle, or off-ramp)
because traffic isn't a very sensitive perceptual system. Nonetheless, the for-

mation of this constraint in movement expresses perception of an obstruction. Of course, traffic as a perceptual system is already composed of individual perceivers, so this model will not tell us how perception happens in the first place; but it puts us inside a moving system to glimpse constraint formation as a perceptual act.

Dynamic systems theorists tell us that bodily perception can be understood in terms of constraint formation. Apparently, Merleau-Ponty was quite fond of tennis. Imagine, then, holding a tennis racket. How do you know how long it is? Carello and Turvey show that one's feeling for the length of a wielded object such as a cane or tennis racket has to do with one's possibilities of moving it about, or rather the way those possibilities are constrained by the actual joint movement of body and racket. Recall their points about illusions discussed in the introduction, specifically, that the scientist is in error when she conceives felt length as referring to a geometrical length measured by a ruler. Felt length does not refer to a geometrical length reconstructed by some sort of inferential process; it refers to something directly there *in* the moving interaction of the body and the object. In the language of physics, this something is called the eigenvalue of the inertia tensor of the object. Put in nontechnical terms, the eigenvalue of the inertia tensor is a set of values that specifies the difficulty of moving something about, its "wieldiness." Felt length corresponds to wieldiness. But note that you can detect wieldiness, which has to do with possibilities of movement, only when you take the racket in hand and move it in a specific way (twiddling it around its long axis won't do, you have to shake it up and down). Wieldiness is a joint result of body and world moving together. What we are perceiving when we perceive felt length is a constraint, a limit on movement, that organizes itself and is manifest within movement that crosses body and world.

This still does not tell us how a body-world system that limits its movement from within is the site of experience—that will have to wait for the next chapter's study of expression. But it gives an initial sense of how perception can arise from constraints.

A BERGSONIAN ONTOLOGY OF CONSTRAINTS

Matter and Memory renews the problem of mind and body by aiming to rise above the turn of experience, putting aside all preconceptions about the division of subject and object. Chapter one of *Matter and Memory* shows how this requires a renewal of the problem of perception.

Above the turn of experience, representationalist doctrines of perception appear to be in error. If we put aside preconceptions and examine the perceiving body in the world, we find that the body and its brain are not the terminal point of a process that records and represents the world, in the manner of a photographic plate that is the terminus of an optical process. The body is never the stopping point of movement; it receives movement in order to move. Perception and action cannot be decoupled—a familiar point by now, endorsed not only by Merleau-Ponty and pragmatists such as Dewey (1929, 1972), but by Gibson, the dynamic systems theorists and an increasing number of philosophers (see Hurley 1998 and Clark 1997), even philosophers such as Dennett (1991), so far as they reject the "Cartesian Theatre" or a "finish line" of consciousness. (Indeed, I would add, following a suggestion of William James, that any account of the body as an evolved organism would have to conceive perception not as a terminus, but as a turning point in efficacious movement; otherwise perception does nothing in the struggle to survive (James 1950, 1: 138).) Perception is not an event enclosed within the perceiver, it is manifest in a moving circuit between the perceiver and the world. Within this circuit the brain is not like a recording device but, in Bergson's metaphor, like a telephone exchange that reconfigures the relation between inward and outward movement. In virtue of this reconfigurability, the body as a whole appears as a center of indeterminacy, selectively reacting to movement. Everything is in a moving circuit that reacts with everything else, but where we observers discover selective indeterminate reactions, there we find perception, at least what Bergson calls pure perception (which is not yet perception as having a subjective or experiential aspect).

Bergson's account of pure perception in chapter one of *Matter and Memory* obviously converges with the account of constraints developed so far. The sort of indeterminacy that we find in the perceiving body arises in the moving circuit that the body forms with things, and it has to do with constraints on movement in this circuit. Not all movements are transmitted through the circuit formed by body and world, and experienced perception is a symbol—we shall end up saying expression—of the body as stopping certain movements, in the way that (using Bergson's analogy) the virtual image seen in a reflecting surface is a symbol of the surface stopping light from moving through it. Perception is due to a constraint.

The convergence becomes more obvious in chapter two of *Matter and Memory*, where Bergson, in anticipation of the role of memory in his project, asks how the recognition of things ever occurs at the level of body and brain. In answering, Bergson invokes what he calls the motor schema, which is quite cognate to Merleau-Ponty's body schema. We recognize things in virtue of a motor schema. But the motor schema is not a cognitive program or neural circuit, an abstract X that can be localized on the side of a representational brain, a schema for matching input with stored representations. The motor schema is a moving pattern immanent within movement, that plays back and forth between body and world, through the body and brain as a differential system that alters movement as it plays across different zones of the body (in the way that light bends when it plays across different media).[8] In being altered as it plays across zones, incoming perceptual movement turns into an appropriate outgoing movement, and it is in this way that the pattern of movement alteration, the motor schema, recognizes things. For Bergson, perceptual recognition is based in something very much like constraints.

Bergson, however, adds a crucial but difficult ontological twist. The motor schema is a phenomenon of limitation, of body-world movement that limits itself. According to Bergson, this limitation within movement is not to be understood as a negative absence, as a restriction on a prior system of possibility, and therefore as something "less" (that is, something less than the possible). The limitation is a positive presence actual in the movement of body and world—it is something "more." In terms of our discussion of constraints: when we understand a constraint as a collapse in degrees of freedom, we take the general degrees of freedom to be the real thing, and the collapse as something less than the real thing, a negative to be understood only in relation to the positivity of general degrees. But in Bergson's view, the general degrees of freedom would be a phantom, something that we construct in the interest of controlling and predicting the systems that we study. The moving arm never collapses merely possible degrees of freedom; those degrees of freedom were never actual in the arm to be collapsed. Indeed, as I pointed out, those degrees of freedom are only ever actual in an arm with dislocated joints. So the arm with its immanent controlling constraint is not to be understood as something less in relation to possible degrees of freedom; the constraint has its own positive actuality in the arm, and that actuality is what lets the arm be and do something more than a system that has greater degrees of freedom.

Bergson's ontological twist follows from his general criticism of the concept of the possible, articulated in "The Possible and the Real" (2002) and also at play in *Matter and Memory*. He argues that we construct the possible by a sort of retrograde movement of thinking in which we pack all variants of actuality as we encounter it into something prior to the actual. We then say that the actual comes out of the possible as a restriction of it, and need to give an account of a causal process that causes the possible to actualize in a restricted way.[9] In Bergson's analysis, the possible is a construction that arises below the turn of experience: it is useful for the purpose of putting things in a framework that allows us to analyze them in terms of their being possibly otherwise, but if we sink to the level of intuition, we find nothing like this abstract possibility that needs to be made actual by the addition of something else; rather, we find a reality that continually actualizes itself by an immanent movement of becoming that restricts itself from within. Constraints are positive actualities immanent within the self-restricting movement of becoming; they are not to be understood as negative restrictions of possibility.

Bergson's point becomes more vivid when we link it to his concern for time. In "The Possible and the Real" he writes that if you "suppress the conscious and the living"—if you suppress all openness and head toward a closed system—"you obtain in fact a universe whose successive states are in theory calculable in advance, like the images placed side by side along the cinematographic film, prior to its unrolling." Nowadays we would use a different metaphor: the closed universe in which everything can be calculated is like a computer program that specifies the relation between successive iterations; the relation between states is specified even before the program is run, unrolled. "Why, then, the unrolling? Why does reality unfurl? Why is it not spread out? What good is time?" (Bergson 2002, 93) If everything that can and does happen is calculable in advance, specified by a program, then what does time do? If we can specify the possible in advance of the actual, and specify the causal process that actualizes the possible, then the unfolding of time makes no difference to the actual, it is a mere index of the cranking out of the film or program. On the contrary, Bergson is convinced that time matters, that it makes a difference: the actualization of things is not specified by a program rolled up in advance, stored in a closed system of possibility; it is inseparable from time. If time is good for anything, it is good as the becoming of actualization.

The dynamic systems theorists begin with a similar conviction. Confronted with the problem of how the body controls itself, perceives, or develops, previous theorists would seek programs or laws specified in advance of bodily control, perception, or development. The dynamic systems theorists, on the contrary, seek constraints that "assemble," come to be, in various orders of time: in the "real time" of a particular behavior, in repetitions of a particular behavior by an individual, in an individual lifetime of development and skill formation. Control is inseparable from the time and movement in which it arises. For example, where other theorists might classify all instances of reaching as being the same, or conceive the achievement of reaching as a fixed stage of development that is the same in all children, dynamic systems theorists such as Thelen and Smith include time as an individuating element in these phenomena. If we examine the ways that children actually reach in real time, we find, as noted above, that they reach in different ways; if we examine the ways that children actually develop in time, we find that they do not at all move through the same 'stages' or move from 'stage' to 'stage' in the same way. "Reaching" as a general category, and "stages of development" or "developmental programs" are fictions, articulations that we introduce into the phenomena in order to solidify the phenomena, to allow for generalizations that enable analysis. The phenomena themselves are rather more fluid, since time does something.

What, then, is the methodological problem with dynamic systems theory? Earlier we noted a tension within science: on the actual historical, empirical side, science notices natural experiments, spontaneous variations within the body's own living framework; on the theoretical side, science installs the body in a prespecified framework. We can now reinterpret this tension in terms of time. Empirically, science, at least the species called dynamic systems theory, is inclined to grasp the phenomena in real time, as inseparable from their actual happening—here science heads in the direction of Bergsonian intuition even if it does not go as far as Bergson. Theoretically, science is inclined to turn actuality into possibility, to abstract phenomena from time and install them in an abstract framework of possibility in which time is simply a variable that is yet to be given a value. Empirically, science immerses itself in the movie of life; theoretically, science rolls up the movie into a program, a system of laws, that is already done in advance.[10]

What Bergson contributes to the scientific account is an ontological perspective, the perspective of intuition, that enjoins us to take time seriously and conceive constraints as positive phenomena immanent within and inseparable from movement that crosses body and world. Taking constraints in their time blocks enclosing them in a closed universe and blocks a logic of solids. Bergson also contributes to the phenomenological account: so far as perception is rooted in constraints inseparable from a time prior to the constitution of the subject, the subject cannot enclose itself in its own temporality. The "unreflective fund of experience" that Merleau-Ponty is seeking sinks us back into a time prior to the subject.

Perception is not based in a schema *added* to the body and world from the perspective of an already established framework, a schema that would already contain rolled up within it a recipe for the division of subject and object. The schema unfolds in real time, as a limit, a constraint, immanent within body-world movement. Qua inseparable from time such a schema is certainly (as Waldenfels would put it) the result of a process of self-organization, and Bergson's ontological perspective moots our temptation to root self-organization in some prior or external framework.

We began with a phenomenologically driven quest for an account of the moving schema of perception as a structure-in-movement. The scientific concept of constraints satisfies that quest, if constraints are reinterpreted in Bergson's ontological perspective, namely, as inseparable from the time of movement and as positive in themselves.

This still leaves questions. First, our discussion takes up basic methodological, conceptual and ontological issues requisite to reinterpreting constraints. But how, really, are we to understand a constraint in the Bergsonian perspective, as a positive limitation in movement? I answer this through the metaphor of folding. Second, what makes a constraint come to be? If we answered this question by appeal to something constituted prior to the time in which we actually find a constraint actualizing itself, we would undermine the whole project. Accordingly, the question will be approached through a discussion of development—of bodily becoming.

CONSTRAINTS AS FOLDS

Obtain a piece of standard origami paper (colored on one side, white on the other). You can flex it in many different directions, it will bend on any axis or line that you choose. Now fold it, pressing the fold crisp with the back of a fingernail. You will not be able to remove the fold, it is a permanent crease in the paper's fibres. Interestingly, folds are asymmetrical: a mountain fold (in which the white surfaces are on the inside of the fold) is different from a valley fold (in which the colored surfaces are on the inside). Each fold is a permanent record of a folding process, of the formation of a 'mountain' or 'valley' in the paper, as geography and geological strata are permanent records of mountain and valley formation.[11] Folds limit the movement of the paper: a fold cannot be removed, and the paper can no longer flex in the same way around the fold. A fold is a limit in the movement of the paper and a record of the temporal process of forming that limit.

Folds limit and affect subsequent folds. (For example, if you want to produce two mountain folds, each running diagonally from corner to corner, meeting in an X in the middle of the paper, you first have to make one fold, then flatten the paper, then make the second fold. If you try making the second fold without flattening the first, your second diagonal will be half a valley fold and half a mountain fold. Folds run into one another, affect one another.) The limitations established by a fold also enable subsequent folds, or novel kinds of folding. (For example, if you flatten out the X-folds discussed above and make a valley fold that runs parallel to the side of the square and through the central X, you can tuck in the sides of the paper, producing a flattened triangular shape called the waterbomb base, which is the base for a number of traditional origami figures. A great deal of origami is (a) folding new figures from folded bases; (b) finding networks of folds that enable new *sorts* of folding, for example, simple folds fold along one line at a time, but a network of simple folds can enable the tucking operation in the waterbomb base, which folds along three lines at once, or more complex squash folds, and so on.)

It is by way of successive limitations, folds, within paper that origami figures—which can be quite complex, ranging from scaly, planar dragons to curvy roses—are produced. What you see in the figure, all of its distinctive lines and shapes, are delineated by folds. It would be easy to conclude that origami figures are made out of folds, but that would be misleading. Unfold an origami figure and flatten the paper out. There you have all the folds, laid out in a complex network on the paper. But you do not have the figure; only an origami master could guess the figure from the network of folds. More, you can't get the figure back by folding along each line in the network of folds, you have to fold them in the proper order, as when the figure was first made (even then, it won't come out exactly the same). Trying to conceive the figure in terms of the networks of folds laid out on paper is like turning from the time of the actual to an abstract possible. The figure isn't made out of abstract folds, it is made out of paper folded in an actual order. The folds record the process of folding. The result of the process contracts the time of folding into an apparent figure that expresses at once the folding process and the folded figure, in the way that a person's distinctive shamble expresses at once her way of walking and the process that led to her walking that particular way.

Crucially, a fold is not made of anything other than the paper that it limits[12]: the fold is nothing other than paper, but as a record of a process in the paper, as a crease, it stands out for us as different from the rest of the paper. Likewise, the origami figure as a whole isn't made of anything other than paper as successively limited by a process of folding, yet the figure stands out for us as different from the paper itself. Finally, the figure—structure—is not achieved by something that joins a set of parts together according to an outside plan; rather the structure results from a process that folds linkages already there in the system. If we are to avoid thinking of limits and structure in terms of a framework constituted prior to or apart from the system, then they will have to have a similar characteristic: limits and structure are not to be understood as a new X added to the system, but as a sort of kink or crease in the system, a crease that at once is a limit and a record of a limit having been formed. The system's recording of its own limit creates structure.

This gives us a metaphor, a vehicle, for thinking about constraints— just as 'field,' 'cell' and 'stage' have provided metaphors for thinking about physics, living beings, or development.[13] Movements of a system prior to constraint formation are cognate to movements of paper prior to folding. Constraints are cognate to folds in the paper, and constraints build into one another in the manner of a series of folds. The strength of this metaphor is the way that folds are immanent within paper, rather than being made of something else.[14] But to do something with this metaphor we need a way of thinking of folds in terms of movement, as immanent within movement. The following provides a preliminary understanding of folds in movement, to be expanded in the section on development below.[15]

Suppose we set up a complex version of an aeolian harp (a musical instrument, the strings of which are activated by wind) on a hilltop, such that winds moving in different directions and speeds produce different notes or chords. (Gordon Monohan installed something approaching this on Gibbet's Hill as part of the 1988 *Sound Symposium* in St. John's, Newfoundland.) For us, the sound of our wind machine is a way of perceiving different winds. But what we are perceiving in the sound of the machine is nothing other than windy movement folded on itself in a complex way, wind divided into streams around strings, setting strings into regular vibration, which vibrations, via the soundboards, vibrate the windy air. Unlike a fold in paper, this sort of fold is in movement. Recalling Bergson's point against representation, and our focus on perception in the crossing of body and world, we should note that the sound is not *representing* the wind, if by representation we mean something that would present the wind in some other kind of 'material,' a duplicate that stands independent of the wind; there would be no sound without the wind, sound is wind made different and audible by folding it through the harp. If our wind machine experienced its own sound, it would be a wind-perceiver. As it stands, it is a prolongation of our perceptual experience, a machine for perceiving wind, as a telescope is a machine for perceiving stars.

We can make sense of constraints within the Bergsonian ontological perspective if we think of them as folds in the movement that crosses body and world. That is, the basic 'stuff' of constraints, of the moving schema, is movement, and movement becomes structure by a complex folding, by a limitation or division arising within movement, in the manner of a crease arising within a sheet of paper. If our wind machine could not only experience its own sound, but bring about the configuration through which it folds the wind, and if that configuration were dynamic, refolding itself to detect different sorts of wind, then that complex folding would be the wind machine's moving and labile schema of perception.

Of course the wind machine gives us a merely mechanical model of folding, because it cannot fold itself (and because it can't, wind and what folds it remain two things). But the body does fold itself, and must fold itself through its development. So I now turn to folding in development.

Before turning back to the body, a remark that takes us back to our initial problem about structure and looks ahead: a distinctive feature of Cartesian and modern philosophy and science is the elimination of the scholastic-Aristotelian concept of "form," of a *sens* in nature; all *sens* is in the subject.[16] Merleau-Ponty is of course pursuing something like form as *sens* in nature when he turns to gestalt and structure; and he later seeks form in being, form in movement, through the figures of chiasm, reversibility, dehiscence. By drawing on a Bergsonian thread in the weave of Merleau-Ponteian philosophy, I reintroduced form in the concept of folds in movement. But a fold is quite different from a form: a fold is not a static, solid being, it is in movement. A fold is not implanted into a cosmos that refers to a mover itself unmoved—Aristotle's cosmos solidifies at its limit. A fold refers to the movement out of which it is folded, generated; and it remains in movement. With Bergson, Merleau-Ponty, and contemporary science of dynamic self-organization, we can make a turn to a cosmos of folds, not forms, of movements, not solids.

DEVELOPMENT

DEVELOPMENT AND THE MOVING SCHEMA OF PERCEPTION

Bergson urges us not to put the possible before the actual, as if stages of actuality could be rolled back up to construct a possible that is waiting to unwind. We must attend to what actually makes itself happen.

When it comes to development, dynamic systems theorists, especially Thelen and Smith, have (at least in the first instance) a convergent position. They criticize previous conceptions of development as the unwinding of prespecified stages. As indicated above, they conceive development as the formation of constraints in movement, and this formation is pervasively dynamic and interactive: development happens only through the infant's dynamic interaction with the world, so it cannot be a program stored up in the infant; they (and other researchers to be studied later) show how development thus emerges in the contingencies, especially the social contingencies, of the infant's interaction with the world. Even if, in sharing a common body and world, they will follow roughly similar patterns, infants will develop in different ways and at different speeds. And of course infants aren't passive vehicles of their development but are desiring beings who can dally or speed up in various areas (the infant who quickly develops a fast and efficient crawl to get around but 'postpones' walking; the infant who begins talking 'late' but begins speaking in full sentences)—which suggests that the current fashion for specifying what children will achieve and when, and building these stages into the marketing of toys, books, and educational programs (at fourteen to sixteen months, baby will . . .) is misguided. Development is not a transition from fixed stage to fixed stage, it happens in process.

Our methodological and conceptual reflections drove us to the conclusion that we must conceive the moving schema of perception as resulting from development in this sense. If we are to keep the schema moving, if it is to be a structure-in-movement, then we cannot refer it to a closed objective or subjective framework established in advance of bodily being in the world. We must refer it, in a Bergsonian manner, to the openness of the time in which body-world movement constrains itself so as to manifest a schema—and this refers us to development as a process that is not programmed in advance. If we were to pursue this we would of course have to refer back to the movement of evolution—but again, not as a movement rooted in a closed system. We shall have to restrict ourselves to development.

THE MOVING SCHEMA AS TWOFOLD MOVEMENT OF THE BODY

We are led, then, to the concept of the moving schema of perception as a twofold movement. On the one hand, movement is the 'stuff' of the schema, since it is within this movement that we detect the constraints that give rise to perception. On the other hand, our question as to how movement comes to exhibit structure refers us to another movement: the movement of *development* that folds body-world movement into a constrained system manifesting a schema. The moving schema is composed *of* the body's movement in the world and is composed *by* the movement of development. The terms *synchronic* and *diachronic* can help here: the moving schema is never a merely synchronic phenomenon, specified by the interaction of the world and a fixed program, revealed in a temporal slice taken through the moment. It is inherently diachronic—"the result of a process of . . . self-organization" as Waldenfels would put it, or, as we saw on the descriptive level, a matter of styles of movement that are habitual. But we cannot separate the synchronic and diachronic aspects: movement synchronically self-organizing in the moment refers us to the diachronic movement behind this self-organization; and the diachronic movement of development is synchronically self-organizing movement limiting, folding, itself. There are not two distinct axes of movement (synchronic and diachronic), but one twofold movement: the twofold movement of a body that grows by moving in the world and moves by growing in the world.

Our origami metaphor helps again. The current configuration of the sheet of paper is cognate to synchronic body-world movement, the successive folding to diachronic development. The structured figure that results from folding is made not of two things, paper and folds, but of one thing, folded paper, that exhibits two aspects (paper and folding process) implied in one another.

It is not the moving schema or body-schema that is the agent or cause of development (see Sheets-Johnstone 1999a, especially chapter 12; Gallagher and Meltzoff 1996). Rather, development is the agent or cause of the moving schema, or more precisely, the two are co-implicated in the twofold movement of the body: a developmental body manifests a schema and a body manifests a schema through its development.

DEVELOPMENT AS FOLDING

The origami metaphor registers a distinctively Bergsonian twist preserved in our conception: development is not the unfolding of an already stored program, but the folding of actual movement from within.

The unfolding model is the traditional one, criticized by Thelen and Smith. It would root the moving schema in a closed, ready-made framework, and leaves us with the problem of what causes the program of development to unfold (which is cognate to Bergson's problem about what would cause the possible to become actual). For Thelen and Smith the latter problem leads to the conceptual absurdity and empirical difficulty of explaining different rates of child development by appeal to some sort of cause that accelerates or retards the unfolding of an already fixed developmental program, as if such a cause could be external to 'stages' of development. This is cognate to the 'Hydra problems' discussed in the introduction and the problems that Merleau-Ponty detects in his criticism of intellectualist and empiricist accounts of learning: the intellectualists cannot say what would keep a priori organization from unfolding; the empiricists cannot say what would prompt a posteriori associations if they are not already waiting to be unfolded (see the section on the development of movement below). The content and process of development cannot be specified independent of each other; the two are co-implicated, and neither can be specified in advance—they specify each other through their co-implication. Thus

Thelen and Smith's pervasively dynamic model, which is in an effort to entirely reconfigure the problem: the content of a 'stage' is not external to the process that causes one 'stage' to lead to another; the internal dynamics of 'stages' develop into new 'stages.'

Instead of beginning with a (mythical) X in which all 'stages' are already enfolded, we begin with the actuality of a moving body. This body does have something generative implied in it, namely, its limited actuality. But structure is not already rolled up into that limited actuality; it is not a controlling X added to the beginning, an X waiting to be unfolded. Structure arises from a limited beginning that becomes more limited by successively folding, limiting, itself.

The moving schema is the result of movement twisting and folding on itself to manifest structure: think of a time-lapse movie (leaving out the hands of the folder) of a sheet of paper being folded into an origami rose; you would see a plane twisting and bulging into something with structure, something becoming out of limit.

DEVELOPMENTAL FOLDS AS CO-IMPLYING UPWARD AND DOWNWARD MODIFICATIONS

We should no longer speak of stages of development, then, but of folds.

In ascending the stages or levels of a building, one leaves previous stages behind, except as underlying support. To build something in stages is to stack layers in a growing pile, as if a stage can be introduced whole from the outside. In the stage metaphor, stages remain relatively external to one another, and the process of adding stages remains relatively external to the growing stack of stages. Finally, when thinking of developmental stages, we usually are thinking of relatively fixed configurations.

Take instead a complex origami figure, say of a dragon, and make an imaginary section through it, say its claw. The claw contains all the folds that go into its development. Those folds are related to one another not as stages stacked on top of one another, but as elaborations of a fold: the first fold that goes into making the claw is there in the final formation of the claw, but folded so as to do something new. More, the folds in the claw are not, finally, local to it, since folds run across the sheet; the folds in the claw are continuous with folds in the body and wing. Folds upwardly modify subsequent folds, are downwardly modified by subsequent folds, and are not local but implied in one another. Folds are not at all like stages. (The fold metaphor also invites thinking of wrinkles or twists on canonical folds—of folds as inherently idiosyncratic.)

The origami paper is meant as a metaphor for body-world movement, not for the material of the body (a weakness of the metaphor, since origami figures look like material rather than movement). So let us study the development of walking as a folding of body-world movement.[17]

Thelen and Smith show that the kicking motion of infants is due to a constraint within infant-world movement. When the infant sets the leg in motion, the leg tends, because of constraints, to fall into a pattern. When the infant is lying on her or his back, the pattern results in a kick. When the infant is held up above a surface that contacts the infant's feet, the very same effort of setting the leg in motion results in a steplike pattern. The steplike pattern is of course crucial to the development of walking. Thelen and Smith's innovative result is their demonstration that kicking and stepping movements arise in one and the same constraint: the development of walking is not due to the formation of an entirely new program or capacity, or the activation of a previously rolled-up program. Walking arises when the constraint that generates infant kicking comes into play in a new way.

Their result arises from their attempt to solve the notorious problem of the "vanishing steps." In the first six months or so infants, when held over a surface, are capable of making steplike, walking patterns, but after, such movements vanish until the onset of walking. Thelen and Smith showed that this phenomenon is not due to loss of or shutting down of a control program; it is due to changes in the density of the leg as the infant grows, to the leg becoming too dense to spring into steplike patterns. The demonstration is simple: if you hold a post-six-month infant so that her or his legs are in a tank of water that buoys the leg, stepping movements reappear. In other words, stepping is due not to something in the infant merely, but to a constraint that crosses body and world.

I shall say that the constraint that shapes kicking and stepping is a basic *fold* of body-world movement. The basic kick-stepping fold upwardly modifies and supports walking, it is folded into walking. Of course it is one thing for an infant to make stepping movements when held up over a surface, another for the infant to make steps of her own when holding herself up against the sofa, yet another for her to step whilst holding herself up. The latter two require postural controls that are not required in the former. That is, walking isn't just a fold of kick-stepping; other folds, say postural folds, are folded into walking.

What leads to the new fold of walking? Crucially, what folds into walking is movement that crosses body and world. The kicks that the infant makes when lying on her back kick into the word, and the world 'kicks' back. As Piaget showed, an infant whose leg is tied with a ribbon to a mobile begins to notice her leg in a new way because of this 'kick-back' (see Acredolo 1985). We could imagine an (utterly inhuman and impossible) experiment in which an infant is suspended in midair such that her legs and movements never encounter anything; such an infant, we would imagine, would never learn how to make walking movements, would never get beyond the whole-body movements with which we began the chapter, in which legs and arms kick/swing in and out in a symmetrical system. It is the world's inherent intrusion into movement that prompts folding of movement. As Thelen and

Smith show, if you hold the infant over a treadmill, it will begin to make asymmetrical walkinglike movements: walking isn't so much a way of controlling the body from our side of things, but a way of bouncing off the world, as a drum roll is a way of bouncing sticks off a surface—you can't quite do the roll without the drum.

A fold, a constrained movement that inherently runs from the body into a changing world and back, develops a new kink, and folds into something new, at the same time transforming intersecting folds. A new organization is folded out of and transforms previous ones. This is the basic course of development. And this developmental folding is social: support of parents and other children, forms of play, even home furnishing traditions intervene in the crossing of body and world. As Zelazo (1983, 1984; compare Thelen 1983) points out, the phenomenon of "vanishing steps" is not quite the same in cultures that have different forms of adult-infant play and that correlatively do not have the expectation that infants go through a relatively immobile, incapacitated stage.

Walking as a new fold also downwardly modifies previous folds. Frans de Waal (2001) observes that Japanese tend to walk from the knee and Westerners from the hip, and that it would be very difficult for an adult from one culture to learn the style of walking of the other. If correct, this means that walking is not the fitting together of fixed substages or components of movement, since substages vary across cultures. The achievement of walking reconfigures the movement repertoire that supports it, as a new fold in an origami figure folds the folds that go into it.

In this view of development, development is not a matter of learning how to control material body parts of an already defined mechanical assemblage, but is the gradual and successive internal transformation of (synchronic) body-world movement through the (diachronic) movement of successive folding, that is, constraint formation. This successive folding internally differentiates and complicates movement of the body, by way of constraint, of limitation. Consider, for example, learning to play the flute or drums; the initial difficulty isn't so much learning to move limb segments that are already prepared to move, but to move fingers or feet as *independent* segments, or to drum them in something other than strictly alternating patterns. The problem isn't like the problem of controlling segments of a loose desklamp so that they swing into place; the problem is breaking up the body into independent segments in the first place. The concept of limb control as regulation of freely moving parts is conceptually backward.

Returning to the opening image of the chapter: The infant develops from moving in a one-beat rhythm, in which arms and legs swing as pairs at the same time, to the two-beat asymmetrical rhythm of walking. How? Not by learning to control the legs and arms as independent elements of a mechanical system. Rather, the infant develops by reacting against worldly interventions such that a basic fold of body-world movement kinks and folds

in a new way. This new fold is supported by previous folds, but also downwardly modifies them, bringing into being new constraints that downwardly
articulate the body, enabling new varieties of folds to develop.

THE DEVELOPMENT OF MOVEMENT AS PERCEPTUAL DEVELOPMENT

In the *Phenomenology of Perception* Merleau-Ponty repeatedly criticizes intellectualist and empiricist accounts of perceptual development. Empiricism,
the doctrine that sensations build into higher units by an associative process,
cannot give an account of how data that was present all along, say an array
of color sensations given to a child, all of a sudden provoke a change in the
child's experience so that it learns the difference between red and blue.
Intellectualism, the doctrine that sensations have a meaning only because we
already have a way of synthesizing them into perception, cannot give an
account of how a synthesizing capacity that must have been there all along
if it is ever to develop, nonetheless develops in a manner contingent upon
sensations external to that capacity. Why would a program that is already
rolled up in cognition unroll only after exposure to certain contingencies?
Would not a synthesizing mind unroll itself? Merleau-Ponty concludes that:

> Empiricism cannot see that we need to know what we are looking
> for, otherwise we would not be looking for it, and intellectualism
> fails to see that we need to be ignorant of what we are looking for,
> or equally again we should not be searching. (PP 36/28)

As Dillon points out, there is a parallel here with the famous seeker's
paradox in Plato's *Meno* (80d), where Meno argues, in effect, that you cannot learn anything new, because if you did not know it at all, you would not
be able to look for it, and if it you did know it, you would not need to look
for it in the first place.[18] Socrates argues that Meno's dichotomy of knowing
or not knowing is false, and Merleau-Ponty argues that the dichotomy implied by empiricism and intellectualism is also false. When a child who
cannot distinguish red and blue learns to see two colored panels as red and
blue, it is not the case that on first encounter the child has two distinct
sensory phenomena but is ignorant of their names, as an intellectualist might
claim. Neither is it the case that the child is given entirely indistinct phenomena, and that exposure to them somehow generates an experience of
their distinctness, as an empiricist might claim.

Conceptually, what must be recognized is that the child has an experience of color that is not like that of adult color, that the panels that we see
as red and blue are for the child two vaguely differentiated or otherwise odd
colors. This color experience provokes the child to learn the distinction
between red and blue, and that distinction resolves the initial vague color
experience. The resolution might be somewhat like a confusing picture snap-

ping into place. As Merleau-Ponty puts it, the colors that the child experiences provoke their own "overthrow," learning to see colors is a process of "making explicit and articulate what was until then presented as no more than an indeterminate horizon."[19]

Collingwood argues, and this obviously counts as a reply to Meno's paradox, that "Establishing a proposition in philosophy . . . means not transferring it from the class of things unknown to the class of things known, but making it known in a different and better way" (Collingwood 1933, 161). Merleau-Ponty's point is that perceptual learning and perception itself are not a matter of transferring things in the world from the class of things imperceptible to the class of things perceptible. That sort of transfer would depend on a ready-made world of objective sensations or subjective ideas in which everything perceptible is already specified.

Perception and perceptual learning are instead a matter of perceiving what is already perceptible in a better or different way. When Merleau-Ponty finally resolves the problem of how the child learns to see red and blue, he writes:

> In the gaze we have at our disposal a natural instrument analogous to the blind man's stick. The gaze gets more or less from things according to the way in which it questions them, ranges over or dwells on them. To learn to see colours is to acquire a certain style of seeing, a new use of the body itself, it is to enrich and reorganise the body schema. (PP 179/153)

I have argued that Merleau-Ponty's "body schema" is to be understood as a moving schema of perception, a structure folded of the twofold movement of the body: developmental movement and movement that inherently crosses body and world. The moving schema is already beyond itself, open to the world and development, ready to run into kinks that develop into new folds. The formation of such folds is a gross reorganization of body-world movement, that rearticulates our exploration and interaction with the world, opening up new regions of perception.

But then the moving schema of perception will not be a possession of a closed subject, it will be an ongoing result of developmental folding and of movement that crosses body and world. The meaning that the schema gives rise to will express the twofold movement of the body: its crossing into the world, and its crossing into the past and future through development.

CONCLUSION

We began with the question "What is the moving schema of perception?" Methodological and conceptual analysis showed that the question was badly put: the moving schema is a structure-in-movement and is not, strictly speaking, subject to "What is it?" type questions. What has been called the body schema is not a possession of the subject but a structure-in-movement. We must keep things open on the side of the perceiver and the world, and seek our schema as arising within movement that crosses body and world, prior to a distinction between the two. Our real question is "Why do such movements appear as schematized in the first place?" Bergson's ontological strategies and the concept of constraints lead to an answer. Body-world movements are constrained, and constraints fold into new constraints. The development of ever more complex constraints, by way of limitations immanent within movement, articulates the body and perception, manifests a schema. A schema is not a transcendental X added to a subject or a mechanism added to a body, it is a complex developmental limitation inherent within the twofold movement of a body that moves by growing, grows by moving.

This answers half of the overall problem: it gives an account of a schema as arising in movement. But all this has shown is how body-world movement, by folding into a complex figure, manifests a schema *for us*, for observers and philosophers. We have remained at the level of what Bergson would call pure perception, perception that does not yet have a subject. At this level we have not shown how the body manifests a schema or meaning *for itself*—and this really means that we haven't even shown how this folding is properly a structure, since it manifests structure, meaning-in-being, for us only. This half-answer is not yet an answer to the problem. Yet it prepares us for what remains: the problem of how there is *sens* in this folding, how a movement that crosses the developing body and the world is the site of comprehension and experience. That will require attention to the temporality, habit, and difference within the body, in virtue of which development as a process of learning expresses something new.

CHAPTER 3

THE TOPOLOGY OF EXPRESSION

DURING THE COURSE OF development, the infant moves from kicking legs and arms together in one overall movement of the body, to walking, an asymmetrical two-beat movement of arms and legs in counterpoint. A fold, a constraint in movement, folds into a new fold. The symmetrical one-beat movement of the infant curls the body into itself, perceptually involves the body with itself and its place. Walking breaks this curl into a line that advances into new places through a body that twists its hips and stretches legs and arms into a linear stride orthogonal to the body's front. A curl around the hips unfolds into a line twisted out from the body, and the infant begins moving in a very different way, indeed in a very different world—the world of the toddler. When the infant toddles into walking, her or his presence spreads out into new places—things must be put away, the stairs become a danger zone, and so on.

A fold in movement generates a new wrinkle of *sens*. But how does *sens* emerge in folds of movement? How is there *sens* in movement for the infant herself? The answer requires a study of expression, habit, and learning, and takes us to the concept of a topology of expression—a constraint on learning specified by the spread-out logic of a body that moves by growing, grows by moving, a constraint that shapes *sens*.

EXPRESSION AND *SENS*

Sens in Movement

One of Merleau-Ponty's greatest discoveries in the *Phenomenology of Perception* is that of *sens* in movement. "[W]hat we have discovered through the study of motility [*motricité*]," he writes, is "a new sense [*sens*] of the word 'sense [*sens*].' " If the empiricists were wrong to cobble *sens* from "fortuitously agglomerated contents," the rationalists and idealists were wrong to constitute *sens* through the act of a pure 'I.' Such an act could not account for the "variety of our experience, for that which is non-sense [*non-sens*] within it, for the contingency of its contents." Rationalism could not account for what I have called the lability of experience, or the way that *sens* crosses into a world prior to *sens*, into an "unreflective fund of experience." On the contrary, "Bodily experience forces us to acknowledge an imposition of *sens* which is not the work of a universal constituting consciousness, a *sens* that clings to certain contents." Everything said so far leads to the conclusion that the contents in question arise in movement: *sens* clings to folds of body-world movement.[1]

Sens in movement is central to Merleau-Ponty's philosophy and its future. As we have seen, Merleau-Ponty's concept of *sens* plays on multiple meanings of the French word: *sens* is not a meaning abstracted from the world, it is meaning directed toward and fit with the world. It has this character precisely because it is in movement; and *sens* could not have the lability discussed in the introduction if it were not in movement. It is because *sens* is first of all in movement, and thence speaking and thinking as elaborating *sens* are first of all in movement, that Merleau-Ponty can later write (in the *Phenomenology*) of a tacit *cogito*, an "I think" that tacitly exists before it comes to explicitly reflect upon itself, and thus root thought in corporeal soil. And what is the project of *The Visible and the Invisible* if not an effort to trace *sens* in movement to its ontological depths, to think of *sens* not as insinuated into being by a reflective consciousness interrogating it from the outside, but as arising in the sinews and folds of a being that opens itself to question in a movement that Merleau-Ponty speaks of as chiasm?[2] As Leonard Lawlor (1998) shows, Merleau-Ponty's discovery of a new sense of *sens* anticipates Deleuze's attempt to find a transcendence within immanence, to find *sens* as an expression that is not outside that which is expressed yet is nonetheless distinct from that which is expressed. But the connection between Merleau-Ponty and Deleuze (and the Bergsonian background of this connection) must be put aside for the moment.

We saw that body-world movement folds into structure. But this just shows from the outside that it looks as though the body is behaving in a meaningful way. The crucial question is: how does *sens* cling to folds of body-world movement? How is structure-in-movement *sens* in movement? How, to set the question against our Bergsonian background, is there something more than pure perception?

EXPRESSION AS SENS IN MOVEMENT[3]

In Merleau-Ponty's analysis, *sens* is inseparable from expression: if his study of motility leads him to a new *sens* of *sens*, to a *sens* in movement, it is because the moving body is already an expressive body. The central claims of Merleau-Ponty's study of expression are that the "*word has a* sens" and "the spoken word is a genuine gesture, and it contains its *sens* in the same way as the gesture contains its." *Sens* clings to the folds of body-world movement because it arises in the gestural movement of expression. To develop this point about *sens* and movement, we need to review Merleau-Ponty's concept of expression, first focusing on the peculiar relation between the expression (the word or gesture that expresses something) and what is expressed. Then we need to turn to gesture.

Merleau-Ponty's concept of expression is critical of traditional accounts that claim that the spoken word is the exterior form of an already determinate interior idea. We often experience linguistic expression in this way: we sometimes know what we want to say or think, and give voice to it through an already defined vocabulary. But Merleau-Ponty considers this a secondary form of speech. Primary speech, in contrast, is a phenomenon that Merleau-Ponty most of all detects in children learning a word for the first time, or in poets or thinkers forging new ways of speaking. Primary speech is creative: the way of expressing a new thought is there 'on the tip of my tongue'; I pace around trying to spit it out; in spitting it out, I clarify the vague something I have been thinking of, I discover with new clarity what I was trying to think and say.[4] (Unless otherwise noted, subsequent discussion of expression concerns primary expression.)

Ultimately, I crystallize my thinking only through finding the words to express it. For a being who does not have what Kant calls intellectual intuition, who works out thought, expression is not like converting an already finished Word document into WordPerfect format, a mechanical translation of completed meaning from one format to another. If expression is translation, it is the paradoxical sort noted by Merleau-Ponty, in which the 'original document' is 'written' only by being translated.[5] Consider translating a text from one human language to another: in 'summing up' a text in a different language, such translation inevitably introduces differences, in effect recreating the source text in the target language, but also elaborating new meaning in both texts and languages. Where mechanical translation shifts completed figures from one location to another in an already defined plane of meaning, and effects no real difference in meaning, primary expression (or translating from one language to another) creates new differences, elaborates a plane of meaning from within. Expressive translation, or simply put (primary) expression, is thus to be contrasted with mechanical translation. Expression changes something that does not yet have a *sens*—*non-sens* (to use Merleau-Ponty's term)—into something that does have *sens*, by elaborating the plane of what I call *sens-non-sens* from within.

A great deal rides on the difference between mechanical translation and expression, both for our project and the philosophy of mind, since a commitment to expression constitutes an attack on representationalism. To show this, I draw a point from Bergson. In the conclusion of *Matter and Memory* Bergson gives a peculiarly insightful criticism of dualism (MM, 225–228). Dualism proposes that each state of mind is nothing other than a material brain state. Each mind-state duplicates the content of a brain-state yet duplicates it in a different, mental form. The problem, according to Bergson, is not that mind and brain are different (the usual focus of criticism), it is that they are not different enough: mind-states *duplicate* brain-states, so how can mind-states be different from brain-states? How can a duplicate nonetheless straddle a difference in being? And what would a mind-state add if it is a duplicate? Either the duplicate is useless (the position of eliminativist materialism) and we have failed to explain the phenomenon of experience; or it is not quite a duplicate but constitutes something more (the position of idealism), in which case we have to ask why experience is bogged down in a brainy-body beyond it. The hypothesis of a duplicate that is nonetheless different from what it duplicates begs the question of the relation of mind and matter.

This dualism of duplicates is allied with the traditional doctrine of representation. Mental representations are supposed to straddle the difference between mind and world by duplicating the represented world in an entirely different, mental form. But if a representation *duplicates* the represented, how is it *different* from the represented, how does it re-present it rather than present it yet again? How do we get to something more than a duplicate? The traditional doctrine of representation endlessly begs this question, that is, begs the question of how a brain-state becomes a representation, becomes something different and more than firings of neurons.[6] The question begged here is cognate to—or is—the question begged by traditional dualisms, namely the question of constituting a genuine difference across different regions of being. In begging these questions, the tradition remains below Bergson's "turn of experience," presuming the difference between subject and object, rather than showing how it first arises. Crucially, below the turn of experience the representational relation between subject and object is one of mechanical translation: representation amounts to a shift of content from one form to another in an already established system. At the turn of experience the relation between subject and object would instead involve expression. By seeing how our *sens* of the world arises in a movement of expression, how subject and object become different by elaborating the plane of *sens-non-sens* from within, through expressive movement, we will reconfigure traditional problems of philosophy of mind and approach the turn of experience.

The key point in this regard is that a genuine expression is not a duplicate of what it expresses. An expression is *different* from what it expresses, since what I am trying to express does not at first have the meaning I discover in expression. Yet what I end up expressing is *not something other* than what I was at first trying to express. This is the paradox: the expression is not other than what is expressed, yet is nonetheless different from what is expressed.[7]

The paradox is resolved by realizing that expression is, logically speaking, a movement. If the expression is not something other than what is expressed, it cannot be placed alongside it, any more than an adult can be placed alongside the child she used to be. The difference between the two cannot be conceived in terms of a plane in which the two would be co-present (as in mechanical translation). Yet the expression is different from what is expressed. Wherein the difference? Not in co-presence, but in the *time of movement*. What is expressed *becomes* its expression, as the child becomes the adult.

Bergson helps make precise the sort of movement in question. Expression is *not* movement as conceived within a logic of solids, a shifting (*transport*) of a thing from one point to another, reducible to positions along an already constituted trajectory and plane—that is the sort of movement we find in mechanical translation. Expression is what Bergson calls a real movement: not the shifting of a thing, but the shifting of a state, an indivisible moving whole irreducible to a series of positions (MM, chapter 4). To invoke our origami metaphor, expression isn't like moving a patch of meaning from the middle to the corner of a paper, from inside to outside in a fixed system. Expression is an indivisible moving whole that stretches across the paper, stressing it, wrinkling it from within; expression is like folding the paper so that a patch that doesn't yet have express form is folded and pressed outward, becoming express as the edge of a new origami figure.[8] (An example might be Aristotle's turning the word *hule*, originally meaning lumber, into a word for matter in general; a concept that did not yet have *sens* in Greek is expressed by stressing Greek from within, 'folding' it into a new philosophical language.) Expression changes the meaning of what it moves and elaborates the plane of meaning from within, the one by way of the other, thus shifting *non-sens* into *sens*, shifting states of meaning. As Merleau-Ponty writes, "Expression is everywhere creative, and what is expressed is always inseparable from it [from expression]."[9]

Crucially, *sens* and *non-sens* are not two different *beings*; they are, as Merleau-Ponty might put it, inseparable, and I have argued that they are inseparable because they are two *moments* of an indivisible expressive movement. If we do not represent but express the *sens* of the world, perception and thinking can neither be cut from their ground in the world nor be remanded to the subject. *Sens* and *non-sens* are not two co-present points, they are related by expression as a movement that expressively translates *sens* within *non-sens* such that *sens* bears within itself the *non-sens*, the "unreflective fund," it translates. *Sens* and *non-sens* are not clear-cut beings, but moments that muddle one another and become different through this muddling. This is in marked contrast to the doctrine of representation as a clean transition across the bounds between *non-sens* (the material world out there) and *sens* (the realm in which a part of the same material world, a brain or processor, is magically said to all of a sudden represent the rest of the world), which doctrine leaves us begging for the magical transition. Traditional problems of philosophy of mind are reconfigured when we locate the relation of *sens* and *non-sens* in the movement of expression.

So far I have shown that *logically* expression is movement: it is the becoming different of *non-sens* and *sens*. But this remains vague. How, really, is expression movement and how does it give rise to *sens*? To answer, I turn to gesture, recalling that for Merleau-Ponty "the word is a genuine gesture" and that the word has a "*gestural meaning*" immanent within speech. (*PP* 214/ 183, 208/179)

GESTURE AND EXPRESSION

I am frying some mushrooms. As I reach over the pan, a cluster of oil drops bursts and spatters my hand; the sharp burning feeling is inseparable from a movement already underway, namely withdrawing my hand, quickly shaking it, and exclaiming "ouch!" The shake-"ouch!" gesture expresses pain, or rather it *is* my way of having pain, of having the event not merely happen but express the *sens* of there-being-pain-in-me. The seasoned chef doesn't say "ouch!" but keeps cooking and in doing so does not have this event as pain in the way that I do.

How does the gesture come to express the *sens* of pain? Here is a plausible story. As an infant, I did not have the word *pain* or the gesture "ouch!"; I did not have the *sens* of pain as a distinct experience with a distinct meaning. Not that I didn't have the experience I now call pain, but I did not experience pain *as* pain. I moved about and sometimes what I did hurt, but the hurt played out in an overall convulsion, in emotional move-ment of my body as a whole. But adults around me would react as I hurt myself, clapping hands to mouth, saying "ouch!," shaking their hand if I had hurt a hand, and so on. My movement followed theirs: shaking the hand and saying "ouch!" is what you do when hurting happens, just as pointing and saying "cat" is what you do when the cat walks by. Of course, prior to this, if I had hurt a hand, I would especially move my hand, but that would be part of my overall reaction, undifferentiated within it. As I began to move in an adult way (and of course adults would never move this way if hand-hurting didn't itself lead to hand movement), as hand-hurting was less and less an overall convulsion, and more and more a stylized shake-"ouch!" ges-ture, the overall emotional color that had previously writhed through my whole body was condensed into the shake-"ouch!" gesture.[10]

In condensing an overall bodily movement into a different movement, the movement of one part of the body, the condensation at once 'sums up' the overall emotion and turns it into something new. The 'summing' and novelty arise by way of each other: the 'sum' figures against the ground of what it 'sums up' by turning the ground into something new, something that can be 'summed up' in a different movement; and the 'sum' is a new figure, something that stands out with its own bounds, insofar as it is inherently related to something different that it 'sums up.' The 'sum,' then, isn't math-ematical, since the 'sum' is something new, irreducible to what it 'sums up.'

A similar 'summation' occurs when bodily movement condenses in a more complex pattern, for example, a shock turns into a startled look and retreat, or a thought, memory, or writing process condenses around a word, as in Archimedes' "Eureka!," Citizen Kane's "rosebud," or, perhaps, Merleau-Ponty's "*sens*." If emotion, for Sartre, is consciousness's way of fleeing situations by transforming them, expression is a bodily 'summation by difference' that lets us handle movement by turning it into something different. (Sartre 1993)

I call this 'summation by difference' *articulation*. Rendering a 'sum' that is incommensurate with yet related to what turns out to be its ground articulates both figure and ground at once, as a fold in paper forms a new figure and ground at once.

This leads to a crisper account of the interrelation of *sens* and *non-sens*. To say that the gesture comes to mean pain is not to say that it comes to mean a pain that had previously been there. Rather, the gesture first of all articulates pain *as* pain by giving me a handle on it. Previously there had only been a shock of movement that overran me. Now there is a way of handling it, namely, running it into a shake of the hand and a vocal "ouch!" What had been *non-sens* runs to ground in a *sens*, is articulated into *sens* and *non-sens*. Shock is articulated into pain grounded in shock. But the pain is not something other than the shock, it is the shock articulated, become different. Instead of convulsing or thrashing at the world, I shake my hand and say "ouch!," letting my pain be manifest to others and myself; or, if I am a chef, I express indifference in sticking with my work. The gestural expression of pain articulates shock into a movement proper to our world, especially to our social world.

Expression is muted where we cannot fold movement into movement proper to our world, where there is shock without pain, happening without a handle, *non-sens* that has not yet run aground in *sens*. Perhaps we could speak here of the interval between death and mourning, between shock and expression. To be in that interval is to be dislocated, to be moved without yet knowing how to move, to be emotive without yet having the proper emotion, to be gesticulating without yet gesturing, to be immersed in a *non-sens* that is nonetheless not yet devoid of *sens*, which is why that interval is so shocking. To cross that interval, to handle movement across it, is expression. Expression is a 'translation' that creates, by articulation, the 'text' being 'translated'; the failure of expression is the failure to even create a 'text' to be 'translated.'[11]

But this would mean, and now we can return to the point more concretely, that *sens* contains within it the *non-sens* it translates, and *non-sens* contains the *sens* translated within it: pain contains shock, and shock contains pain. This deepens the point that expression is not a mechanical translation between points on a plane. It is more like an articulatory convulsion in which points already muddled and implied within one another have their differences become express in a new way. Expression is not a movement from pure *non-sens* to pure *sens*, but a movement within what I call *sens-non-sens*.

Here we should recall our Bergsonian background, in which perceptual recognition is not a matter of adding meaning to matter (a magical addition begged by representationalism) but of removing movement from the body-world circuit, that is, folding and constraining. *Sens* is not a ready-made, self-subsistent ingredient *added* to the body, it is a movement of *sens-non-sens* articulated into *sens* by folding movement from within. Body-world movement is thus the native tongue of *sens*; the web of *sens* follows the articulations and condensations of body-world movement. Reworking a Bergsonian word, I shall say that *sens* is *contracted* out of body-world movement, and thus contracts a 'taste' of its moving native tongue. The word *ouch!* contracts shock: there are not two things, shock turned into pain and *then* "ouch!" as a word for pain, an abstract sign added from thin air; gestural expression *is* the having of the pain. The word is the shock contracted into sensible form, and so it retains something of the movement from which it is contracted, giving a taste of shock in verbal form, as the origami figure retains something of the proportion of the paper from which it is contracted, giving a visual 'taste' of planar geometry in figural form. Indeed, the exclamation point is almost part of the spelling of "ouch!," and gives a little taste of shock; the one who utters "ouch" in flat tones is the ironist or comic, not the one in pain. As Sheets-Johnstone and Lakoff and Johnson show in much more detail, our language in general bears many traces of its origin in movement (Lakoff and Johnson 1999, Johnson 1987, Sheets-Johnstone 1999a).

But expressive articulation generates meaning more on the side of the body than on the side of the world. If it is like Bergsonian perceptual recognition, it is affective.[12] In Bergson's account of perceptual recognition, incoming movement repeatedly "translates" back and forth across different zones of the body and goes back to the world in different form. For example, in listening, movements of hearing and speaking cross over, 'scanning' hearing with speaking. By repeated translation through my body, the movement of sound becomes the very different movement of a body listening for words as discrete units. The "translations" here are not expressive but what I call bodily translations. Bodily translation is like routine (nonpoetic) translation from one language to another, in that it involves shifts from one established region of meaning to another, but the 'language' in question is that of the moving body. The 'motor language of hearing' translates, across the body, into a 'motor language of speaking'; in translating between two different, already established 'languages,' the one cuts up the other; hearing is 'scanned' by its differences with speaking, in the way that French is 'scanned' by its differences with English when we translate computer manuals back and forth. Through repeated bodily translation, perceptual recognition turns sonic movement back into a different perceptual movement *toward the world*. In contrast, expressive articulation translates movements of the body into different movements *within the body*: the shock of the oil is 'scanned' and articulated by the gesture of my hand; the movement of a shocked body translates, through the body itself, into the very different movement of a body tenderly moving pained parts.

Perceptual recognition and articulation depend on bodily translation, and bodily translation is due to folds that constrain body-world movement, folds that generate differences when movement crosses a body. The shake-"ouch!" gesture begins in a shock of movement and folds this shock into new movement, articulating shock as something different. But in the case of primary expression the gesture does not just run through existing folds, the movement of shock creates new folds in the body. So expression involves two entwined temporal orders: the order of a gesture (the shock of the oil folding into the shake-"ouch!" movement); and the order of learning to gesture (shock gradually folding into constrained movement that turns shock into gesture). The two orders intertwine: movement on the temporal order of learning generates the fold at play in instances of gestural movement, and instances of partial gestures generate the learning process. In both orders the overall movement is expressive: within a gesture we find a beginning in *non-sens* and an ending in *sens*, but the overall arc of learning also begins with *non-sens* and ends in *sens*. It is in learning, specifically learning habits, that we will find a link between expression, *sens*, and perception.

The account of gesture puts flesh on our bare-bones account of expression. I continue to speak of the shock of movement, playing on two different senses of "shock": as a sheaf or tangle, as in a shock of hair, and as a disturbance. A shock of movement is an as yet inarticulate tangle of movements, a moving disturbance, *non-sens*. Yet as a disturbance that translates through a *limited* body, through a body that isn't just moved but *moves itself in self-limiting ways*, shock is already moving to *sens*. Expression is the movement in which *non-sens* folds into *sens*, in which shock is articulated in a 'summation by difference' that turns what it 'sums up' into something new. Expression is thus a movement that articulates *sens* within *non-sens*. *Sens* thus contracts something of the *non-sens* from which it is articulated. Not only does *sens* cling to the folds of movement, the folds of movement cling to *sens*.

Two questions remain. First, the above does not claim that certain kinds of movement *cause* sense, but that descriptively *sens* is found in the articulatory movement of expression. Articulatory movement is our way of making sense of our moving being in the world in the way that emotional movement, for Sartre (1993), is our way of changing our relation to the world. But how, in detail, does a particular folding accrue *sens* and accrue the particular *sens* that it does? This will require an account of learning as contracting *sens* from other bodies in the social world and one's own body in the natural world, and will point us back to nature as a movement in which *sens* always already inheres.

Second, in the case of gestures or words, expression goes 'from the inside to the outside.' But our target is perception, in which expression goes 'from the outside to the inside,' in which what is expressed is the world, not ourselves. It should already be clear that perception and expression fit together, that wielding the tennis racket expresses our *sens* of its felt length, that wiggling the cork expresses our *sens* of its springy unity.[13] This follows from the turn to perception as inseparable from movement: if perception is not cut off from movement, then perception cannot be based on representations cut off from the world; if perception is not a mechanical duplication of outside *non-sens* in inside representations that magically acquire *sens*; if it is a movement that crosses body and world; then this movement as giving rise to *sens* is the movement of expression. I do not represent the world, but express its *sens*. Perception, though, is not quite the gesture studied above. How does perception involve expression?

To answer I turn to a study of habit, drawing on the connection to learning remarked above, but also recalling that the moving schema of perception as an ensemble of styles is habitual: the folds that constrain body-world movement are habitual.

HABIT AND EXPRESSION

If gesture is a creative, expressive movement that generates *sens* from shock, habit is a way of freezing body-world movement, stereotyping it, so as to preemptively articulate shocks as having *sens*—even if inappropriate. There is the stop sign, I have hit the brakes. Hitting the brakes 'sums up' the stop sign but the 'summary' figure is quite different from the ground that the 'sum' inherently points to.[14] It is in this sense that habit articulates *sens*. But how does habit accrue *sens*, and how does *sens* figure in perceptual acts based on habit? The answer hinges on the point that habits are never entirely frozen; they are on the verge of thaw and change, and thus express the *sens* of a relation to the world.

A while after I moved from my parent's home, they redid the front walk, raising the flagstones at the bottom step of the porch, to keep water from puddling and freezing in the winter. For a long time, on leaving their house after a visit, I wrenched my back on the bottom step. I was not descending material stairs in the present, but the habit stairs of my youth, taking too deep a step at the bottom. Like an extra step at the top of the stairs in the middle of the night, the shallow bottom step was a shock. When stair-stepping habits are appropriate to actual steps, habit removes such shocks: you don't deal with the shock of each step, a series of step-shocks freezes into a habitual movement in which you bounce up or down the steps in a rhythmed lope. Yet the very same habit, because it freezes over individual steps, makes possible a new kind of shock, namely overstepping the bottom in a jolt to the back, or overstepping the top in a jolt to a gullet falling through a phantom step. New shocks are the basis of changes of habit. Habit as freezing out shock contains the seeds of new shock that lead to thaw and reform.

The relation between habit and shock indicates a link to perception. I couldn't tell you the height of the steps at my parents' house, but evidently I perceive, in some sense, their rise. Habit is a kind of frozen perception. Yet this 'freezing' precisely enables new perceptual sensitivities. If I were sensitive to all details of each step, I would never get anywhere and would be incapable of perceiving stairs as general climbing surfaces. Habit is ambiguous: it renders us insensitive to actual situations, but is thus the basis of our power of perceptual generalization, of skipping over detail, of treating situations the same way even if they are different; and, as a determinate insensitivity, habit is the basis of further sensitivity. Habit is a kind of frozen armor that at once dulls and crystallizes sensitivities.

Habit as insensitivity-sensitivity is thus a counterpart to gesture. Gesture is a present folding of movement that expresses my relation to the world right now; gesture articulates a *sens* proper to the moment. Habit is a frozen folding of movement that expresses a general sensitivity to the world, a *sens* not quite sensitive to the moment. If gesture articulates *sens* across the arc of a gesture, habit articulates *sens* across the arc of habit acquisition, beginning with the *non-sens* of shock, and ending with the acquisition of habitual armor.

But so far we remain in an outside perspective. The moving schema of perception is habitual armor. To return to Bergson, the moving schema is akin to an optical medium that limits the movement of light. When placed at a sufficient angle to incident light, light does not pass the medium at all, it reflects, and as Bergson writes, the virtual image that *we* see "symbolizes" the medium's activity of limiting optical movement across the medium-world interface (MM, 37). Similarly with the body: for us looking on, the habitual, schematic character of bodily movement "symbolizes" the body's activity of indeterminately limiting body-world movement, and thus "symbolizes" perception. But for Bergson this is just a "symbol" of *pure perception*, perception that has its locus in the object reacted to, that is not yet a locus of experience in a subject. *We* see a schema that "symbolizes" perception, that for us expresses a meaningful relation between the body and the world, but that is not enough to show that perception—something with *sens*—is happening *for the being* manifesting this schema.

To solve the problem of how there is something more than pure perception, Bergson appeals to pure memory. Perception proper arises in the intersection of pure memory, that is, *durée*, time; and pure perception, that is, material movement. The point of intersection is the body: the body is the point at the tip of the famous "cone of memory," where memory stabs the plane of moving matter. Pure perception and pure memory, body and mind, matter and durée are entirely different in kind, but to be sure there is an affinity of durée and matter, as Bergson shows in chapter four of *Matter and Memory*.[15] Durée contracts the rhythm of matter. For me to experience each electromagnetic oscillation in a burst of red light, my moving encounter with red light would have to be slowed down tremendously; but it would take me hundreds of thousands of years to experience each oscillation in the burst as a distinct event, for me to distinguish red light from other light on the basis of the quantity of oscillations per unit time. The perceptual experience of red contracts all these oscillations with their distinctive rhythm into a quality. Durée is thus in contact with the rhythm and time of the world, or rather it contracts that rhythm into something different, contracts quantity into quality. It is this contraction that gives perception *sens* from within, that turns pure perception into perception. Bergson's entire solution to dualism turns around the point that durée contracts quantitative rhythm into some-thing qualitative. Yet he insists that durée is different in kind from rhythmic, moving matter—no doubt in an effort to free thinking of matter.

Habit, in Merleau-Ponty's sense, poses a challenge to Bergson's division of durée and matter. For Bergson, habit is a simple mechanical process that, by repetition of movements, 'contracts' complex movements into simple ones, without retaining any of the past, and for Bergson in general the body itself has no temporal depth, it is just matter in the present. Habit on its own could not generate anything different in kind from mechanical movement, and this is why the movement of the body acquires *sens* only when the body is stabbed with pure memory.

If one of Merleau-Ponty's great discoveries in the *Phenomenology* is *sens* in movement, another—and it is really just another side of *sens* in move-ment—is the temporal depth of the body, especially as manifest in habit. In stepping down stairs that no longer exist, in going through a stop sign, in having a phantom limb, my bodily movement insists on retention of the past and protention of a future; my movement is not just a displacement of matter, but a being in time that has a *sens*.

We detected this temporal depth of the body in habit as insensitivity-sensitivity. Described from the outside, the movement of habit acquisition begins with *non-sens* and ends in *sens*. But that articulation of *sens*, expressed in the arc of habit acquisition, does not vanish into present routines, it is not just apparent from the outside. We are faced with it in the volatile balance of insensitivity-sensitivity intrinsic to having a habit; the articulation of *sens* and *non-sens* achieved over the arc of habit acquisition is contracted into a habit that threatens to return to insensitivity or to turn into new sensitivity. My habit is not entirely in the present, but teeters between past and present, thus confronting me with the *sens* expressed in the arc of habit acquisition (in the way that the arc of my gesturing confronts me with the *sens* expressed in the gesture).

In acting from solidified habit in the present, my perception indeed almost occurs in the object to which I am responding, in the manner of Bergson's pure perception. I hardly notice the stop sign that I am stopping for; further, I almost don't notice that I have noticed the stop sign, I am on 'autopilot,' riding a habit to work (see Russon 1994); my perceptual response goes back to the thing upon which it reacts, leaving no trace in me, leaving me pure of having perceived. But in the shock of realizing I have gone through a stop sign, the commitment to the world frozen in my habit as balance of insensitivity-sensitivity is cracked, thawed, and thrown back at me: the commitment is expressed not just for the outside viewer, but for me. I am not a mirror, nor am I a telegraphic exchange (Bergson's metaphor) routing movements in the present; I am a habitual being, and a habitual being at once freezes over and forges meaningful commitments to the world, the one by way of the other. The forging of meaning is not reduced to the present, but retains its past, retains its momentum toward the future, and comes alive in the present when habits thaw and reform.

In short, having a moving schema based in habit expresses in and for the body a relationship to the world, a relation that has a *sens*. Habits are not dropped into our laps, they are an *achievement*. The *sens* achieved in acquiring a habit is contracted into present habits, ready to be thrown back in express form when habits crack and thaw. A mirroring medium does not experience its relation to a point outside, it just reflects light back, and the virtual image left behind by that reflection "symbolizes" this limit to the outside observer. But a cracked mirror does not insist that it reflects a virtual image. We do. My arm is not a mere motor mechanism. As a habitual way of relating to the world, fringed with the balance of insensitivity-sensitivity, my arm "symbolizes" a certain way of being in the world, and if it should crack I may still insist on that way of being in the world—hence, according to Merleau-Ponty, phenomena such as the phantom limb. Bergson reduces habit to a mechanism in the present, and so for Bergson, *sens* can arise only if the body is stabbed with the cone of memory; but Merleau-Ponty finds a temporal dimension within the habitual body—the body stabs itself with memory. So the body can manifest *sens* within itself. This *sens* is always implied in habits, and becomes express when habits crack.

In detecting meaning in the temporality of the body, Merleau-Ponty commits meaning and thinking to roots in moving nature. This, as suggested below, can work only if nature is no longer an inert sphere of matter but a nature that moves and articulates itself. We shall be led to this point about nature if we return to a question posed above: It is one thing to show that in general a gesture or habit expresses *sens*. But how does a gesture or habit acquire the particular *sens* that it expresses? To answer I take the time of habit back into the time of habit formation, of learning.

LEARNING AND *SENS*

HABIT AS A SCALE OF FOLDS, AND LEARNING

In what follows I expand the concept of habit to cover a scale of learned movement patterns. Just below the lower fringe of the scale, not really belonging

to it, are those folds of movement with which one is born—natural constraints of the moving body. Above that are the basic, learned movements
of the body, for example, walking, grasping, reaching, sitting, and the slightly
more idiosyncratic inflections of these moving patterns contracted in learning them in specific situations, for example, one's unique style of walking, of
going up and down specific stairs, and so on. Habit in the usual sense—I call
it habit proper—falls somewhere in this range. Above this range are skills—
more complex and specific movement repertoires that not everybody learns,
such as driving and ballet. Above that I include habitual forms of secondary
expression acquired through the cultural milieu in which we learn language,
dialect, lingo, usage, and so on; and the even more idiosyncratic quirks of
rhythm and gesture that testify to our own individual paths of learning.
Above the higher fringe of the scale, not really belonging to it, are movements of primary expression that are not stereotyped but creative.

It should be clear that there is an ambiguity in locating a given learned
movement pattern on this scale: isn't a given person's ability to do ballet, for
example, both a skill, a stylized expressive repertoire, and a site of idiosyncratic quirks of balletic expression? Yes, and a full analysis, if possible, would
depend on the individual case and require many subtle distinctions. The
point of conceiving habit as a scale is not to establish a quantitative ranking
but to draw basic learned movements, habits proper, skills, styles, and idiosyncratic quirks into a continuum of learned bodily movement, whilst punc-
tuating the continuum with a differentiating principle that reminds us that
not all instances of learned bodily movement are the same.

There are at least three interrelated differentiating principles at work
in the scale. First, complexity. Folds higher on the scale are folded out of
folds lower on the scale, and are in that sense differentiated as more complex. But we must recall that in the case of folding, complexity is not a
matter of accretion, of stacking independent units on lower units, but of
folding the lower in a new way. So a gain in complexity both upwardly
contracts lower folds into a higher complex, and downwardly modifies lower
folds. Learning ballet contracts something of the way you walk and stand and
thence your quirky style of walking, and at the same time it downwardly
modifies your walk and stance; a similar relation holds between the quirks of
your balletic expression and your initial palette of ballet movements.

This upward and downward overlapping accounts for the ambiguity
noted above. The points on the scale aren't independent of each other,
ranked according to an outside measure of degree. Points on the scale differentiate by overlapping, and this movement of differentiation generates a
scale susceptible of coordinate ordering by both degree and kind, in which
differences in kind are nonetheless irreducible to differences of degree. This
is what Collingwood (1933) would call a "scale of forms." But I call this
particular scale a scale of *folds*, since habits are folds, and the metaphor of
folds (unlike forms) directly captures the overlapping that yields the peculiar

confusion of degree and kind belonging to the scale. (The difference be-tween intensive and extensive magnitudes, noted by Kant and developed by Deleuze, would also be helpful here, and so too is Hegel's discussion of the logic of magnitudes and measures.)[16]

The second differentiating principle, related to the first, is of individu-ality and idiosyncrasy. At the low end are folds shared by all bodies; higher in the scale are more individualized folds. All sheets of paper are roughly the same, but in folding they become more individualized, turning into dragons versus roses, with individual roses looking different because of quirks in fold-ing. Developing complex folds of movement is not a matter of unrolling a rolled-up program, of jumping to a new point on an established scale, but of a process of successive folding that contracts the movement of learning, with all its quirks and detours, into present movement. So more complex folds will also be more individual, idiosyncratic.

The third principle, related to the second, is of independence. At the low end the folds we have are dependent on nature, on our natural bodies. Above that, the folds we learn depend on our social sphere, since we depend on others in acquiring kinetic abilities. But as we move from basic habits to complex skills, we become more independent of a fixed nature and a social sphere, more inclined to choose who we are going to learn from, and eventu-ally begin to teach ourselves to move, and to learn things independent of other individuals. Individuality of habit couples with independence of learning.

Two notes: First, acquiring more complex habits is not a matter of transcending the body, of approximating to a disembodied agent. (Feminist critics, for example, argue that Merleau-Ponty has this view of our relation to the moving body.)[17] Learning is rather a matter of developing one's own body in one's own way, of sinking into to it as one's own, which would include sinking into it as a being with her or his own movements and imperatives. Second, I illustrated the scale with examples that could be construed as 'stages' in a linear development from infancy to adulthood. But this is for the sake of exposition. It is misleading to think that devel-opment means linear movement up the scale, or that movement up the scale can be achieved only through linear development—that would repeat the error of 'stages.' Isn't it the case that the child begins by trying to express her own individual moving, desiring relation to the world, but that requires abilities such as walking that impose certain simplifications and generalities? In this case learning isn't a linear progression up the scale, but a leap up it, where the leap becomes stable only when novel movement becomes stereotyped and general, that is, by dropping back down the scale. And doesn't the development of complex artistic expression begin by break-ing up stereotyped complexes? In a scale of folds where differences up-wardly and downwardly overlap and modify one another, the concept of linear progress up the scale is complicated by the peculiar upward and downward dynamics of actual learning.

The important point is that learning involves movement on the scale, even if the movement is not linear or progressive. Learning is something like a diachronic version of Bergson's motor schema. The motor schema is movement that recognizes things by playing across different zones of the body, synchronically. Learning is a movement that plays across differences in successive foldings and unfoldings of habit, diachronically, generating *sens*, as we will see, by contracting *sens* up and down the scale, either from other bodies, or from one's own body.

SKILLS AND DELIBERATE LEARNING: CONTRACTING *SENS* FROM THE SOCIAL BODY

Moving and perceiving are two sides of the same coin. We arrived at this point by analysis of perception and its moving schema. But the point is already clear to those who teach or learn complex skills. Driving instructors do not just teach learners how to move the wheel and accelerator, but how to perceive the traffic world, the one by way of the other. As novelist David Foster Wallace vividly shows, tennis isn't just a matter of swinging a racket but of perceiving a 'gamey' geometry of the court, of learning the angles, vectors and ways of seeing that give advantage in tennis as a moving game of chess (Wallace 1996, 1997). Learning to play tennis is learning the *sens* of the tennis world. But how do I learn this *sens* if I do not already have it, if I would already need that *sens* to move and perceive in such a way as to be exposed to that *sens* in the first place? Wouldn't learning such a *sens*, a sensible structuring of the moving world, be a bit like learning the basic structure of space, which, as Kant shows, is impossible unless you possess that structure a priori?

Bergson gives a wonderfully insightful account of learning a skill in *Matter and Memory*. Herewith a version of it, drawing on the key insight that learning a skill is a process in which movements are recomposed by repeating their decomposition, what I call a synthesis that proceeds by repeating an analysis.[18] I do not see the tennis instructor doing a backhand and then immediately reproduce the movement as a whole. To do that, I would already need to be able to do the backhand. But that is precisely what I cannot do, what I am trying to learn. So the instructor breaks the backhand into fragments, and I learn how to perform the fragments, by deploying or modifying habits, folds, that I already have. Still, I have not learned the backhand if I perform it as a series of movement fragments. That sort of fragmentary, choppy movement is characteristic of the learner, or of the comic—I am thinking of Jacques Tati as M. Hulot—who draws out humor in human movement by unhinging it from within. It is not until fragments slide into a smooth whole that I have learned the backhand. How do I achieve the smooth whole? Precisely by doggedly repeating the choppy fragments in a sequence that follows the smooth whole modeled by the instructor, until the fragments start flowing into one another in my own movements.

I am a being who gets to play tennis only by *learning* how to. I cannot directly or instantaneously copy the moving figure manifest in the instructor's moving body. That figure must be unfolded into a network of folds, analyzed, either by the instructor, or by me trying to break things down. But the folds revealed by analysis are fragments of a whole, folds implicated in one another in the instructor's body. The folds retain something of their co-implication. As I repeat fragmentary folds in my body, these implications are activated, and the folds gradually fold back into a whole, are synthesized, in the way that someone playing with an unfolded piece of origami, by following folds hinged into one another in the paper, may fold it back up (although it won't come out exactly the same). Learning a skill is not a direct transfer of moving wholes from instructor to learner, but a 'synthesis by analysis': it is only by repeating, over and over, analyzed movement in my body that I synthesize the complex movement of the instructor's body. Crucially, the synthesis by analysis is conducted within the movement of bodies. (Being able to learn or re-jig movements just by watching or talking is characteristic of experts well past the simple stage of acquiring skills.) Skill acquisition depends on synthesis by analysis and on the interrelation of the bodies in which alone this synthesis by analysis occurs.

What is transferred in skill acquisition is not just a way of moving, but a *sens* of the world. In learning the backhand, I learn how to approach the ball, court, and world, I learn a whole attitude and orientation to the world, a *sens* that I did not yet have. I do not gain that new *sens* directly, as if handed it ready-made and entire. When I first step onto the court, I glimpse a *sens* in the instructor's way of moving, but I do not yet have it. (How did the instructor see what was going to happen? It seems almost magical!) But in learning, an aspect of the instructor's moving schema of perception is unfolded along the lines of moving bodies, analyzed; and when I play and replay that analyzed movement in my moving body, I refold it, synthesize it, and begin to acquire a new *sens*. I do not already need to have the *sens* to learn it, because I never seize *sens* entire from the instructor. In some sense, I learn the *sens* from *myself*, from moving in a certain choppy way and having it fall together in my own movement. I cannot directly seize the *sens* of being Cary-Grant-like, that seems vague and mysterious, if distinctive; but if I catch and repeat fragments of Grant's expressions, the minimal mouth move-ment that seems as crucial to his manner as tautness to a drum-roll, I start feeling Grant-ish, and other gestures snap along, sharpening a rhythm of screwball repartee.

Returning to the discussion of Merleau-Ponty, Collingwood, and Plato's *Meno* at the end of the previous chapter, skill acquisition is not a matter of transferring something from the class of the things without *sens* to those with *sens*, but of having *sens* in a different and better way. Vague *sens* analyzed and played out in my body becomes clear through a synthesis conducted in my own body.

The movement from vagueness to clarity is a synthesis by analysis, which has an ontological structure cognate to 'summation by difference,' to what I called articulation, and to 'bodily translation.' (Here we are already beginning to see an underlying ontology.) But articulation involves more or less spontaneous folding of body-world movement. In contrast, skill acquisition depends on and is constrained by a *sens* vaguely outlined in another's body, and by the commonalities of moving bodies in which synthesis by analysis takes place.

This provides a partial first answer to the question: how does a habit acquire the particular *sens* that it expresses? In the case of a skill, I contract *sens* from another body into my own. A particular *sens* clings to the folds of my movement because I acquire my skilled way of moving by unfolding and refolding folds of another moving body.

But that defers the question. How does a body have a particular *sens* in the first place?

Habits and Natural Learning: Contracting *Sens* from One's Own Body

In learning a skill from an other I begin with a vague *sens* in another body and end up with that *sens* sharpened in my own body. In more basic cases of learning—what I will call natural learning—our own bodies offer the vague *sens* that prompts an analysis in movement. Such an analysis amounts to a breakdown of our moving relation to the world. In getting past it by a new synthesis, we sharpen and contract a *sens* from our own bodies.

It is a fact about us that, unless and until we become incredibly skilled and versatile, we need to learn skills by repeating and following others. Related to this is the fact that we need to learn how to move about. We have to learn how to roll over, sit up, crawl, stand, walk, ascend and descend stairs. Nobody offers us analytical instruction in learning these movements, nobody provides a template of delineated movement fragments (in the manner of a tennis instructor), even if others help out in crucial ways. Rather, the world and others draw us into new engagements that provoke a breakdown of movement, an analysis that reveals a new, vague *sens*, and the consequent repetition amounts to a synthesis that sharpens a new *sens*.

The infant reaches out for a toy or an other's hand, drawing on the *sens* of her reaching, extending body, falls over, tries again, falls over, and again. A stable fold of movement that lets the infant reach a little ways from the body intersects with the world in encouraging a broader reach, but falls apart, exposing a new vague *sens*. Fragments of movement formerly folded into an inseparable whole fall apart, a leg and hand that had formerly always extended in sync with one another begin to move separately, the leg providing stability, the hand stretching out. An existing *sens* of the body crosses into the world so as to provoke an analysis. In repeating the analysis, new movement fragments fall together in a new way, and the infant acquires not only a new way of moving, but a new *sens*. In learning a skill, an other's body provides a vague *sens* together with its analysis; when repeated in my body, the analysis lets me sharpen a new *sens*. In natural learning, the world that crosses into the body provokes this vague *sens* and its analysis; repetition in the body once again synthesizes the new *sens*.

This helps answer the question how a body comes to have a particular *sens* in the first place: *sens* is contracted out of the body itself in learning to move in a provocative natural and social world.

The question as to why the body itself has a vague *sens* that can be provoked into sharpening would take us into questions about the very nature of the body and of nature itself. Such questions cannot be pursued here, and are no doubt the sorts of questions that Merleau-Ponty was trying to pursue in *The Visible and the Invisible*, which is not just a turn to the philosophy of being of Heidegger, but to the philosophy of nature of Schelling, or that Bergson was trying to pursue in *Creative Evolution*. One cannot develop a philosophy of perception that overcomes traditional dualisms without also rethinking life and nature.

The concept of nature demanded by everything said so far is one in which nature is no longer a ready-made whole with crisply specified laws, but is itself a movement from vague organization to clear organization. Nature itself would not be the unfolding of an already achieved synthesis, would not be rightly analyzed on solid lines. Nature itself would be a synthesis by analysis, a fluid, moving whole, the very movement of which breaks up into partial movements that retain a trace of the movement from which they unfold and thus in the very movement of breaking up fold back together so as to generate new movements. A feature of such a nature would be that parts of it already overlap one another and reflect one another in different forms, that is, the relations of synthesis by analysis, summation by difference, and bodily translation would reflect the ontology of nature. Merleau-Ponty is searching for such an ontology in *The Visible and the Invisible*, with his pursuit of resonances, a narcissism of the other, and in this pursuit he is going back to Schelling's "wild being," to the "identity philosophy" which seeks the difference of subject and object as unfolding from their identity.[19] But we should not forget Hegel. In his earliest book, *The Structure of Behaviour*, Merleau-Ponty writes that the phenomenon of life appears "at the moment when a piece of extension, by the disposition of its movements and by the allusion that each movement makes to all the others, folded back upon itself [*se repliait*] and began to express something, to manifest an interior being externally" (*SdC* 175/162). Here Merleau-Ponty is conceiving expression through Hegel's philosophy of nature, via Hyppolite, who, it is worth remarking, is one of Deleuze's inspirations.[20] My analysis shows that expression is something like the folding mentioned in *The Structure of Behaviour*, but it is not extension that folds, rather *movement* itself folds from within. A shock of movement washes through being, overruns a body that limits movement, breaks up in translating across a body, and by the allusion that each movement in the shock makes to all the others, the shock folds, effecting a summation by difference, an articulation. So perhaps in his earliest philosophy Merleau-Ponty is already thinking of nature as a movement that differentiates by way of folding itself into a different sum, which is perhaps also what Renaud Barbaras means by desire (Barbaras 1999, 2000). Realize, though, what such a summation by difference in the folding of movement amounts to: an inside is expressed in an outside, pain is expressed in the gesture; but the outside is equally expressed in the inside: the painful gesture expresses the shock of the world, as the painting (to draw on Merleau-Ponty's *Eye and Mind* and "Cezanne's Doubt") expresses the look of the mountain. This reversing of inside and outside in expression is, I think, what is meant by chiasm.[21]

In any case, if we wish to find a *sens* in movement, without falling into a logic of solids, and if we wish to answer the question why there is *sens* in the first place, then at the level of the living body, I think we shall have to say that *sens* belongs to a moving body that needs to learn how to move, that learns from others, and that can learn to move differently, that can teach itself to move differently, that itself stumbles upon and encounters differences in ways of moving. Most of all, a body of this sort will have to be conceived as desiring, else it would never learn. A being that did not need to learn how to move, that could move in only one way, that never stumbled, that did not desire, would not have the sort of labile *sens* that we detected in perception, but a crystalline meaning that would transcend movement, the sort of meaning urged by representationalism or to be found in the mind of God. On the other hand, the movement in question here is a movement of learning, a movement that implicates itself in what we might call the social and the symbolic: it would be wrong to say that certain movements of bodies on their own cause *sens*; rather *sens* is contracted in moving bodies that are part of larger movements, social movements, symbolic movements.

And so perhaps we return to Hegel here, detecting a fleshy matrix for Hegel's logic of recognition: a body that needs to learn to move from others is a body that is operating as a bodily "I" that is "We," and a body of this sort depends on a bodily "We" that is "I," a social body that helps—and thus also possibly hinders and does violence to—the movement and growth of individual bodies.

The *sens* of space is shaped by this fleshy matrix from which we contract *sens*. If there is a specific *sens* in movement, a *sens* that is not plucked from thin air but is worked out, expressed, in movement itself, it is because a body that needs to learn to move in relation to the world and to other bodies already has, in its relation to the world and others, a vague *sens* that constrains the contraction and sharpening of *sens*, a vague *sens* that always traces back into movement that can never be fully solidified or completed as a point of origin, but that trails back behind us in movement that exceeds us.

THE TOPOLOGY OF EXPRESSION

The fleshy matrix from which we contract the *sens* of space is constrained by a specific logic of interrelated parts and movements that spreads out over the place of the body into the social and natural world. I shall call this constraining logic the topology of expression. To begin, a couple of general points about my concept of topology.

In *The Roots of Thinking* Maxine Sheets-Johnstone has many insightful discussions of the topology of the body. These discussions are geared to thinking about the way that topological properties of the living body become a phenomenological template for behaviors and concepts, for example, the mouth as opening becomes a template for concepts of inside and outside, the movement of teeth and different topological properties of craggy molars and bladelike incisors become a template for grinding and chopping tools, the rhythm of bipedal motion becomes a template for counting. Her focus is on topology in terms of shape characteristics of body parts, and relations that remain invariant through bodily motion; her (very critically qualified) model is topology as a science that studies shape characteristics that remain invariant through certain stretching operations.

My interest is not so much in shape characteristics of body parts as in the logic of relations between parts of the body as a spread-out place that is nonetheless a unified whole, the "original here" discussed in the introduction. This interest stems from a small remark by Merleau-Ponty immediately preceding his discussion of the illusion of the double marble and his point that the "theory of the body schema is already, implicitly, a theory of perception" (PP 239/206). Merleau-Ponty writes that "The thing, and the world, are given to me along with the parts of my body, not by any 'natural geometry,' but in a living connection comparable, or rather identical with that existing between parts of my body itself" (PP 237/205). This is clearly coupled with an earlier remark that if we describe the spatiality of the body we find that "parts are not spread out side by side, but [are] enveloped in each other" (PP 114/ 98). That is, the geometry of the world, the structure of lived space, is not reflective of a mathematical geometry, but of a living, 'phenomenal geometry' of the body. The lived body, we could say, stands to lived space in an articulatory relation: the lived body 'sums up' space in a form that is different from but not other than space, since the two cross one another. The lived body 'sums up' space as lived space. Again we are confronted by the ontology I noted above, and the concept of bodily translation: in the body, zones and movements envelop one another, translate one another in very different forms, and when movement repeatedly translates through the body, the body translates the world. But the 'phenomenal geometry' of such a translating or articulating body is not that of classical topological descriptions of the body. It is not even defined by the sorts of meanings that Sheets-Johnstone discovers inherent in shapes of body parts as figuring in movements like putting food in one's mouth, chewing food, and walking. Merleau-Ponty points us to a more fundamental 'geometry,' one in which the most basic unity of the body is at stake: the body "is not presented to us in virtue of the law of its constitution, as the circle is to the geometer," "it is an expressive unity which we can learn to know only by taking it up," that is, by *living* the body. What counts in this expressive 'geometry' of the body is the way that life takes up parts spread out alongside one another and envelops them in one another through movement as a unified whole that expresses an attitude toward the world. So the 'geometry' in question has to do with fundamental facts about the way parts work together in the movement of an expressive body.

In other words, the living body is a special sort of place, with a special topology. As noted in the introduction, all the parts of the body are absorbed into one original and unified 'here.' The logic of parts and wholes that would apply to any other place (*topos*) does not quite apply in the place of body. The body has a different topo-logic (place-logic), a living, phenomenal topo-logic, in which parts are not beside one another, but envelop one another in movement. More, the topo-logic of the body extends into a larger place. As Edward S. Casey shows in *Getting Back into Place*, the body is, in Casey's term, inherently "implaced": to be is to be in place. Casey shows that our sense of place inherently has to do with a coupling of body and place; for example, left-right and ahead-behind stem from the moving interaction of the body and place. That is, the topo-logic of the body would stem not only from the peculiar logic of parts and wholes in the lived body, but from the body's relation to place. I agree. The phenomenal topo-logic of the body, as shown in the next chapter, runs between the body as a special place and the larger place in which the body lives. We have already seen that the social place of the body is vital to learning, and subsequent chapters show that more fundamental relations to place, for example, to the earth as a place of residing, already figure in the relation between parts and wholes of the body. But if we are not to turn the living geometry of the body into a possession of the subject, and thus close the subject to the world, violating the method outlined above, place must already anticipate the sort of geometry of envelopment or bodily translation that we detect in the body. We shall see this below.

The topology of expression is the topo-logic of a body crossed over with place, conceived as a constraint on the developmental and expressive process of the body, a constraint that shapes the *sens* that we contract from our body moving and growing in place. If learning to move expresses *sens* in our bodies, that learning is constrained by the spread and implacement of our moving bodies. The topology of expression thus designates the living intersection of spatial and temporal, fleshy-placial and developmental-habitual, aspects of the living, moving body. It is a concept for thinking of *sens* as arising in a moving, growing body in place. The concept is fleshed out in subsequent chapters.

CONCLUSION

Bergson's account of perception, of how there is something more than pure perception, of how there is *sens*, depends on the lightning of pure memory striking the plane of pure matter in the singular point of the body. *Sens* depends on a leap across differences in kind that nonetheless have an affinity. Our pursuit of *sens* in movement took us in another direction, into the time of expression, of gesture, habit acquisition and learning, and thence directed us to the topo-logic of the implaced body, a topology that constrains the expressive movement of learning. In the topology of expression, what Bergson would call matter and memory intersect in a mutual constraint. In a body that moves by growing, grows by moving, and is spread out in place, *sens* is contracted from the mutual constraint and co-implication of movement spread in place and developmental movement stretched in time. In effect, the concept of the topology of expression plunges us inside that turning point where, in Bergson's account, the cone of memory stabs the plane of matter. But instead of a featureless point, the body is an open wrinkle of place and temporality overlapping one another, waiting to unfold and refold in a movement that sharpens new *sens* by contracting it from vague *sens*. *Sens* is not to be traced back to an already constituted origin outside of *sens*, it is not caused to come into being by such an origin; rather *sens* arises in a continual movement of becoming, and the concepts of articulation and the topology of expression help us gain insight into this movement by tracing constraints on this movement from within.

The chapters of part two explore this topology of expression, or rather aspects of it that I call topologies, showing how our *sens* of space is contracted out of it and how spatial *sens* depends on the social.

PART II

THE SPATIAL SENSE
OF THE MOVING BODY

CHAPTER 4

ENVELOPING THE BODY IN DEPTH

I AM WALKING DOWN the hill toward my house. As I move toward it, it turns different faces toward me. First I see only its west side, with the north face tucked in behind, hidden, although obviously there. As I get closer, the north face swings into view, and the west side contracts behind until all I see is the north face; and then the east side makes an appearance, and so on, as I move past and around the back of my house. For my moving, seeing body, the house is not there all at once, its faces dance by, swallowed up and enveloped in one another.

This experience belies the traditional claim that visual depth perception reconstructs, from two-dimensional arrays of data, spatial properties of a fully present solid object in space. And it belies the claim that the object of perception is a fully present solid thing. Within perception, a fully present object is mythical. As Husserl, Merleau-Ponty, and others point out, we never perceive a thing as fully present all at once; things are present through limited perceptual aspects.

Does this mean we are never presented with solid things? No, it just means that some form of quasi-absence inheres in solidity. In fact, Merleau-Ponty argues that this quasi-absence is definitive of perceived solidity: solidity is manifest as an inexhaustible quasi-absence that is continually replenished during perceptual explorations. My house is solid, I live in it, it is there at the bottom of the hill. But I am a small, finite being-in-depth, I perceive the house from the limited place of my body, I cannot encompass the house all at once. So my house has hidden sides, sides that are quasi-absent, but are nonetheless present as the sequel to visible sides. The hidden sides belong to the perceptual envelope of the house. Imagine that my house is replaced with a film-set façade. At the top of the hill I see the west side, but as I move closer the envelope of my house sadly fails to unfold into something more since it is just a façade. But the west side of my real house unfolds into the north face, there is a sort of continual peristaltic movement in which sides unfold into new sides and consume sides past. This is palpably revealed in a stop motion or overcranked film of a house or a building going by: the faces of the building rhythmically swing into and swallow one another, giving a sense of a solid building spinning in space around its corners, like a dancer spinning around feet that periodically tamp down into the ground. I perceive my house as solid not because I see all of it at once, but because it inexhaustibly hides and reveals itself in a peristaltic flow that couples with my movement around it.[1]

Our perception of unified solid things in depth does not refer to replete geometrical solids, but to the envelopes of things, to what Edward S. Casey calls, following William James, their voluminousness. We perceive either the outside envelope of a thing's volume, as when we see a house from the outside, or the inside envelope of a thing's volume, as when we perceive a room from the inside. And we perceive such envelopes as a flow of parts that continually unfold into and envelop one another in movement.

The flowing, voluminous envelope through which we perceive the solid pith of things is key to depth perception, since depth perception is a matter of perceiving solid things that are separate from us. Place is also key, since it enables our explorations of the inexhaustible envelopes of things. I show that the way that parts of things envelop one another is correlative to and constrained by the way body parts envelop one another in movement, and is further constrained by the larger place in which movement happens. Together these two constraints specify what I call the topology of enveloping: if we look into the point in which the body crosses with the world, we find that it has a topo-logic of parts that envelop one another in relation to larger place. Our movement with the world is folded through this topology and thence expresses a *sens* of depth, in the way that a shock folded through the gesture expresses a *sens* of pain.

THE TOPOLOGY OF ENVELOPMENT
AND THE PROBLEM OF DEPTH

Transforming the Problem of Depth

A brief, dialectical review is in order, to see how our study of the moving body transforms yet retains aspects of the traditional approach to depth.

Traditional inferential accounts conceive depth perception as the reconstruction of an already specified distance between ourselves and things. Imagine a computer model of a scene of perception. The positions, surfaces, and volumes of the body and things around it would be fully specified. From this specification it is possible to construct the two-dimensional images projected on the retinas of the body in the model, which is the business of computer engines for running simulations or 3-d computer games. Depth perception is the reverse process: reconstructing the three-dimensional model from the two-dimensional retinal images. Inferential accounts presuppose what Merleau-Ponty calls a ready-made world in which all things are fully present, but the body accesses only limited aspects of the ready-made world, and so must reconstruct the full presence of things from limited aspects.

The introduction showed that this leads to circles and a brittleness of perception, and thence to problems explaining the lability and meaning of depth perception. At bottom, the problem is the presumption that depth perception is *nothing more* than the reconstruction of solids from 2-d retinal images. It is not. After sessions in flight simulators, highly trained pilots, capable of spinning jets through spirals and landing them on stormed-tossed aircraft carriers, get "simulator sickness": they tend to crash their cars, become nauseated, and so on. After simulator sessions, they are forbidden to fly real airplanes or drive their cars. Simulated images are of course very similar to real images, otherwise they could not be used to simulate the flying of real planes. But then why is it that after flying real planes, and seeing roughly the same sorts of images as in the simulator, pilots *do not* tend to crash their cars, become sick, and so on? The answer suggested by previous chapters is that perception is not a matter of reconstructing a ready-made world from limited aspects, it is a matter of moving in the world in a limited way. You don't see with your eyes, or at least not just with your eyes, you see with a moving body that crosses with the world, and what you see expresses limitations of that crossing. Simulators introduce drastic and artificial limits on body-world movement, sever the crossing of body and world, and thus disturb perception.[2]

Ecological psychology repairs inferential accounts by repairing the crossing of body and world. But it tends to reduce that crossing to optics, physics, and so on, to laws specified in advance of the crossing of body and world. Installing the crossing of body and world in a framework of laws institutes a new variant of the ready-made world, and makes it difficult to account for the lability and *sens* of perception.

Instead of installing perception in ready-made frameworks that start from a closed body or world, we sought a point at the "turn of experience," a point where body and world are open to one another, not yet distinct. In this point we found movement. Body and world form a moving circuit, and movement in this circuit folds, specifying an overall constraint, a moving schema of perception. Body-world movement folds because the point in question is not featureless, but has a topology that constrains body-world movement from the start. When we learn how to move, from ourselves or others, a *sens* implied in that topology is contracted into our movement, becomes express. This chapter enters into that point in more detail, tracing a topology of envelopment within it, and showing how the *sens* of perception expresses this topology.

But we should not just discard traditional accounts and traditional problems. We should learn from them. Even if the tradition arrives at the wrong answers, or misconceives problems, the tradition points to genuine problems that help specify the topology we are seeking:

(1) The problem of separation by contact: The most basic problem of the tradition is how we get from what is given in the body, say retinal images, to perception of things separate from the body. The problem becomes a false problem when the given is reduced to the terminus of a movement entering the body, as if the given, once given, could be detached from the body-world movements that give rise to it; as if light, once it hits the retina, turned into a pixel to be processed; as if that pixel were not a continually changing symbol of a limited relation between body and world, in the way that the virtual image in the mirror is a symbol of the stoppage of light. On the other hand, visual perception of course has something to do with light moving on the retinas. The true problem behind the false one is that perception involves givenness, givenness dependent on a primordial, moving contact with things. Yet perception takes that contact as a separation between us and things. This is precisely what happens at "the turn of experience." The true problem specifies a fundamental, almost analytic, constraint on perception: before we perceive things separate from us, we must have a pre-objective, moving contact with things. The body as place of perception crosses into a larger place of things.

(2) The problem of unity through spreading: Another traditional problem is how we get from a multiplicity of bodily givens to unified perception. The problem becomes a false one when the unity and multiplicity are abstracted from their embeddedness in the crossing of body and world (for example, turned into the synthesis of data, or reduced to a fixed ecological law). The true problem is that our primordial contact with things is given in a spread-out body that contacts things through a multiplicity of parts and movements. The true problem specifies yet another constraint: if there is to be perception, a moving, spread-out body must move as one.

(3) The problem of place: This is another side of the problem of separation by contact. Although the given occurs in me, what I perceive is placed outside me. I do not see images on my retina, but things outside me. The 'pink elephant' is a hallucination not merely because it is the wrong color, but because I cannot place it outside me, it just floats through the room with blatant disregard for place. The traditional problem is how something given in the body is experienced as something placed outside the body. Once we move to the turn of experience, the problem becomes a false one: perception was never a collection of givens in me, but a limitation in a circuit of body-world movement; perception goes back to and refers to outside places because it is movement in the world; where the tradition can imagine the perceiver is a brain in the vat, at the turn of experience and in the phenomenological life-world, the perceiver is a moving being in a place.

So the problem is no longer how perception refers to a place of the per-ceived. The true problem is how the place of the perceived acquires the *sens* of being independent of the body-world circuit. This is Bergson's problem of how pure perception becomes perception proper. Put otherwise, at the turn of experience, we are beyond the skepticism that would cut the subject from the world, we are committed to perception as moving in the world. The 'inside' is already stretched outside itself, the place of the body already moves through the place of the world; the problem is how this primordial contact that crosses over with the world acquires the *sens* of a relation between an explicit inside and outside. We shall encounter this as the problem of how primordial depth becomes objective—and the answer will depend on the permanence of a place beyond the body.

Things and Place

The last problem occasions some preliminary remarks on perception, things and place.

The difference between real things and pink elephants is that real things occupy place and they present, as Merleau-Ponty urges, an inexhaust-ible wealth of different aspects. The pink elephant not only disregards the place it floats through, its front side doesn't open onto a back side, and so on. It looks as if we have two separate criteria for the reality of the thing: (1) occupying place; (2) being inexhaustible. But the inexhaustibility of the thing is coupled with its being in place.

A work of art by James Turrell, *Atlan* (1986, installed in the Musée d'art contemporain de Montréal), makes this vivid. Walking into a darkened room, you view what looks like a rectangle of light projected on the wall, a strange blue light, perhaps from a video-beam projector, and you wonder why the video has stopped playing, or what *really* you are supposed to be seeing. The whole experience is obscure, ambiguous, and vague. So you wander around. You discover there is no projector playing the beam. As you move, you perceive that the rectangle doesn't sit right; there is something strange, disturbing about it. I would put it this way: your movement provokes a queasy question as to the being of the rectangle, it directly provokes onto-logical unease. Eventually, you discover there is neither a flat rectangle nor a wall behind it: there is a rectangular hole in the wall, and behind it a ganzfeld, a uniformly lit room (in this case lit with ultraviolet light). Where you perceived a flat rectangle, there is nothing.

Yet you perceive something there. Even when you *know* there's really nothing there, even when your nose is an inch from the plane of the wall, the perception of a flat rectangular surface persists. On a reflective level this is clearly disturbing, but before that there is a prereflective, perceptual dis-turbance that drew you into exploring the room and rectangle. This can be seen in others too: people walk in, look for a moment, look puzzled, wander,

go up to the hole, and seem surprised. Wherein the prereflective disturbance? A real thing in a place changes in concert with surrounding place
as you move around. Turrell's rectangle, on the contrary, is exhausted in a
glance, it keeps on staying the same, it is featureless and doesn't change
even when you stick your nose up to it, whereas the place around it (the
surrounding walls, the room) is constantly changing and never exhausted
by movement. Turrell's rectangular surface is the intersection of a real place
and a ganzfeld that approximates to no-place (by removing the spread-out
difference that is the signature of place). The rectangle appears to be no-
place, and a thing that is no-place is not really a thing. Turrell's piece
shows this in another way: when you or a person beside you pushes (that
is the feeling) an arm through the rectangle, the arm appears to lose its
reality, to not be right, as if threatening to dissolve into a zone of non-
being. A thing, an arm, that appears no-place loses its thingliness, as if its
inexhaustibility is exhausted when put into a region that exhausts spread-
out difference. Experience of Turrell's piece strongly confronts us with a
tight coupling between the inexhaustibility of things and the inexhaustibility of the places in which we move and explore things.

Here we should recall Gibson's emphasis on the environment, and his
point that real environments have texture, and so on. In a way, Turrell's work
shows that perception of inexhaustible things is grounded in the inexhaustible features of environmental places. If we need to move to see a solid thing,
we could say that the environment has to return the favour in kind, by not
merely being a featureless space, but by being movement spread out and
solidified as place: real rooms record in solid, spread-out form the movement
of building or painting, real fields record in solid, spread-out form the movement of growing plants or of shifting dirt. Place is roughed up by movement.
A ganzfeld, on the contrary, manifests no difference; it is place ground down
and smoothed out by the artist, homogenized by the bouncing of light; it is
created by movement that obscures itself, and so presents no field or room
in which things can appear for our moving body.

Living things depend for their life on the aspects they manifest in the
world. If the reality of my house is manifest for me in faces that swing into
and envelop one another, the reality of a frog or fish is, for that animal, the
various faces with which it faces the world. As the work of zoologist Adolf
Portmann (1961, 1967), scholar of art and vision James Elkins (1996), and
philosopher Evan Thompson (1995; see Thompson, Palacios, and Varela
1992) show, what we see of animals is what they evolve to display to other
animals, and this display evolves in relation to the place an animal inhab-
its. Animals display masking camouflage that hides them in their environment, or markings that distinguish their role in the environment, or colors
geared to the eyes of other creatures (for example, flower colors co-evolve
with the eyes of bees). Animals with transparent bodies (fish, frogs, and so
on) have their interior organs wrapped in sacks (something not found in

opaque-bodied animals), suggesting in another way that animal bodies evolve to be seen.

Living things explicitly manifest something implied in our perceptual experience: that things are perceived in place, that the first unit of perception is not even a figure-on-a-ground (as Merleau-Ponty argues), but a thing-in-a-place. We too are evolved, living, moving beings, and we too have evolved to be perceived in places and perceive others in places, so it should not surprise us that our perception is geared first of all to thing-place relations.[3] (Our places and ways of being in them are, though, clothed in cultural significations.)

In any case, these testimonials from art and evolution are echoed in everyday experience. Our attention is grabbed by things that are "out of place." Things that are in place fit so well that we do not even notice their dependence on place except, perhaps, in the moment when something that vanishes into background place becomes apparent as a thing, for example, an empty doorframe that vanishes into the layout of a house is newly perceived as containing a sliding pocket door, or a snake appears where formerly one had perceived a tree branch.

All the above indicate a complicity between things and places. As Merleau-Ponty notes, an existential condition of perception is our "setting of co-existence" with things.[4] I am urging that this setting has to do with place and movement: things have their reality in aspects that inexhaustibly envelop one another, and so our setting of co-existence with them is a place that enables the movement of exploring their inexhaustible envelope.

THE TOPOLOGY OF ENVELOPMENT

Our dialectical review of the tradition left us with a new version of the problem of depth: how spread out movements of a body moving in the world become unified in such a way as to give a *sens* of things placed outside the body. What makes this possible? Rather than answering by specifying empirical factors, brains, bones, and so on, I answer by specifying a concept. This is what Kant does when confronted with a similar question, namely, "What makes spatial experience in general possible?" Kant does not answer by speaking of eyes, and so on, rather he analyzes the fact so as to specify its conceptual condition: if spatial experience is possible, we must conceive its possibility in terms of an a priori pure intuition of space. Kant's analysis exhibits his right to invoke such a concept, it gives what Kant (1929, A84–92/B117–124) calls a transcendental deduction of the pure intuition of space. Aristotle would call Kant's process of moving from observed facts to underlying principles insight (*epagogé*; see Kosman 1973). Whether we call the process transcendental deduction or insight, we are moving from facts back to a concept that lets us grasp what makes those facts possible, and it is a procedure that we shall follow in the rest of the book in order to trace topologies of spatial perception.

What we have before us at the moment is a much more concrete description of spatial experience than the one Kant begins with. Our description specifies constraining relations (separation by contact, unity through spreading, relation to place) that belong to any spatial experience of things. What makes such experience possible? I answer: a certain topo-logic of the body, what I call a topology of envelopment. The answer is a concept that captures all these constraints as implicated in one another.

To begin exploring this concept, recall that grasping a marble or seeing with two eyes means having two fingers or two eyes work as one. This might seem accidental, contingent on the special demands of gripping or binocular vision. But perception of anything requires that multiple zones of the body work as one. Merleau-Ponty argues that the figure-ground relation is the "very definition of perception" (PP 10/4) and argues against reduction of perception to punctiform sensations. J. J. Gibson's ecological psychology likewise enjoins that no constellation of discrete sensations could in itself give rise to the perception of unified things. If there is to be perception, a moving engagement with a figure on a ground or a thing in a place, zones of the body cannot be independent, but must envelop one another in a complex co-implication, in the way that multiple aspects of a thing, or things and places, are co-implicated, complicit. As Merleau-Ponty puts it, in the body "parts are not spread out side by side, but [are] enveloped in each other" (PP 114/ 98). I am arguing that this is a *logical* requirement of perception, a transcendental yet existential condition of it, if you will. The condition of spatial experience is not, as Kant would have it, a pure intuition of space that immediately allows us to intuit an A and a different B as co-present and alongside one another. The condition is rather a topo-logical envelopment of zones of the body, an envelopment that couples with the enveloping surfaces of things in places.

We are used to the thought—which goes back to Aristotle's *On the Soul*—that if we are to see, there must be zones of the body responsive to the proper object of vision, that each modality of perception requires a complicity between body and world in that modality. No doubt Merleau-Ponty's concept of reversibility begins with this thought. I am pointing out that perceiving things in places (which is requisite to a sense of depth and space) requires a more general modality of body-world coupling: the zones of our body must envelop one another in the way that aspects of things envelop one another. The topo-logic of the body and the topo-logic of things are, we might say, the reverse of one another, are coupled. The topo-logic we are describing is not of the body merely (a possession of the subject), but is of the body crossed with the world.

Drawing on Merleau-Ponty's concept of "envelopment," I call this topo-logic a topology of envelopment. On the side of the body, the point of this concept is that zones of the body must function together, have a unity that is spread out, as the envelope of our atmosphere spreads out over the Earth, or as petals or scales envelop one another in enclosing something within, or as notes envelop one another in a melody, or as dancers moving together describe an envelope of movement. Discussion of envelopment in things is deferred for the moment.

With respect to the body, I use the term *envelop* in a purely descriptive sense, to designate functional unities of spread-out zones. I make no claim that zones literally extend some tenuous, miraculous envelope over one another. I am not interested in explaining how zones envelop one another, any more than Kant would be interested in explaining how it comes about that we have a pure intuition of space. My purpose is conceptual, to show that there must be such a topology of envelopment, not to say how it comes about.

I speak of 'zones' of the body, to address a conceptual difficulty. Everything said so far aims at avoiding the logic of solids. The body is a developmental being whose functions fold out of body-world movement, and we should not think of the body as an assemblage of parts, since what 'parts' are depends on folds of movement. A hand is a prodder, and a grasper, and for a doctor tapping on your stomach, it is a way of feeling things inside a belly. All of these functions depend on development, habit, learning, practice, on folds of movement. Strictly speaking, we should be speaking of *movements* enveloping one another. But in the end it is too difficult for us to think in terms of 'pure' movement; more, the movement in question is not 'pure,' it is of a moving body. I intend the term *zones* to address these problems. Zones are functional regions of a moving body. In prodding, a finger moves as a zone of poking that couples with the elasticity and rigidity of things; in grasping, multiple zones (flexible yet rigid manipulating fingers) envelop one another in a zone of tactile manipulation that couples with the unity, wiggliness, and so on of things; when two hands move in joint exploration, grasping zones envelop one another in a zone composed of body parts that are not materially contiguous but nonetheless function as a unified zone of exploration. Zones are neither simply identical with nor reducible to contiguous material body parts: a cane is a zone of prodding, and chopsticks a zone of grasping, as is an artificial arm, whereas an arm caught in anosognosia is no longer a grasping zone; for a trumpeter, fingers, lips, upper body, and ears are the forefront of a new zone of trumpeting; for a cetologist, hydrophones tethered to the ocean bed and linked by the Web become a zone of hearing. It is the movement of zones and the envelopment of zones that is important for perception.

The word *zone*, in short, is meant to capture the concept of movements distributed over regions of the body and its prostheses. (Alternately, the concept conceives folds of movement as surfacing in regions of the body or its prostheses.) It should be clear that 'zone' and 'envelopment' are complementary concepts: a zone (a finger, say) already is the envelopment of moving regions in one another, and is the basis for further zones that envelop one another and create new zones. For all these reasons, I speak of zones, rather than parts (Merleau-Ponty's term), enveloping one another.[5] (I also suspect that the concept of zones enables an interpretation of Deleuze-Guattari's (1983, 1987) concept of "the body without organs," which would be a body in which folds of movement have not yet surfaced as distinct zones—but of this I am not certain.)

It is worth noting that what is here conceived as "envelopment" is a focal issue in the life sciences. Evolution is often discussed as a story of the sporadic, yet progressive, development of complexity: first primitive proto-cells draw a boundary in the primordial soup; then prokaryotic cells arise, in which molecular complexes have differentiated functions; prokaryotic cells infect one another, giving rise to endosymbiotic eukaryotic cells in which bounded organelles work together; then different germ lines unite as complex multicellular organisms (Margulis 1981, Buss 1987). But the development of complexity is *not* a mere increase in the number of parts. The parts work together, envelop one another in a whole. Or, at least—since some consider the organism less as a unity than as parts or cell lines in an intra-dermal war—the problem of envelopment is serious and central.

The biological problem of the unity of parts side by side in space is complemented by a temporal problem. When I gaze into the night sky, I am looking back into the past: what I now see of a star N light-years away is what happened to that star N years ago. Since stars are different distances away, I never see what is happening to all stars at one particular moment in cosmological time. From the point of view of neurology, the situation is rather the same for the brain 'looking out' at its body, only speeded up. Neural signals take time to travel from periphery to brain, but they all have different distances to travel, and therefore take different amounts of time to reach the brain. The brain receives signals coming in from different parts of the body, but these signals are from events at different points in the past, as light reaching the star-gazer is from stars at different moments in the past. If I touch my toe, the signal from my hand will arrive in my brain before the signal from my toe, since it has less distance to travel, yet I experience both events as happening at the same time. As well, neural signals within the brain travel different distances from one area to another. A desktop computer and the Internet make use of central clocks to properly sequence and coordinate the processing of events that happen in different regions of space at different moments of time. There is no such time-stamping clock in the body, yet we nonetheless experience our body, which is spread in space and time, as one body. How is this the case? Daniel Dennett (1991, Dennett and Kinsbourne 1992) convincingly argues that the problem is badly put if it seeks what he calls a "finish line of consciousness," some one place in the brain that captures what is going on in one instant across all of the brain and body. In other words, the unity could not be reduced to a point in space or time, but inherently envelops spatial and temporal events in a process, what Dennett calls a "multiple drafts" model of consciousness.

Whatever the solution, the problem is vital. A body moves and spreads in space and time, but nonetheless is one body. The topology of envelopment conceives this as a basic topo-logic of the body, a topo-logic that couples with the envelopment of surfaces in things, where this topo-logical coupling is crucial to perception. We now have to shift from what Aristotle would call insight into this concept, to demonstration: showing how we can grasp the phenomena in terms of the topology of envelopment.

PRIMORDIAL DEPTH AND THE BODY AS PLACE

THE INNER ENVELOPE OF PERCEPTION

My body is a moving being whose zones envelop one another in perceptual movement. But my movement crosses with the world. Zones of my body do not envelop one another in an entirely spontaneous manner, this envelopment is taught me by the barbs of a world that draws zones of my body together in relation to things. A suitable metaphor is of an elaborated phagocytosis: in phagocytosis, a particle impinging on the cell-wall provokes a flow of matter that envelops the particle and pinches the envelope in a vesicle. In perception, a thing impinging on the body draws the body's zones together in an activity oriented around the impinging thing, enveloping the thing in perceptual explorations. I feel a sting on my neck, I start moving my fingers over it; a thing is put in my hand, and I start gripping it. I perceive by enveloping things in explorations; perception is never punctiform. Of course perception, unlike phagocytosis, does not consume things. The thing's reality is its inexhaustibility, and this inexhaustibility is precisely the provocation and guide of enveloping explorations. Even when I am spontaneously exploring something (rather than being goaded by the barbs of the world), the thing is an accomplice in enveloping explorations: the marble, for example, guides and supports my pincing, rolling movements; Turrell's rectangle, on the other hand, is a poor accomplice.

Zones envelop one another within a perceptual process that envelops things in explorations, generating an envelope of movement. Envelopment in the body thus crosses with a topo-logic of things whose aspects inexhaustibly envelop one another. What I have called the topology of envelopment is not, as I noted before, actual in the body merely, as a static structure, but is actual in movement that crosses body and world. This body-world movement, as constrained by the topology of envelopment, generates what I call the inner envelope of perception, an envelope of exploratory movement. Put another way: a body whose zones envelop one another in exploring the envelopes of things is limited to explorations that envelop one another. Perception is not a matter of collecting sensory data that would then have to have a spatial sense added; the topology of envelopment already limits the body to an envelope of explorations that pinches around things, an inner envelope of perception that already generates a spatial sense.

To contrast, Kant conceives the pure intuition of space as the transcendental condition of spatial intuition. As such, this pure intuition immediately and statically specifies the structure of space as a manifold of co-present intuitions. Note that pure intuition thus wears two hats: (1) it is the transcendental condition of intuition, and as such is not intuited; (2) it is the fundamental organization of spatial intuition, and as such is at least liminally intuited. Hence the tension in the very concept of a "pure intuition," of an intuition that is not intuitively given. The inner envelope of perception wears the second hat: spatial experience is not structured by an abstract manifold, but by many movements folding into one moving envelope. This inner envelope, though, is not immediately and statically specified; it is generated in movement by way of a prior limitation on movement, namely, the topology of envelopment. Where Kant's analysis of spatial experience points him back to a single and immediate concept, a pure intuition, that wears two hats, we have discovered a twofold, mediated concept: the topology of envelopment as played out in movement that generates an inner envelope of perception. It should be clear how this twofold mediated concept responds to the problems of lability and ready-made worlds discussed in the introduction.

With the concept of the inner envelope of perception, we return to the theme of the intrinsic organization of perception. Berkeley was right to say that perceptual organization is intrinsic (rather than being captured in premises for inferences). But Berkeley repeated the problem of the ready-made world when he turned that intrinsic organization into the language of God. We have now discovered such a language moving in the flesh: there is a deep grammar of the flesh, namely envelopment, the folding of many zones into one; the movement of this deep grammar crosses with things, generating further structures, envelopes of movement that arise in the interplay of body and things. There are different grammars of enveloping spongy things and hard things, rigid things and floppy things, things underfoot and things in hand, and different sorts of grammars of envelopment can give a different *sens* of things.

But what does this inner envelope give us in terms of the *sens* of things in depth? Not very much. The inner envelope is an envelope of pre-objective things, of things crossed with the body, things that have no objective status on their own, that can be felt as minuscule or enormous, near or distant depending on the way you handle them—a piece of rosemary stuck in a tooth feels enormous until felt with fingers. The inner envelope generates the bodily space that Merleau-Ponty refers to at important points in his discussion: "Experience discloses beneath objective space, in which the body eventually takes up place, a primitive spatiality of which [objective space] is merely the outer envelope and which merges with the body's very being. To be a body is to be tied to a certain world, as we have seen; our body is not primarily in space: it is of it" (*PP* 173/148). Our body is *of* space, not just dropped into it as into a container. Why? Because it moves, and the deep grammar of bodily movement generates an inner envelope of perception that already has a spatial *sens*. Why does that inner envelope remain primitive? Earlier I argued that the inexhaustibility of a thing depends on the thing's relation to place. But in the case of inner envelopes, things are related solely to the place of the body. This just gives us primordial depth. To get to objective depth we need a larger place that holds both body and things—the deep grammar of the body needs to cross not just with things but with places.

First, though, we have to answer the question how, really, movement in this envelope "gives us," expresses, a primordial *sens* of depth.

Primordial Depth as an Expression of the Inner Envelope of Perception

Merleau-Ponty writes that "Every external perception is immediately synonymous with a perception of my body, just as every perception of my body makes itself explicit in the language of external perception" (*PP* 239/206). The mutual envelopment of fingers in a grasping hand is made explicit in the feeling of the continuous envelope of the marble grasped in hand, and vice versa. We can now see that this is because body-world movement is constrained by a topology of envelopment. Our sense of primordial depth is expressed, I shall say, in terms of the inner envelope generated by this constraint. Primordial depth does not express centimeters, and so on, but enveloping movement in the way that, for Berkeley, distance expresses the grammatical relation between terms in God's visual language of nature. To show this, I draw on the analysis of gesture, articulation, expression, movement and *sens* in the previous chapter.

Where shock is expressed as pain through gestural movement, things explored are expressed as things in primordial depth through moving envelopes of exploration. The movement in which zones envelop one another and thence envelop things in explorations is constituted by a tensed separation between the body and things. I feel the cork *here* and *now*, but this feeling is constituted by an anticipatory wiggling stretched, tensed, in space and time. This stretched process constitutes a *sens* of a separation between me and things, a *sens* contracted from the *sens* of a pre-objective 'thickness' of a body that moves and perceives only by stretching over, enveloping, space and time. Shock folded through a limiting body becomes express as pain. Encounters folded through this 'thickness' of enveloping movement become express as a thing in primordial depth. Primordial depth becomes express through enveloping movement (the inner envelope) that accomplishes this folding, as pain becomes express in the gesture that folds shock.

Put in terms of articulation ('summation by difference'), our movement articulates the thing in terms of the inner envelope through which we explore it. The thing has an inexhaustibility that could never be captured in the body, but is nonetheless 'summed up' in the rather different form, in the shorthand, if you will, of enveloping explorations. Our *sens* of primordial depth expresses the depth of things in terms of the spatio-temporal 'thickness' of the enveloping movement through which alone we 'sum up' inexhaustible things in exhaustible form.

When, in the middle of the night, I tumble through the extra stair at the top of the flight, the step that I fall through is not N centimeters high; the depth of the stair step is 'summed by difference,' articulated and expressed, in the 'thickness' of my steps, in a spatio-temporal distension defined by my rhythm and gait. If I am slowly probing my way up the steps, I experience a fall through a short distance; if I am hurling up to get the ringing phone, I experience a fall through a stomach-jolting distance; this difference does not directly correlate with the height of my feet above the top landing. When I search for my glasses in the middle of the night, they are hugely distant until I feel my hand brushing into the region of my bedside table, and then my glasses are somewhere in the near distance; when I grasp them, they are non-distant. Perhaps, too, this analysis accounts for the felt difference in the size of things in hand and things in the mouth; my molar feels huge; it seems as expansive as a craggy rock held in hand; perhaps this is because my tongue is so much more sensitive than my hand, because a greater 'thickness' of explorations is 'summed up' in its movements, than in the movements of my hands.

In these examples I am thinking of something like Turvey and Carello's "wieldiness," a movement pattern that 'summarizes' felt length in the different form of wielding, a movement in which the body couples its own wieldiness with the wieldiness of things and thus 'translates' length into a movement pattern. In feeling things in primordial depth, in feeling things as rounded-out, voluminous beings in primordial depth, the body couples its own enveloping movement with the enveloping surfaces of things and thus 'translates' primordial depth and volume into a movement pattern. Primordial depth is thus articulated in the moving language of inner envelopes of perception.

At this level, depth has a *sens* that does not smoothly quantify along a scale of objective measures, but is qualitatively articulated by the rhythms and sweeps of my enveloping body. All that is expressed is the *sens* of a pre-objective, primordial depth, in which we might be able to, for example, specify broad distinctions between the hugely distant and the near, as in the example of my glasses: the hugely distant expresses an opening or extension of the enveloping body in relation to the thing, while the near expresses a closing and retraction. But our sense of primordial depth could not on its own, as Edward S. Casey (1991a) argues, give us a sense of objective depths between ourselves and things. With primordial depth we are caught in the realm of the strange, plastic, and suddenly transformative depths that haunt us in dreams, in states of half-waking.

Recall, though, that perception is never a miraculous transfer of things from the category of things not perceived to things perceived, rather it is a development from vague to clear perception. Primordial depth expresses depth in terms of envelopes of movement required for exploring things attached to the place of the body. But for a body that can detach from things in a larger place, this vague *sens* leads to a *sens* of objective depth.

OBJECTIVE DEPTH IN LARGER PLACE

THE ENVELOPES OF THINGS

In passing I have already talked about things as having envelopes. In his article " 'The Element of Voluminousness': Depth and Place Re-examined," Edward S. Casey makes the insightful point that for Merleau-Ponty the mutual envelopment of *surfaces of things* is a crucial motive for depth. Casey (1991a, 12) notes that Merleau-Ponty's notion of the envelopment of surfaces (*PP* 304–306/262–265) is strikingly similar to Gibson's notion of the layout of surfaces as an affordance for depth.

Before proceeding to objective depth, a few remarks on the concept of envelopment in the case of things. The sides of my house push out into new sides, and consume sides past, as I move around my house. This means that when I am standing still, the west side of the house excludes yet envelops the north face: the west side 'sweeps away' the north face, and thus envelops it in its sweep. If this envelopment were not somehow perceived in the side of the house facing me, then the house would appear as a mere façade.

The way in which faces of things envelop one another is coupled to the mutual envelopment of zones of the body, the two envelopments are correlative facets of the topology of envelopment. When I wiggle a marble, the outside observer might claim that two separate digits are touching two separate hemispherical surfaces, but this is accurate only if the digits do not move as one, as in the crossed fingers of the illusion of the double marble. With uncrossed fingers, digital zones envelop one another. The same holds for the surfaces of the marble: the marble's surfaces are enveloped in one another, but not because of anything directly given in the marble. The sides of the marble envelop each other when I explore the marble with grasping fingers, but not when I explore it with crossed fingers, in which case the sides appear as surfaces of two ghostly marbles that have little to do with one another. In normal vision the faces of my house envelop one another in a way that motivates me to see the house in depth when I move around it; but when I let my eyes go cross-eyed, the two surfaces float out, they no longer envelop one another, but are relatively indifferent to one another. It is as if the sides of the house (that I *know* are there as the envelope of one solid thing) fall outward and flatten.

It is not because surfaces (in and of themselves) envelop one another that I touch or see a thing as being in depth. My enveloping look or touch draws aspects of things into an envelope that motivates further enveloping looking or touching of the thing as a voluminous thing in depth. There is a deep complicity between my body and things.

Objective Depth as Expressing Movement in the Outer Envelope of Perception

My placing of a thing in bodily space, however, could never make a thing *be* a thing whose surfaces envelop one another for me. The thing solicits me as occupying its own place, in my explorations it keeps on drawing me into turning it about and exploring its envelope. While my explorations draw its surfaces together in an inner envelope of bodily space, the inexhaustibility of the thing goes beyond bodily space, it goes back to the thing in its own place.

For me to encounter this inexhaustible aspect of the thing, I must be able to leave the thing in its place or turn about the thing in its place, to *not* exhaust it in enveloping it. Without this sort of movement in place, objective perception would be impossible, and indeed it is a feature of perception that it becomes less convincingly real when the body is immobilized. It is when I am immobilized that colors flatten out so that they do not belong to surfaces of a thing in its own place, but "diffuse around objects and become atmospheric colours" (PP 308/266). Or, as we saw with Turrell's rectangle, when a thing is exhausted by being no-place, it appears unreal. To perceive a solid thing unified in depth, movement is required, either of the body, or the thing, or both, and in all cases what is required for this movement is a *larger place* that holds body and thing together and yet separate, so that it is possible to adopt a moving relation to things in places, so that it is possible to not have the thing be exhausted by the enveloping movement of the body.[6]

Larger place is in fact a constraint on perception: even the constitution of primordial depth depends on a place that holds the body and thing *together*, thus allowing the body to have a relation to things in the first place. But the very same larger place grants the *separation* of the body from the thing, so that the thing is not encrusted into and exhausted by the body. This larger place is the truth of the tensed relation between the body and the world, of the impassable 'thickness' of the body. Without larger place, no body, no inner envelope of perception. Encountering a thing within the inner envelope of perception already requires immersion in a larger place that opens contact with the thing. It requires what I call the outer envelope of perception. The inner envelope thus seeps into the outer envelope.

Movement in the outer envelope of perception articulates the inner envelope of perception, 'sums up' things in the inner envelope in 'different' form. If primordial depth expresses the 'thickness' of an inner envelope generated by movement in the place of the body, objective depth expresses the 'thickness' of an outer envelope generated by movement in a larger place. Things have the *sens* of being in objective space because perception is not only folded through the enveloping movement of the body, but through movement of a body that moves around things in place.

For example, the movement of my eyes toward the thing both unifies the thing and places it within bodily space, giving it a primordial depth. But this movement of my eyes also shows my detachment from the thing, and thus puts the thing in its own place. More precisely, the thing continually 'peels' away from me as zones of my body envelop one another in explorations that envelop the thing. This becomes explicit when I move around the thing, or it moves relative to me, and it stays detached from me: the mutual envelopment of bodily zones is inexhaustibly demanded by the thing and constantly places the thing at a certain primordial depth, in which it 'peels away' from me. The thing thus surpasses me and demands a unity in which *its* zones and surfaces peel back, envelop and consume one another in its own place. This would be opposed to a unity in which a vague surface in primordial depth undergoes systematic color changes, or in which surfaces rotate away from me in a quasi-objective space. The latter experience sometimes occurs when looking is detached from visual movement through a place, for example, when watching the landscape passing by through the rear-view mirror from the passenger side of a car, or similarly, when watching a film in which trees at the side of the road are shot at medium distance from a moving vehicle, without showing the ground. The landscape seems to float by and rotate away in an abstract space, rather than placing itself as a solid thing. (Examples are to be found in Stan Brakhage's *Vision in Meditation* series, or Michael Snow's ↔ and *La région centrale*, in which the horizon of the earth seems to peel back into a sphere as the camera swoops around in circles within circles.)[7] This sort of abstraction, achieved by way of film or mirror framing, exhausts the thing, turns an inexhaustible thing into an envelope. In contrast, in moving around a thing in place, the inexhaustibility of the thing is not dissipated, but constantly replenished, it can only be 'summed up' in the different form of a thing whose envelope 'peels back' into its own place. Compare this with primordial depth which sums up things in an inner envelope. Turrell's rectangle cannot be 'summed up' in the form of an envelope that 'peels back' into its own place, because its surface does no enveloping, does not differentiate as you move, but envelops itself all at once; but neither can it quite be placed in primordial depth, because you move around it in place; it is inbetween, neither a solid thing nor mere floating color, but color, light, verging toward a solid.

What gives a thing its own *sens* of place and thence a *sens* of objective depth is the way in which its primordial depth in relation to one's body is continually exhausted and replenished as one moves about it—unlike, for example, the unchanging, unplaced, ambiguously sized and permanently remote moon that seems to pursue one in one's car as one crosses the night-time landscape, or to pursue Woyzeck through his torment. If I could look at my house as being placed solely in bodily space, as not demanding a detachment from me within a larger place, then it too would lack the solidity of a thing in place, it would hover about and follow me around as does the moon. (A film that puts this to somewhat comic effect is John Smith's *The Black Tower*, in which the eponymous tower seems to pursue the spectator's viewpoint across town; again, the film frame, which cuts things from place, is crucial to this effect.)

This account amounts to an answer to the problem of place, to the problem of how things acquire the *sens* of being in their own place. It is crucial to note that this answer depends on place as primitive. In shifting from the inner envelope to the outer envelope, from primordial depth to objective depth, we are echoing the shift between Bergsonian pure percep-tion and perception proper, between perception that vanishes in things perceived, and perception that includes a sense of the experienced differ-ence between perceiver and perceived. How can we do this without memory? On the one hand, we are appealing to the previous chapter's concept of the body and expression, to a body that is not simply matter, but a habitual, moving being stretched in time. On the other hand, we are appealing to a place that is in some liminal sense external memory, place as difference spread out and recorded, place as interacting with things so as to expose the inexhaustible differences of things and also enable the summing up of things in different form.

When Bergson speaks of the circuit of body-world movement in the image system, he speaks as if looking into a cosmos devoid of place, in which a point P is to be located only in relation to the body; he focuses on a circuit of movement, but the circuit is anchored in the body insofar as it is only the body that limits movement (Bergson's account is notably body-centric). But once point P is in a place—not an abstract point in a cosmos but a thing in a textured, differentiated space that records and sediments movement—the point P also stands as an anchor of movement. The movement of perception is limited not just by the body, but by what happens when we move around a thing in place. Turrell's rectangle has no 'memory' of itself, no way of exposing a record of sedimented movement as we move around it, and so our perception almost takes place in it, almost fails to express the *sens* of a thing in its own place. Things in our world are not featureless points dropped into a featureless space, they are things made or grown in place, and such things bear a record of their making comple-mentary to the record born within the place around them. Animals make this explicit in one way, made things in another way, and this textured relation in place is crucial to things becoming express as things for us in the fullest sense. This point, and the point that place is external memory, draw on and speak to Casey's work on place.

PRIMARY AND SECONDARY SENSES OF DEPTH

The above analysis must be complemented by a distinction between primary and secondary senses of depth, a distinction modeled on Merleau-Ponty's distinction between primary and secondary expression. The former is creative, original, spontaneous, the latter conventional.

So far the analysis has focused on depth perception in the primary sense. Body-world movement is constrained by a topology of envelopment. Where the body serves as the place of movement, movement generates an inner envelope. This envelope 'sums up' and thus expresses the depth between us and things, not in the language of Berkeley's author of nature, but in the 'language' of constrained movement. Something as voluminous as a marble is expressed in one kind of enveloping movement, something more voluminous by another kind of enveloping movement. Similarly with things in objective depth, only here the enveloping movement is movement in the world, in larger place. Envelopment is the basic gesture of the 'language' of depth.

Here we have a cognate of primary expression, a spontaneous gesture that contracts and expresses a *sens* implied in the topology of envelopment. How far away are my glasses in the night? The distance is expressed for me in the movement of trying to envelop first my nightstand and then my glasses.

But this sort of gesture becomes habitual. The height of the steps becomes correlative to my habit of sweeping along stairs, the size of my room is encapsulated in the envelope of movements I use to traverse it. Moreover, new things appear as already summed up and thence sized up by envelopes of movement. The pile of books already roughly appears as sized to my enveloping hand, the distance across the curbside puddle already roughly appears in terms of my enveloping stride, the distance to the upper shelf of the cabinet in terms of my reach. If the expression of depth depends in the first instance on envelopes generated in actual movement, these envelopes later become conventional, habitual, implied in our relation to things.

As we acquire habits, as we learn to move, a thing already appears as detached from the body with respect to the way that the body *can* handle the thing. The thing reflects our habit of handling it: the cork is wigglable, the sponge is pokable, and even young infants reach out ready to explore these possibilities of things.[8] It is as if an envelope of movement were already coiled within things, and perception expresses this coiled movement, not an actual envelope generated here and now. This suggests an interpretation of Merleau-Ponty's concept of motor-perceptual maxima.[9] Objective depth is, according to Merleau-Ponty, perceived "in terms of the situation of the object in relation to our power of grasping it," that is, of grasping as 'summarizing' our handling of a thing in a place. The maximum of grip, of motor-perceptual

notivates perception of a closer distance, and increasing dis-
ses the fact that "the thing is beginning to slip from the grip of
 is less closely allied with it" (*PP* 302–303/261). In other words,
eptual maxima are habitual envelopes of movement, envelopes
d maximal handling.

r *sens* of depth thus expresses movement envelopes in two different
registers. In the primary register, by actually moving things about, we are
contracting and making express a *sens* implied in the topology of envelopment. Such movement begins with something whose depth or distance from
us does not yet have a sharp *sens*, and ends with a movement that makes *sens*
of the thing as being voluminous, and thus as being in depth. Examples: after
putting on skis for the first time, getting a sense of how far they extend in
front and back of you by shaking them about; getting a sense of how big your
teeth are when they first grow in by running your tongue over them, and
being astonished when you later take them in hand after they fall out; learning how to judge distances when moving in a forest at night for the first time.
In the secondary register we develop habits of practiced movements, 'standard envelopes,' further contracting and explicating a *sens* implied in the
topology of envelopment. Examples: a dancer who sizes up a new stage in
terms of strides and movements; a driver who maintains following distance
not in terms of meters, and so on but in terms of a space of movement
between cars.

We would have to add that the conventional expression of depth
becomes even more conventional with the development of extrabodily
measuring systems. But we thus arrive at the intersection of lived space and
objective space, a topic for the conclusion of the book.

CONCLUSION

We have looked into the point in which body and world cross, and have
found that it is not quite a point. It has an inner texture, a topo-logic of
envelopment, of stretching across space and time yet remaining unified, a
topo-logic coupled and crossed with the envelopes of things. Given this
constraining topology, body-world movement generates envelopes of perception: an inner envelope in relation to the body as place, an outer envelope
in relation to larger place. The crucial result is that our *sens* of depth does
not express the terms of an order provided by a Berkeleian divine language,
a Cartesian geometry, or a Kantian pure intuition. Our *sens* of depth ultimately expresses a deep grammar of body-world movement, a topo-logic of
envelopment; or rather, this deep grammar constrains body-world movement
so that it generates envelopes, and our *sens* of depth is first of all expressed
in terms of these envelopes. The native tongue of depth perception consists
of envelopes of body-world movement. As a pain is something shocking
flung away by a reacting gesture, as a short thing is something easily wielded,

so a small thing is something easily enveloped, and an objective thing in place is something that keeps on being enveloped and enveloping itself, and so on. A taste of this native tongue is contracted in habitual depth perception. It is a labile tongue: it goes back to envelopes of movement that can be disturbed, that have to be relearned, and so on. And of course deploying conventionalized, habitual envelopes requires a certain attitude: it is one thing to perceive depths and distances on the 401 Expressway when you are alert and confident; it is another when you are tired, unfocused or shaken up by crazed truck drivers.

Here we have our response to the tradition: the *sens* of depth is based not in divine grammars, geometry, cognitive structures, but in envelopes of movement generated in body-world movement constrained by a topo-logic of enveloping. Such a *sens* is obviously rooted in the crossing of the body and world, and is labile. We would have to add (returning to the previous chapter) that such a *sens* could be discovered only in an expressive body, and in a nature in which movement gives rise to expression.

A new theme emerged in passing. The topology of envelopment crosses body and world, crosses the body with things and larger places. This suggests the theme of *care*. Heidegger, in his existential analytic of Dasein in *Being and Time*, argues that what is existentially constitutive of our being is care, roughly, a pre-objective existential comportment that inherently enwraps our being in something greater than ourselves. If our being were not fundamentally care, then there would be no world and no objects.

Our study suggests a pre-objective, bodily care, *a care in movement*. To say that the topology of enveloping stretches our body in space and time and roots us in place, is to say that bodily movement is constitutively wrapped up in a pre-objective care for things in places. The moving body 'translates' things in terms of its own movements; I perceive the marble's volume by lending it a hand; the price of 'summing up' its inexhaustible envelope is moving a body in a specific way, such that the body's inexhaustible depth is also 'summed up' in an envelope of movement, such that a hand that can also type, play, sign, and so on is partially exhausted in grasping and doing nothing else[10]; in turn, the marble 'gives up' something too in being 'summed up' in this way. The topology of envelopment says that the encounter of inexhaustibly voluminous bodies and things plays out in enveloping surfaces; in the point where world and body cross, we do not quite have complete volumes meeting, but volumes moving together to generate envelopes. The body, with its being stretched through time and space, lends existential ballast to this envelope of meeting, lends its 'thickness' to this envelope, and in turn this lending is demanded by the differential ballast of things in places. Put otherwise: If I never did care to lend the marble a hand, to handle it, it would not quite become perceptually present as a thing with enveloping surfaces; but the marble with its surfaces provokes this care in me, is already on the way to caring for itself in its way of sticking together. If, as Merleau-Ponty might put it, I see the mountain, it is the mountain out there that makes itself be seen in me. I am complementing Merleau-Ponty's thought of reversibility by thinking about it in terms of body-world movement, and by thinking that this reversibility is a marker of a care in movement, whereby body and world give themselves to one another in order to move back and separate. At bottom, perhaps it is care in movement that keeps us from falling into Bergson's appeal to pure memory: we do not need to stab the body with memory to have it experience, because the body is already outside itself in care, and care is already sedimented in place.

With this last point we return to the theme of place, but it now intersects with the theme of care. It is larger place that grants the possibility of care in movement and a *sens* of objective depth—this is what our critical discussion of Bergson and place amounted to. As Casey argues, *"place grants depth"*—depth belongs to place (Casey 1991a, 14). More, Casey remarks that the cultivation of place *"localizes caring,"* and this suggests an intimate connection between care and place, one that would be rooted in the body (Casey 1993, 175). As well, David Michael Levin (1999, 1985) draws a connection between place, movement, and care in his discussion of the body in Heidegger, when he discusses the *Legein* of the *Logos* in terms of the layout in which we move about.

It would seem that the topo-logic of a body that senses depth is not merely a topology of functional envelopment but of caring in movement, care in place. This point will be deepened in the next chapter, where I show how the body's emotional and caring relation to itself in place informs the *sens* of up and down.

CHAPTER 5

RESIDING UP AND DOWN ON EARTH

At my feet ticklish
and hard like the sun, and open like flowers,
and perpetual, magnificent soldiers
in the gray war of space,
everything ends, life definitively ends at my feet,
what is foreign and hostile begins there:
the names of the world, the frontier and the remote,
the substantive and the adjectival too great for my heart
originate there with dense and cold constancy.

Always,
manufactured products, socks, shoes,
or simply infinite air,
there will be between my feet and the earth
stressing the isolated part of my being,
something tenaciously involved between my life and the earth
something openly unconquerable and unfriendly.

—Pablo Neruda, from "Ritual of My Legs"
in *Residence on Earth*

WE ARE IN A CURIOUS CONFLICT with the earth upon which we reside. We are bound to it, yet are separate from it; there is "something tenaciously involved between my life and the earth," yet this something is "openly unconquerable and unfriendly." The conflict concentrates in the legs and feet, which are, as we might say in English, foot soldiers in the "gray war of space," the zone where push comes to shove. A gray war, because unending and self-defeating, because we cannot conquer our residence on earth, because we are rooted on earth. Yet we are not rooted in one spot, in the manner of a plant; we move about. Neruda's "infinite air" is not simply a sign of unsurpassable distance, but of an unsurpassable rhythm of a life dragged out on earth, a pedal rhythm transformed but never undone by manufactured products, shoes and socks.

Neruda turns us from world to earth. One's body is not merely crossed with a world, but crosses the earth. Earth is thus not merely a planetary body suspended in astronomical space, it is a larger body crossed with one's own. In this chapter I detect an integral relation between body and earth by studying the unearthed body, the body floating in weightlesness. The study reveals what I call a topology of residing, a topo-logical constraint in body-world movement. The topology involves posture and has an emotional *sens* concerned with being on earth. I show how our sense of up and down, of orientation, refers to movement constrained by this topology.

RESIDENCE ON EARTH

From the start, our topic has been a moving body crossed with the world. But even before we turn to the testimony of the poet, it is philosophically and empirically clear that the moving body moves not just in any sort of world, but in an earthly world, a world that is not devoid of place but laden with it.

The claim that movement depends on earth is central to Aristotle's philosophy, as is clear from *On the Movement of Animals* and the way that his philosophy of nature keeps coming back to earth as the central orienting place that makes movement intelligible.[1] In book two of *On the Soul* Aristotle writes:

> Empedocles is mistaken in his account of [growth], when he adds that the growth in plants, when their roots spread downwards, is due to the fact that earth naturally tends in this direction, and that when they grow upwards, it is due to the natural movement of fire. His theory of "upwards" and "downwards" is wrong; for up and down are not the same for all individuals as for the universe, but the head in animals corresponds to the roots in plants, if we are to identify and distinguish organs by their functions. (II·4·415b29–416a6)

Up and down and are rooted in a functional, topological relation between a living body and the larger body upon which it lives, and this topological relation correlatively invests zones of a living body with functional specificity. In book two of *Parts of Animals* Aristotle observes that: "plants get their food from the earth by means of their roots; and this food is already elaborated when taken in, which is the reason why plants produce no excrement, the earth and its heat serving them in the place of the stomach."[2] The *sens* of a living being's body (what is stomach, what is head) crosses with its *sens* of place (what is up, what is down) in a complex topological relation. Body and place are implied in one another.

We can see this in our bodies. Our feet have their *sens* in the earth, their evolved function inherently refers to some place against which they push, in the way that roots refer to soil. The earth is the stomach of the plant, an external yet integral nutrient resource. We aren't plants, we carry our stomachs with us. For us the earth is rather a different kind of external resource. As electric current moves only by going to a ground that sucks up excess electrons, we move only by having the earth push back against our excess push. The earth is an integral part of the circuit of body-world movement, and a body cast into empty space with nothing to push against (and no excess matter or energy to throw away) is soon dead because incapable of the self-movement requisite for getting food and other external resources. One's body depends on outside bodies, and so one's movement must cross with a larger body that enables movement in the outside.

I call this larger enabling body, whatever it may be, "earth." In everyday terrestrial life, earth is in fact the Earth, the singular planet upon which we live. But it could be something else, say a spaceship. Husserl has remarkable thought-experiments in which he imagines how a spaceship could serve as what he calls "earth-body," and how a space-colonist's sense of orientation would be rooted in different earth-bodies as she moves away from Earth, moves between the stars, and begins approaching her destination planet (Husserl 1981). What Husserl calls earth-body, I call earth. I distinguish between earth, the larger body (whatever it may be) on which we move, and Earth, our singular planet. In keeping with this distinction, I capitalize the term *Earthly* when it is meant to designate our situation on our singular planet Earth.

I introduce the concept of 'excorporation' to help capture the sort of relation in which something that remains external to the body is nonetheless vital to it. One's body crosses with the world, and incorporations are a familiar phenomenon within that crossing: shoes, clothing, canes, glasses, other prostheses, cars, and so on, are incorporated into one's moving body. Incorporations are labile, since the threshold between body and world is labile. Excorporations are like incorporations, but remain in place beyond the threshold of one's body: the stairs at my parents' house that are counterpart to my habit body, my house as place of residence, my office as place of memory, with things to do distributed about in it, are excorporations of my body. I often get to leave excorporations behind, even if I depend on them or return to them. But there is one excorporation that permanently haunts me, that follows me insofar as I keep on having to leave it behind, that pursues me through the landscape as the Moon does through the winter's night—the landscape itself, or rather earth, whatever it might be.

We are, as Neruda would put it, resident on earth. This is not a merely empirical characterization of us, it is a deep and necessary feature of our being.

PHANTOM EARTH

The rest of the chapter studies the topology of our crossing with earth—the topology of residing—to reveal an emotional *sens* that colours our *sens* of up and down.

It is possible to reveal a connection between orientation, the body, and emotion by studying our words for 'up' and 'down,' their cultural and cross-cultural connotations, and our experience of Earthly orientation and emotion. Work of this sort has been carried out by Gaston Bachelard (1964), Erwin Straus (1966), Edward S. Casey (1993), Sue Cataldi (1993), and Ernst Cassirer (1955), and is also to be found in Lakoff and Johnson's (1999) linguistic-corporeal analyses, which are prompted by Sheets-Johnstone's (1990) work on the body as corporeal template.

I want to take this connection back into the movement of the body, take it toward that turn where body-world movement turns into the experience of 'up' and 'down.' Here we run into a problem noted by Merleau-Ponty: our experience of 'up' and 'down' is so fundamental that we cannot catch it "in the ordinary run of living because it is then hidden under its own acquisitions"; we are always past the turn. Merleau-Ponty's response is to "examine some exceptional case in which it [up or down] disintegrates and re-forms before our eyes." He does this by studying experiments by Stratton and Wertheimer in which psychologists varied the subject's visual relation to what I call earth via the device of lens and mirrors.[3]

The microgravitational experiences that arise in spaceflight and training for spaceflight present a new and deeper possibility for such "disintegration." In Stratton and Wertheimer's experiments, it is just the visual field that varies, but in microgravitation—hereafter called "weightlessness"— the entire crossing of body and world varies. Crucially, weightlessness decouples orientation from the gravitational field, letting us see how orientation emerges in a body *moving itself* in relation to the world, rather than in a body (or its organs, for example, the inner ear) *being moved* by gravitational acceleration.

Correlatively, in weightlessness earth appears as an excorporation of the body. Husserl's imaginative variations and the actual experience of astronauts studied below show that even when the Earth is absent, even in weightlessness, certain surfaces and regions appear as earth. The earth is determined not so much by what something outside one's body *is*, as by the movement that the outside world *affords*. In the absence of Earth, which holds one down, one's moving postural attitudes nonetheless 'adopt' certain surfaces and regions as earth, as affording moving, residing, and orientation. The body, I shall say, earths itself, using *earth* as a verb, on analogy with the verb *ground*, as when we say that something grounds a circuit. (The OED reports usages of *earth* as a verb: in gardening, it means covering the roots of a plant with earth, and in electronics it is equivalent to grounding.)

This suggests that in Earthly situations earth is not simply a thing outside one's body, but counterpart to ways of residing. Indeed, this seems to be the case: people reside in different ways, whether it is the sailor whose sea legs find stability in a churning ocean, or the mountain climber solidly bedded down on her narrow slip of rock hundreds of feet in the air, or the mechanic beneath the car, or the academic hurtling between conferences in the no-place system of aircraft aisles and airport lounges. In all these situations, residing is determined by habitual bodily movement in place, by body and earth moving against one another. In contrast, the weightless body floating in midair cannot move in place since nothing moves back against it, yet the floating body has a *sens* of up and down. Significantly, this *sens* is reversed when the experimenter pushes the head of the floating body, that is, when the world resumes movement against the body. But in the absence of outside movement, earth is still counterpart to residing, the body earths itself.

There is an analogy here with the phantom limb. When a phantom limb appears, we learn how a living limb is not simply an organic function, but correlative to a habitual way of moving in the world. When Earth is cut off by hurling the body into weightless conditions a 'phantom earth' appears, and we learn how earth is not simply a physical function, but is the moving counterpart of a habitual, moving body. As with the phantom limb, phantom earth is a deeply emotional and existential matter.

LACKNER'S POSTURE-ORIENTATION EXPERIMENT

The case of orientation perception in weightlessness that I study is given in an experiment first conducted by psychologists Lackner and Graybiel (1983; also see 1979), and then explored in a more thorough manner by Lackner (1992). The experiment reveals a remarkable relationship between the weightless subject's bodily posture, the subject's position in relation to the architecture of the aircraft, and the subject's experience of the orientation of his own body and of the aircraft. The relationship was surprisingly uniform across subjects, but exhibited some systematic variations that suggest it is due not to 'built-in' factors but to habit or development. My analysis of Lackner's experiment inherently involves a fair bit of detail. So I first present the experiment and its results, criticize objective interpretations of it, and then develop my own interpretation.

A few observations about method before beginning. Philosophy and especially phenomenology are at a disadvantage in working from the results of current psychology because the demands of experimental method—of inserting the subject into a framework of repeatability—often erase the identity and subjective experience of individuals (even if the developmental, longitudinal studies of psychologists such as Thelen and Smith challenge aspects of this practice). In contrast, earlier work extensively records first-person reports; for example, Stratton's (1896, 1897) experiment (which is a classic study of orientation, and a touchpoint for Merleau-Ponty) is a long first-person report on Stratton's *own* experience. Lackner's experiment also abstracts from the details of the environment in which it is conducted. I am at a disadvantage in giving my interpretation since there is data missing, and I tried to make up for this in various ways that would require confirmation from experience. On the issue of subjective and objective language: I say "the subject felt X" as a shorthand for "the subject reported that he experienced his body or the aircraft as being in such and such an orientation." Significantly, the language of feeling leaks into Lackner's write-ups: one gets the impression that his subjects really felt the world turning upside down and rightside up; and other experiential terms and descriptions creep in (for example, subjects experience orientations as being more or less "distinct" or "compelling"—hardly 'objective' criteria).

Finally, I am studying Lackner's experiment to approach the turn of experience where 'up' and 'down' first arise. So the language of 'up' and 'down' should not be used in specifying the independent variables in the experiment (postures and orientations of the body in the aircraft, and so on). There is some conceptual difficulty here. (I have to speak of ceilings vs. floors, and mightn't these be 'up' and 'down' in disguise?) The more pressing problem is that leaving out 'up' and 'down' is awkward—perhaps precisely because 'up' and 'down' are so fundamental.

THE POSTURE-ORIENTATION EXPERIMENT AND ITS RESULTS

To the experiment. (I integrate detailed experimental data into the text by summarizing it in indented blocks. Unless otherwise noted, the following material is summarized from Lackner 1992, Lackner and Graybiel 1983, and Lackner and Graybiel 1979.)

Lackner conducted a series of experiments on subjects (all male) who were put aboard an aircraft that flew in parabolic trajectories, which produces periods of microgravity, that is, what I call "weightlessness." [4] This is the standard technique for producing relatively long-term weightless conditions without sending a spacecraft into orbit and was, for example, used to film some weightless scenes in the film *Apollo 13*. I use the data from a number of different experiments, but my main concern is an experiment I call the posture-orientation experiment.

In the posture-orientation experiment, experimenters positioned subjects so that they floated weightless with the long axis of their bodies parallel to the long axis of the aircraft, with their arms by their sides. Subjects were tested with their bodies in a variety of postures and orientations relative to the craft, specified by a combination of the following variables (see figure 1, page 135): (1) gaze toward body/gaze forward/gaze away from body (I use *gaze* to designate direction of the head and eyes together); (2) face ceilingward/face floorward; (3) head forward/head aft.

Case B: In case **B**, with face floorward and gaze toward body, subjects felt vertically upside down in a vertically-oriented aircraft. Within this case, when the subject's head was aft, the aircraft felt tail down; with head forward, the aircraft felt nose down (that is, the subject felt the aircraft to be oriented in this way).

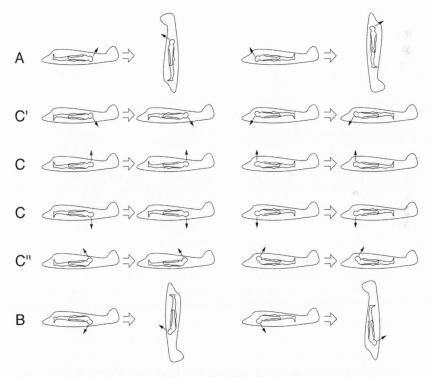

Fig. 1. A diagram representing the results of Lackner's posture-orientation experiment. The left figure in each pair represents the subject's 'actual' orientation in the aircraft; the right shows the 'perceived' orientation of the subject and aircraft. The labels of the cases are given at the beginning of each row. (Diagram adapted from Lackner and Graybiel 1983, with permission of the Aerospace Medical Association. I am grateful to Dan Donaldson for producing this diagram.)

Variability across Individuals, and Group N: Lackner reports that of thirty-one subjects, twenty-two found that they could consistently change their orientation as described in case **A** and **B**. But four subjects experienced changes in orientation only in case **B**, not **A**. That is, they did not feel vertically upright in condition **A**. I call these four individuals members of group **N**.

A CRITICISM OF OBJECTIVE OR CAUSAL INTERPRETATIONS OF THE POSTURE-ORIENTATION EXPERIMENT

The posture-orientation experiment, I argue, is not to be characterized objectively or causally. Orientation has a *sens*, is phenomenal, in Dillon's sense of the word (see chapter one), and depends on movement that crosses a postured body with the world.

(1) Mere posture does not determine orientation. For example, the movement of the gaze away from the body results in an experience of being upright only when the face is ceilingward, not when it is floorward. Since the subject is weightless, the only difference between these two postures is the meaning of the architecture that the subject is looking at.

(2) On the other hand, the influence of posture and gaze direction is not reducible to looking, is not simply a matter of seeing this or that by looking here or there. While the latter interpretation may be suggested by the posture-orientation experiment, other results show that simple *direction* of eye-gaze toward or away from the body influences the *sens* of up and down, since in some cases it has an influence *even when the eyes are closed*.

In a related experiment, the same subjects were floated in the aircraft with their eyes closed; twenty-three of thirty-one felt no sense of spatial anchoring. The remaining eight continued to perceive the same orientation with respect to the aircraft when they closed their eyes, although less distinctly. Seven of these eight stood out in another way: when floating free of their seats, they could make themselves feel upright by directing their *closed* eyes at their feet or past their forehead. I call these seven individuals members of group **S**. In related results: (I) When entering zero gravity, sixty-six of sixty-eight blindfolded subjects strapped into seats (rather than free floating) felt upside down. (II) Twenty-seven nonblindfolded subjects strapped into seats reported that directing their head and eyes at their feet or deviating their eyes toward their forehead made them feel upright.

(3) Visible architecture does not determine orientation on its own, since, keeping the architecture the same, different orientations are felt when gazing up, down, or ahead.

(4) The known orientation of the craft relative to the Earth is also not determinative of orientation: in case **C**, the orientation of the craft could be construed as providing a framework for the orientation of the subject, while in cases **A** and **B** it seems that the orientation of the craft follows from the subject's experienced bodily orientation, yet in a way that depends on the head-forward/head-aft variable. There is no uniform correlation between felt orientation of the body and felt orientation of the craft.

All the objective elements that the third-person observer can specify are internally related within the subject's experience of orientation. It is not just the objective value of these elements that varies, but their linkage in a system of relations, and within this system the sense of each variable is internally related to the sense of other values. So it is best not to explain the subject's experience in terms of causal relations between independent objective elements, but to interpret it in terms of shifts in an overall system.

(5) But this system involves *sens*. This is suggested by the fact that the subject's experience of orientation is, in the rather horrifying term I introduced in chapter one, non-ontonomic. It does not obey the law of things, rather it is phenomenal:

(a) Changes in orientation were felt not as abrupt transitions, but as a fading from one orientation to another, without any apparent physical rotation of the body or aircraft, in which the initial orientation feels less and less "compelling" and the new orientation more and more "compelling." In another experiment, some subjects described this transition as a telescoping motion in which the feet moved down and the head moved up internally through the body. As Lackner notes, this is physically impossible, and again suggests to us that the felt body has a *sens*, rather than being a representation or model of an objective body (see chapter two).

(b) In cases **A** and **B** there was "a compelling visual illusion of elongation of the aircraft"—the subjects reported that it seemed as if they "were looking down or up a long tunnel."

(c) Lackner also reports that (in experiments other than the posture-orientation experiment) the "inversion illusion," the "illusion" of feeling upside down, was experienced in different ways by different subjects: (i) self inverted, aircraft inverted, (ii) self inverted, aircraft upright, or (iii) self upright, aircraft inverted. In case (ii), some subjects reported objects in the visual field as left-right reversed, while others reported that the visual field was normally oriented but they were upside down while viewing it; in case (iii), subjects reported objects in the visual field to be up-down and left-right reversed; and in cases (ii) and (iii), subjects who experienced a left-right reversal commonly misreached when pointing or grasping.

(d)   Finally, in some cases subjects reported a "dissociation" of the visual field, in which parts of the visual field were upright and others upside down. Most extraordinary is that in some instances this was tightly correlated with what could only be called the subject's *meaningful* relation to the environment: "when the subject was reading a dial, *the numerals on the dial could seem upright and the rest of the instrument upside down*" (Lackner 1992, 808, emphasis mine). Felt orientation is not a matter of rotations of overall visual or kinesthetic fields, but of relations to meaningfully or pragmatically segmented fields.

(6) On the other hand, there is strong evidence that the phenomenon is not merely intellectual or subjective. The response was uniform across subjects in most respects (see the exception of group N, above), and orientation was experienced as beyond the control of the subject. Only one subject could change his felt orientation by imagining himself in a particular orientation, and this occurred only when he was floating free of his seat. Otherwise felt orientation could be changed only by changing posture and gaze direction, or donning prisms that "invert" the visual field.

In sum, these points suggest that the experienced orientation is neither purely subjective nor reducible to the objective world of things, but is in that middle region of the experienced world that Dillon labels the phenomenal. More, it suggests that the moving relation between a postured body and the visual scene is central.

To give an example of how a causal account is inadequate to the phenomena, I briefly consider Lackner's own interpretation of his results.[5] Lackner suggests that the subject's experience of orientation is due to a dynamic reorganization that reinterprets and gives new weights to the different sensory, motor, and cognitive factors that "singly and in combination, synergistically specify body orientation in relation to gravity and to the ground or support surface" in the everyday situation (Lackner 1992, 809–811). But there is a problem here, and I think Lackner tacitly acknowledges it. To fit the results within a linear causal framework, you have to claim that factors work singly and in combination, and in a linear framework this is a somewhat contradictory conjunction. The interpretation I offer cuts through this contradiction by arguing for a holistic, circular relation, having to do with limited body-world movement.

Lackner also suggests that the different relations between the orientation of the self and the orientation of the environment in the inversion illusion may be due to the fact that self and visual environment are "independently represented and mapped by the nervous system." But this hypothesis requires some binding mechanism to account for the systematic interrelation of the orientations of self and environment, which would lead to problems explaining the genesis of this binding mechanism from mappings that must originally be separate: the mappings must be both independent and interrelated. (This is really another version of the "singly and in combination" problem.) And the separate-mappings hypothesis could not explain the meaningful, non-ontonomic dissociation of the visual field in which numbers on an instrument dial appear upright while the dial appears upside down. Taking results of experience (independent felt orientations of self and visual environment) as principles for explaining that experience is an instance of the experience error, or is at least too hasty. If we are going back to the turn of experience, then we cannot appeal to such a division between self and environment.

Here we should also recall our earlier discussion of illusions. Merleau-Ponty and Carello and Turvey argue that very often philosophers and scientists are in error when they call certain phenomena illusions, because they are falsely insinuating a referent of perception, one that can be objectively measured, rather than noticing what perception really refers to. It is not as if in Earthly situations orientation perception is a matter of "correctly" recovering an objective up and down, but then goes haywire in weightlessness because an objective up and down disappear, leading to illusion. One of the advantages of studying something as profound as orientation is that orientation is clearly not something given in itself; it never has a simple objective referent: which way is up depends, to some extent at least, on the way one becomes involved with things. In weightlessness this is obviously true: when one is floating weightless, many different objective orientations could equally be considered up. In general, there is no fully objective yardstick for orientation—ask a kid who insists that today is upside-down day. Yet still there is an 'up,' even in outer space. But the referent of 'up' is not an object, it is something cross between body and world, something in movement, something not out there on its own. And this 'up' that one senses in body-world movement really matters. When Skylab astronaut Joseph Kerwin loses his sense of 'up,' he feels as though he is falling, and reaches out to grab onto something. 'Up' in outer space is no mere illusion, it has as much of a grip on Kerwin's life as it does on Earth. It is striking how body-world movement figures here: either you move in the world (you grab on), or you are moved in the world (you fall). (Kerwin 1977)

An objective, causal account of the posture-orientation experiment, that tries to pin orientation perception on a ready-made world or ready-made cognitive structures or capacities, will not do. The referent of 'up' is neither in the world nor in the body, but in movement that crosses the two.

A POSTURAL INTERPRETATION OF LACKNER'S EXPERIMENT

My overall interpretation of Lackner's result is as follows: Body-world movement is constrained by a topology of residing rooted in postural articulations
of a body evolved on Earth. Movement constrained by this topology gives
rise to postures of residing. The referent of 'up' is postures of residing, postural movements.

The interpretation is organized around an analysis of posture. Lackner
shows that posture is crucial in the experience of orientation in weightlessness. In our conceptual framework, which conceives perception as arising in
movement that crosses the body and the world, this fact leads to an insight.
In Lackner's experiment subjects did not move themselves into place but
floated free and were moved into place by experimenters. Indeed, it appears
that the subject's hands were passively resting alongside the body. Body-
world movement seems to have been cut off. But even a subject floating free
in space and moved into place draws on habitual patterns of movement that
cross body and world: looking, seeing, maintaining a posture, being prepared
for further movements and explorations—witness astronaut Kerwin's preparedness to reach out and grab when he feels as though he is falling. Posture, as preparedness for movement, is a moving relation to the world, even
if it involves no noticeable locomotion. We could hardly say that the athlete's
pose in the starting block or the sniper's absolute stillness has nothing to do
with movement just because it does not involve *moving about*.

I treat the three different postures in the experiment, gaze away from
body, gaze toward body, and gaze forward, in that order. For each posture,
facts about posture and felt orientation (in relation to all the other data)
prompt an insight into a general and habitual *sens* of the posture. To develop
these insights I draw on Earthly experiences, and attend to the topo-logic of
our bodies, the way the articulation of our bodies allow us to turn toward and
away from ourselves and our rootedness in place. I expose an emotional,
concernful *sens* of posture: the three postures are emotionally significant
because they open, close, and rest the body in the world and thus pose very
different concerns about our moving relation to the world. Having gained
insight into an emotional core, in each case I go back and show how the
insight helps make sense of the facts.

'UP' AND THE OPEN BODY

I begin with cases **A** and **C'**, with the posture in which head and gaze are bent
back and away from the body. When looking at the ceiling (case **A**), the
subject felt upright in a vertically oriented craft. When looking at the floor
(case **C'**), the subject felt horizontal in a horizontally oriented craft.

My insight here is that the topo-logic of the body is such that tilting
the head and gaze back at once opens the front of one's body, the trunk, to

the world, and turns one away from a moving involvement with one's body. (I use the term *trunk* to refer to the torso plus legs; I also deliberately play on the arboreal connotations of the term.) Tilting one's head away from one's trunk does this to a much greater degree than just tilting one's eyes. With the head tilted back, one's trunk is not only open but *vulnerable* to the world, since the trunk is hidden from view and one gives up moving involvement with the world in front. To deliberately assume this open posture is to thematize the vulnerability of one's body and to show that one is not concerned about it. Throwing the head back is a gesture that accompanies laughter, or contemplation, or indicates a carefree attitude that neglects the weight of the world. I call this the open posture.

To assume the open posture is to show with one's body that one is unconcerned with the surrounding world in which one moves, and with things moving toward oneself. But this precisely hides the sort of concern inherent in the being of a body that moves in the world. To be unconcerned is not to have no cares at all, it is to be in the fortunate position of not having to be concerned about one's concerns. (I use *concern* as a synonym for *care*.) When one is unconcerned, one gets to put one's head back and relax. To assume the open posture is to be *able* to experience one's body as unconcernedly resident on earth, even to *assert* this unconcernful residence. One who moves, laughs or dances with head thrown back shakes off (or escapes, avoids, runs away from) earthly cares. One who claims triumph over the world not only tilts the head back but lifts the arms over the head, as if daring the world to attack, as if making the body even more vulnerable in contempt of the surrounding world. The open posture claims a conquest in Neruda's "gray war of space," disowns its resident vulnerability on earth, as if the body can earth itself.

In short, the open posture turns a primordial concern of body-world movement, namely residence on earth, into an unconcern. But this is really a matter of displacing concern rather than eliminating it. Whereas residing is usually a movement that seizes one from the outside (a larger body, Earth, holding one down), the movement of opening one's posture displaces that outside movement through a movement of the body itself, 'sums it up in the different form' of bodily posturing that claims to earth itself, rather than being earthed from the outside. The open posture thus expresses residing as a movement in one's power. The *sens* expressed in the open posture would belong to the natural body (since it follows from its topo-logic) and is, as we see in studying habitual expression, contracted into habits.

If this postural *sens* is habitual, we would expect it to persist even if the everyday globe of Earth is cut off. As a phantom limb, the correlate of a certain possibility of moving, can persist when a limb is not present, phantom earth, the correlate of a certain possibility of residing, can persist in weightlessness. A phantom earth would not obey the law of things, it would be phenomenal and correlative to one's habitual ways of residing. If so, a subject who adopts the open posture might feel uprightly resident on earth, without being objectively upright according to or by cause of any external standard. Uprightness would not refer to any larger body, but to habitual postures of residing that express the body as being "on top of things," and to an earth correlative to such a posture. This, I suggest, is what is happening in the posture-orientation experiment.

Consider those subjects (members of group S) who can change their sense of orientation by changing eye direction. When strapped into their seats, they felt upright when looking up past their forehead. When floating outside their seats, members of group S felt upright when they turned their eyes past their forehead with their eyes *closed*. For members of this group, a movement of the eyes, a postural movement, even without visual input, was sufficient to give a *sens* of up. In my interpretation, this is in virtue of habitual postures of residing and the correlative *sens* of up and down expressed by such postures.

But posture is directed toward a surround, so let us turn to the posture-orientation experiment and see what happens when subjects have their eyes open and are visually engaged with their surround. Postures of residing imply a relation to earth, and so we should expect that the *sens* of posture gives a *sens* to the surround, gives the surround a role as earth. Subjects in the open posture felt upright when looking at the ceiling (case A), but horizontal when looking at the floor (case C'). Gravity is out of play, so the difference between the floor and ceiling cases must stem from their visual role. Interpreting this role is key, but it must be remembered that it is not independent of posture (compare cases A and C' with cases B and C''). In offering my interpretation, I am at a disadvantage since I do not have a good description of the ceiling or the floor (should the two surfaces even really be called floor and ceiling?), nor do I know how far the subjects were away from these surfaces, or the history of the individuals (which is important, since members of group N did experience inversion in case B, but did not experience themselves as upright in case A). So I have to fill in the blanks by imaginatively drawing on Earthly experience.

Imagine being in the open posture, floating weightless along a surface that looks like the the floor of an aircraft. One's posture puts one's gaze ahead of one's body and habitually expresses the power of residing as being at work in one's body, as being unconcernedly secured behind one's gaze. Residing is a background power taken care of in one's trunk, and the floor appears as the earth correlative to such residing. This gives an overall feeling that approximates lying along or being held over a surface, as when looking out over an edge or floating over a river bottom. This interpretation assumes that the look of the floor, together with the feel of residing occurring in the trunk, motivates the sort of experience I just described. This would make sense of case C'.

Imagine being in the same posture but looking at the ceiling (case A). The ceiling might not appear as a horizontal surface that affords residing;

perhaps the ceiling, which is probably arched rather than flat, and perhaps ribbed rather than continuous, cannot support this meaning; or perhaps the fact that one is looking at a ceiling enters into perception, and while it is semihabitual to lie or crawl along or over a support surface, or even to float over it in water, or survey it from a ledge, we have no such habits of residing in relation to ceilings. In this case (as with the previous case), one's posture expresses the power of residing as unconcernedly taken care of behind one's gaze, in one's trunk. But in this case the earth that supports residing is nowhere to be seen. Recall my argument, though, that earth is not a thing: it is correlative to the movement of residing, an excorporation integral to the moving body. The earth must be somewhere. So it arises in some phenomenal, non-ontonomic, way, and in the only region where it can: behind the gaze. I claim that in this situation rather than being earthed by some visible surface out front, the body experiences itself as taking care of earthing, or perhaps the way to put it is that earthing is taken care of in the region behind one's gaze, in a plane behind the body (which happens to be an airplane in the experiment). Not only residing but earth become a function of a bodily power behind one's gaze. This interpretation hinges on the claim that the floor can play the role of earth, but the ceiling cannot. (Or rather, it aims to interpret the difference between cases C' and A in terms of the difference between floor and ceiling. Note that the interpretation could be tested by making ceiling and floor be visually uniform, by putting different images on ceiling and floor (for example, sky versus ground), and so on.)

Perhaps the overall feeling of this situation approximates a habit of clinging to a vertical surface or climbing or even 'diving' upward. This might make sense of the fact that the subject perceives the aircraft as elongated, like a long tunnel. The aircraft elongates because it has the meaningful role of something that the body is traveling up.

In case C' the floor appears as earth, and the felt orientation of the body follows that of the craft—the craft establishes earth. In the case being considered here, case A, earth appears in the region behind the gaze of the body and the orientation of the craft follows from that of the body—the body establishes earth. The body is upright, and when the subject's head is aft, the tail of the craft is upright; when the subject's head is forward, the nose of the craft is upright. Here it is interesting to note that when experimenters pressed the subject's head, the subject felt upside down, that is, when the body is moved from the outside, it can no longer establish earth, and things turn upside down. It is tempting to say that an outside push shows the body's posturing to be a fraud.

Granted my assumptions about the role of the floor and ceiling, the above interpretation makes sense of case A. But these assumptions would need further exploration.

It may be objected that the phenomenon is based not in postures of residing (overall moving relations to the world) but simply on the direction of the eyes. The head is at the upper end of the body, and when our eyes point in that direction, we habitually feel as though we are looking up, so the direction in which we look is up. But first of all, this begs the question of 'up,' since it equates it with a simple vector across the body, and we, following Merleau-Ponty, are trying to figure out how 'up' is constituted in the first place, which is why we are pursuing this strange disturbance. Second, in the *Phenomenology of Perception* Merleau-Ponty points out that it would be a mistake to equate the direction of the head with 'up,' since Stratton's experiment (in which the world is visually inverted but the subject nonetheless eventually comes to see it as upright) shows that these vectors can be inverted; further, the world does not turn sideways when we lie down. More, this equation would not explain why the body as a whole is experienced as upside down in case **B** of the posture-orientation experiment; if the head is supposed to mark the direction of up, why would looking toward one's feet invert the body, rather than just giving one a feeling of looking down at one's feet? The equation would also not explain why subjects experience themselves as horizontal in case **C**, rather than just looking forward, and why, in some experiments mentioned below, looking down at the body also causes a feeling of being upright. These replies indicate a basic problem with the objection, namely that it tries to isolate factors that need to be understood as internal to one another within the overall crossing of body and world.

A Conceptual Framework: The Topology of Residing, Earth, and Orientation

Now is a good time to consolidate a conceptual framework.

As in the case of depth, orientation perception is not rooted in an a priori intuition or a fixed, immediate principle; the principle is twofold and mediated by movement. In depth perception, a topology of enveloping constrains body-world movement, generating envelopes of movement that are the referent of depth perception. In orientation perception, a topology of residing constrains body-world movement, generating moving postural relations to the world, ways of residing, that imply a relation to earth. Postures of residing on earth are the referent of orientation perception. Where the *sens* of the topology of enveloping is contracted from the very basic constraint that zones of a body must work as one, and that things perceived have enveloping surfaces, the *sens* of the topology of residing is contracted from the natural postural articulations of a body evolved to cross the earth, a body that can turn toward or away from itself in turning toward or away from the world. The 'language' of orientation, the order within movement that gives a *sens* of depth, arises in the movement of a body that can be concerned for itself, and that is concerned with itself in place. Orientation thus has a concernful and emotional aspect.

'DOWN' AND THE CLOSED BODY

We have seen how posturing as being unconcerned with one's residence on earth gives one a feeling of being up. Interpretation of cases **B** and **C''** shows, in a parallel fashion, that posturing as being sunk in concern for one's residence on earth gives one a feeling of being down. I abbreviate many details spelled out above; these can be carried over by the reader.

Tilting one's head toward one's body closes one's body in on itself. This closed posture is protective and concernful, it turns one away from moving involvement with the surrounding world, and brings one into a moving relation with one's body and roots in the world. One looks down at one's feet, and there one notices what Neruda calls "the isolated and solitary part of [one's] being." Just as the unconcern of the open posture hides one's concerned relation to the world, the self-involvement of the closed posture hides the fact that one is concerned not just with oneself, but with one's residence on earth. The closed posture, like fainting in Sartre's analysis, is a postural, emotional attitude that affirms contact with the world precisely in turning away from it (Sartre 1993, chapter 3). It folds one's involvement with the world into one's involvement with oneself, as if that involvement could be 'summed up in different form.' It is a movement of bad faith, if you will: as if hanging one's head in shame is really the way to address the shameful thing one has done in the world; as if putting someone on the spot by shaming him, getting him to curl into his own body, really invites a response. If there were no others, no earth beyond oneself, nothing to worry about as one moves about on earth, then a hang-dog posture would express no shame, or concern, or anything at all. But one moves on earth, and even if there are no others actually present, hanging one's head is a way of expressing concern with one's situation, or shame at one's way of being in the world, or just simple care for the way one is moving about on unsteady ground.

This is carried over, by habit, in the body cut off from Earth. Tilting one's gaze toward one's body expresses concern for one's body and residence on earth. In weightlessness we would expect that this posture would express the *sens* of being rooted on earth, as was the case with the open posture. Indeed, members of group **S** felt upright when strapped in and looking down at their bodies, and also floating outside their seats with their *closed* eyes turned toward their bodies. Here it is important to note that both the open and closed postures produced a feeling of being upright when subjects were either passively strapped into seats or floating with their eyes closed: when the body is not actively engaged with the world, concern or unconcern for one's residence on earth, expressed in posture, can be sufficient to give one a feeling of being upright.

Things change when the subject visually engages with the world. With face ceilingward, subjects felt horizontal in the aircraft (case **C''**), but with face floorward they felt upside down, not upright (case **B**). Recall that the closed posture is like the open posture in implying a relation to earth. But the open posture expresses unconcern for the earth, implies earth as a power at one with the body's power of residing. In contrast, the closed posture implies earth as a region of concern, antagonistic to the body's power of residing. Further, the open posture implies earth and the power of residing as being behind the gaze, whereas the closed posture implies both as a visible concern.

It is important to note that in case **B**, subjects experienced the transition to feeling upside down when their gaze turned to the point where they could *see* their bodies physically separated from the deck. I interpret this in the following way. When one hangs one's head in shame, looks at the ground, or is miserable about one's life, one is occupied with one's residence on earth as manifest right in one's moving body (rather than being behind one, as in the open posture). The closed posture expresses the body as taking care of residing, albeit badly. When the subject sees there is no earth supporting this residing, that the body is floating in midair, the earth implied in residing goes somewhere else, into the region that is not seen, into a region ahead of and against oneself. The subject experiences this as being upside down, not "on top of the situation," in the sway of an outside power. The slump of the head in Earthly situations sometimes expresses that the whole world is against us. It is almost as if the weightless situation literalizes this. On Earth we say we feel "down," dejected; in weightlessness, with no apparent earth to hold us up, we do not just feel emotionally down, we feel ourselves as actually being upside down. One is reminded here of the moment when Dante and Virgil climb up Lucifer's body out of Inferno (*Inferno*, Canto 34). At the midpoint of Lucifer's body, Virgil has to rotate 180 degrees, at first looking to Dante as though he is climbing with his feet first; but then it turns out that past this midpoint 'up' and 'down' have reversed their sense, so that Virgil is climbing headfirst. Or rather, it turns out that all along everything has been upside down in Inferno: Lucifer now appears to be hanging head down into Inferno with his feet in the air. Dante the poet is drawing on a connection between moral baseness and being upside down; I am suggesting that the posture that habitually expresses moral baseness, shame, and so on gives one a feeling of being upside down, in conflict with the world, suspended by an outside power.

Subjects do not feel as though they are falling, yet they feel inverted. I interpret this as the feeling of earth being there but working against oneself. Thus the vector of upside-down orientation follows from the vector of the body. So the orientation of the aircraft follows the orientation of the body; as in case **A**, the body anchors orientation, not the craft. Perhaps the subject's experience in this situation is akin to a phenomenal version of diving or falling, or being hung upside down, and then we can suppose that the aircraft's elongation into a tunnel makes sense of the situation (as in case **A**).

At this point I speculate on the experience of members of group **N**, who felt upside down in case **B**, but did not feel upright in case **A**. One possibility is that the members of group **N** have a much more intellectual, less emotional relation to their bodies than the other subjects. They feel upside down when they see their feet floating above the floor, but emotional aspects of bodily postures are not sufficient to change the meaning of their bodily relation to the world. In a way, they behave as if inferential models of perception are true. (Merleau-Ponty makes a similar claim about the individual Schneider: according to Merleau-Ponty, Schneider has a conscious, intellectual relation to his body, he reasons about his body, rather than directly living its *sens* (*PP* part 1, chapter 2–3).) Or perhaps they have some training that makes bodily orientation into an intellectual, technical issue for them, for example, training as pilots, high-divers, or gymnasts, in which case orientation perception could to some degree become a matter of sight. A second, perhaps related, possibility is that the open posture of the body has not acquired the same meaning for them as it has for the other subjects. This could be due to their personal history. Members of group **N** might be the sort of individuals who assert bravado by hurtling into situations without any concern for damage to the body. Or maybe, on the moral and emotional register, they are not prone to shame or feeling responsible to outside powers, which has some relation to recklessness. Some mixture of these possibilities might account for the experience of each of the members of group **N**. But it is not possible to give a firm interpretation without further evidence.

The above gives an account of the experience of subjects whose gaze is toward the body and whose face is floorward, case **B**.

In case **C″**, with face ceilingward and gaze toward the body, subjects can see the gap between their feet and the ceiling, and they feel horizontal. As in case **B**, one's posture expresses residing as being taken care of by the body. The key to interpreting this case would seem to be that when one is seeing the ceiling (rather than one's feet floating over the floor), the earth can be located behind oneself in a surface counterpart to the ceiling. In case **B** earth is nowhere to be seen, and there is nothing implied in the scene that would make sense of floating feet, so earth is located in a region antagonistic to the body, turning the body and craft upside down. In case **C″** an unseen surface behind the body earths the body. The orientation of the body would thus follow the orientation of the craft, that is, of the floor which appears as the unseen earth. This would make sense of case **C″**.

THE HORIZONTAL AND THE RESTING BODY

I have already covered several conditions in case **C**, where the body is experienced as horizontal, namely, **C′** and **C″**. In the remaining conditions in case **C** (the two center rows of the diagram), the subject is in a gaze-forward posture. The subject's arms are by the side of the body and the subject has been moved into place by the experimenter.

When one hangs one's arms at one's sides and does not actively move, but looks at what is in front, one's whole front becomes open to moving interaction with the world. But one still has a forward and downward residential involvement with earth, so long as one is working to stand up. When one gives up this work and rests, one gives up active movement and passively opens oneself to the world in front. In situations where one has weight, it is only when one is lying on something that one can rest in this way and still be involved with the world. In this resting posture one's residing relation to the earth is beyond the periphery of one's vision and is not of concern, it is rooted in earth behind the plane of the body. This resting posture expresses a relative patiency of residence, as if one is cradled by earth.

This posture, then, expresses a restful residence that implies earth as behind one and on one's side. In weightlessness this might give the feeling of being horizontal. In Lackner's experiment this happens when the subject is either face floorward or face ceilingward. We can presume that in this situation the subject postures himself as residing in relation to an earth not in his power, that holds the subject as either looking up at the ceiling, or as looking down at the floor, in which case the orientation of the body would follow the orientation of the craft that earths the body. The difference between this case and case **B**, in which the subject feels upside down, has to do with the fact that the subject's posture is restful, rather than concernful, and the subject is not visually preoccupied with the relation between body and earth. This would make sense of the remaining conditions in case **C**, but here I would want a better account of why the ceiling can support the meaning of the resting posture, going back to the floor/ceiling issues mentioned in case **A**.

'Up' in the Working Body

My contention so far is that the referent of orientation perception is not an absolute up or down, or an up or down specified by static neurological or cognitive structures, but postures of residing that are generated in body-world movement constrained by a topology of residing. So far I have been looking at a floating, weightless body that does not move about in its world. The *sens* I detected does not stem from movement in the sense of locomotion and doing things, but from movement in the sense of being moved, staying in place, and being emotional. I detected an emotional *sens* in our relation to place, an emotional *sens* expressed in postures that open and close us to earth around us.

What of the body that moves about and does things? In everyday situations, when one is involved with movement out front, one experiences oneself as residing through one's trunk, in a way modified by one's relation to earth: for the writer writing on a table, the body resides as up; for the automechanic working under the car, the body resides as horizontal. One would expect that if the weightless perceiver, unlike Lackner's subjects in the posture-orientation experiment, can become involved in moving about and doing things, then the habitual meaning of that moving activity, rather than just posture, would determine the *sens* of up and down: the referent of up and down would just be not postures of residing, but what can be done. This would be similar to Merleau-Ponty's finding in his analysis of Wertheimer's experiment, namely that the upright is geared to the subject's ability to establish a habitual relation to the visual world: the world comes to rights for Wertheimer's subject after the subject becomes habituated to a room that is visually rotated forty-five degrees from vertical, after the subject, as Merleau-Ponty puts it, is able to live in this odd world.

That this is the case in weightlessness is shown by astronaut E. G. Gibson's report that on his Skylab mission:

> . . . being upside down in the wardroom made it look like a different room than the one we were used to. After rotating back to approximately 45 degrees or so of the attitude which we normally called "up," the attitude in which we trained, there was a very sharp transition in the mind from a room which was sort of familiar to one which was intimately familiar. (E. G. Gibson 1977, 24)

When E. G. Gibson rotates his body to within forty-five degrees of the attitude in which he trained, he can engage in his *habitual* involvement with the wardroom, and this means that his moving engagement with the world implies earth, something that supports habitual body-world movement. So he undergoes a phenomenal transition to feeling upright, one that snaps from zero to forty-five degrees, from the strange to the familiar, without intervening stages. We should conclude that it is the body's habitual crossing with the world, its grip on the world, and not the objective direction of parts of the body on their own, that determines 'up' in this case. But on the other hand, the crossing of body and world *does* depend on the objective attitude of parts of the body: Gibson experiences the room as familiar only when he is positioned within forty-five degrees of his habitual attitude.

Another Skylab astronaut, Joseph Kerwin, reports that he could play with his sense of up and down by rotating his body, turning walls into ceilings and vice versa (both walls and ceilings were work surfaces in Skylab). By rotating his body in a manner that gives up his habitual commitments to fixed attitudes, and playing with different attitudes, Kerwin set up different sorts of moving involvements with the craft and gave different determinations and meanings to his residence on earth, thus changing his sense of orientation. On the other hand, Kerwin also tried playing with closing his eyes to "make everything go away," but the first time he tried this he reports that his instinct was to "grab hold of whatever was nearest and just hang on, lest I fall" (Kerwin 1977, 27). Severing the crossing of body and world cut off the possibility of being earthed, and set off an experience of falling. The extraordinary point here is that throwing the body into space is not enough to cut off the sense of a supporting earth: you have to go farther, and cut off the moving interaction of body and world. On the other hand, perhaps this is just the flip side of a familiar Earthly phenomenon: the actual Earth 'spins' and goes 'topsy turvy' when our moving relation to it breaks down, as in a shock that cannot be grasped. Even on Earth support is not simply given in the ground, it is a matter of being able to move.

Finally, the sense of orientation in weightlessness depends not only on bodily movement, but on what the world affords to the moving body: according to Lackner and Graybiel, "one of the things that bothered Skylab astronauts most was a lack of a structured 'visual horizontal and vertical' in the docking adapter of their spacecraft" (Lackner and Graybiel 1983, 50). Other experimental data, I think, can be understood along similar lines. (See Gurfinkel, Lestienne, Levik, Popov, and Lefort 1993; Gurfinkel and Levik 1991; Mittelstaedt and Glasauer 1993.)

When the body moves itself about in the weightless world, 'up' is specified by a grasping relation, similar to the one that Merleau-Ponty discovers in his analysis of orientation. This might be specified as a topology of grasping, based in habitual active movement. But when the body is moved in a weightless world, moves only by posturing and seeing, 'up' is specified by postures of residing that point back to an underlying topology of residing, and to an emotional register of our postural relation to earth.

REPLIES TO OBJECTIONS

One possible objection to the above is that it is not predictive, and thus lacks the objectivity found in scientific account. To an extent it is true that my interpretation is not predictive. My focus, in any case, is on interpretation. Nonetheless, a kind of prediction is involved: I am predicting that certain topological constraints and habits are at the basis of the phenomena. Specifically, I predict that the body's habitual postural relation to itself has a significance that colors our sense of orientation. Science may want more specific predictions. But I should note that (on the basis of study of Heidegger, Merleau-Ponty, Straus, and others) I did, in my own course of research, predict that moving, habitual and postural relations would influence the sense of up and down in weightlessness, and expected some of the observations that the Skylab astronauts made about their moving relation to their environment. Philosophical-phenomenological insight can lead to hypotheses and predictions that are in a sense testable.

When it comes to prediction, the problem is that I am interpreting the phenomena as meaningful, and if they are meaningful, they are subject to interpretation, and are inherently labile. Moreover, the sort of *sens* that I have been pursuing—*sens* contracted through habit and movement—is inherently individual. So we should expect variations in *sens*. Indeed, I am not prepared to predict that the *sens* of up and down will unfold exactly as specified above, just that the postural and other factors detected above will play some role, even if the role is reversed or neutralized. To the scientist, this will look like the invention of a closed discourse that claims to explain everything even if predictions turn out to be reversed (the sort of accusation brought against Freud). But I am not, finally, interested in prediction, I am interested in interpretation. Why can the difference between ceiling and floor, and so on, this posture or that, be the difference between feeling up or feeling down?

What is really at stake for me here is not so much my account of Lackner's results, but the insight that the *sens* of up and down is rooted in a moving, postural relation to the world, and has an emotional color behind it. I argued for a particular, detailed configuration of this emotional-postural relation, and I suspect that elements of it are fundamental. But the relation is not the same across all bodies—the exceptions in Lackner's experiments already show that. And I suspect that the very configuration of the experiment, the very sort of moving body that you already have to be to get into the experiment (male, prepared to be hurtled about in an aircraft, perhaps training for the air force), and the questions posed to the subjects (given the long-term practical interests of the experiment) have an impact on the sorts of experiences reported, and thence shape the details. All of the above invites another layer of questioning, especially from feminist scholars (see Code 1995; Grosz 1995; Duncan 1996; Ardener 1993). But given that only air forces and space agencies conduct such experiments, and given their current configuration, such questioning would be demanded by any appeal to extant data on weightlessness.

The goal of my interpretation is to gain insight into an emotional-postural relation to the earth at the core of felt orientation, not by appeal to literature, poetry, or emotional experience, but by appeal to the experience of a body moving in weightlessness. What is evident to the poet who reads a relation to the earth in socks, shoes, and the experience of one's legs, becomes evident in the unearthed body, complements the poet's insights.

It might also be objected that we need not refer to anything quite so elaborate to explain the phenomena. A simple input/output matrix would do the trick of explaining Lackner's results.[6] The problem is that we would have to explain why and how the difference between floor and ceiling, which does not seem like the sort of thing that would be encoded for any evolutionary reason, would figure in this matrix. And we would have to explain why the matrix goes together in this way. Why would the variables in the matrix be divided from one another in this precise way and give this precise output when the body is hurled into weightlessness? We also would have to explain why and how output varies across individuals. And we would have to explain how the output correlates with phenomena such as the perceived elongation of the craft, and so on. In short, it seems that the input/output matrix model is just too simple, and leads to a Hydra of ad hoc corrections. Lackner himself does not turn to such a model, because he is puzzled by the role of the floor/ceiling architecture in the phenomenon. The interpretation I offered grasps all the elements as standing in mutual motivating relations, so that the experience cannot be modularized and pressed into a matrix.

Suppose, however, that science could identify some sort of complex neural network that explains the phenomenon. In any such account, posture, head position, and so on would be important factors. This would leave two questions: Why does head position and so on have such an important role in relation to the environment? And why have neural networks developed such that their dynamic activity in the novel condition of weightlessness specifies the sense of orientation uncovered by Lackner? Presumably an answer to these questions would turn to evolution, but the condition of weightlessness could not have had any influence on the evolution of a terrestrial creature. So an appeal to evolution would have the form of explaining why certain phenomena ensue when gravity is curtailed. But then the phenomena and their neural basis must be comprehended in terms of a body for whom gravity and thence earth matter. I am arguing against the procedure of reducing the phenomenon to a weighted network of abstract activation levels. The activation levels matter to a body evolved in a gravitational environment and reference to a gravitational environment must be brought along. Whatever is beneath the phenomenon, it must be understood in terms of a moving body crossed with earth, a body that carries its relation to Earth along with it. This is what the concept of the topology of residing aims to do: to understand 'up' and 'down' not in terms of the isolate body, but in terms of the body's residential relation to earth. To attempt to understand the phenomenon of the unearthed body without reference to earth would be like trying to understand the color of a polar bear without reference to the Arctic; both are terrible mistakes.

A little thought experiment will help make the point. Imagine an intelligent creature whose body is a sphere with eyes and arms distributed evenly across its surface, that respires and ingests through diffusive processes distributed across its surface. We would not imagine that this creature would have evolved neural networks that would duplicate Lackner's results—it could not have, because it has neither the neck nor the postural possibilities of the human body. Human astronauts report discomfort in weightless conferences if their heads are pointing in different directions; sphere-creature astronauts would not have this problem. Even if we could identify some neural network that produces Lackner's results, we would not be explaining anything unless we understood why that network had evolved, and that would mean attending to our body not as an isotropic sphere, but as having certain symmetries and asymmetries, as being articulated by a neck, as evolving through a life in which the way one faces the world matters quite a bit. Our analyses cannot proceed in abstraction. And if we refuse abstraction, then we cannot isolate factors and put them back into a matrix to see how they interact. We must instead see how gaze, posture, surfaces, and bodies go together in a moving body that crosses earth.

THE TOPOLOGY OF RESIDING, AND FACING OTHERS IN PLACE

The purpose of studying Lackner's results is not simply to interpret orientation in weightlessness, but to gain insights into Earthly orientation. The main insight is that felt orientation does not refer to axes of 'up' and 'down' inscribed in things or the body, but to patterns in body-world movement, moving patterns of grasping (when the body is allowed to move about) and moving patterns of residing (when the body does not move about but still postures). Orientation perception likely refers to a complex of both movement patterns.

Let us focus on residing. Our result is that the deep grammar of residing, the topo-logic of a jointed body, is a constraint that generates meaningful movements of residing that are the referent of felt orientation. But this is not the end of the story. Analysis of the topology of residing and the topo-logic of the jointed body deepens the points about concern, place, and emotion treated above.

Where the topology of enveloping stems from the fundamental necessity that zones of the body move as one, the topology of residing stems from the topo-logic of a body jointed so as to be able to face itself, to see itself and be involved with its place, or face away from itself and its place. Throughout his philosophy, Merleau-Ponty invests a related topo-logic, the ability of the the body to see and touch itself, with metaphysical significance, and dwells on the phenomenon of double touch, in which a hand ambiguously and complexly reverses between the roles of touching and being touched. In "Eye and Mind" Merleau-Ponty imagines what our body would be like if it could not touch or see itself: "Such a body would not reflect itself; it would be an almost adamantine body, not really flesh, not really the body of a human being" (OE 20/163). Although the ability to touch and see one's body is not sufficient to bring about humanity, it is necessary for humanity: imagine what it would be like to have no encounter with one's own body, to not be able to perceive oneself as a fleshy finite creature mired in a larger place. One would experience oneself as invincible, as vanishing from the world, rather than as a fleshy being spread out and open to the world. Such a being, I would think, would not have a *sens* of 'up' and 'down.'

Interpretation of Lackner's experiment draws attention to a further aspect of the bodily topo-logic that so entranced Merleau-Ponty. The body is not merely in touch with itself, but can face itself. The fact that the face and head are attached to the body by a neck that allows the face to turn toward and away from the body has metaphysical significance with respect to our experience of orientation. If the previous study of the topology of enveloping ultimately took the hand as its exemplar, finding metaphysical significance in the topo-logic, the deep grammar, of a hand in which zones envelop one another, the study of the topology of residing finds its exemplar in the face, or rather in facing, in turning the face here and there, in the deep grammar of flesh facing itself through others. (In fact, perhaps the body's ability to touch and face itself is linked with the topology of envelopment, since, in effect, facing and touching oneself make explicit the way that zones of the body envelop one another; perhaps these two topologies are to be traced back to one underlying nature of nature, of movement.)

But we already know that the face and facing have profound significance. Although we should not and cannot reduce bodily life to the face, perception, expression, eating and breathing, speaking and hearing 'live' in the face. I do not need to make much of an argument for the centrality of the face: it is long evident in philosophy, from Plato, to Hegel, to Levinas, Deleuze and Wittgenstein; it is evident to artists; and it is evident in everyday life, in the way that people are present through their faces.[7] In this context it is extraordinary to note that a simple movement of the neck allows one to face oneself, or away. And in the very movement of facing oneself, one faces away from others; and conversely, one needs to face away from oneself to face others.

Since the movement of facing oneself is the reverse of the movement of facing others, the postures discussed above have their *sens* not merely in the way one faces one's *own* body and residence on earth. Where the reversibility of one hand touching another unfolds in an interior network, the topo-logic of facing reverses through one's residence on earth, reverses into others who can and do "get in our face," whom one can face or not face. Indeed, in facing oneself in shame, something curious happens. One turns one's face to oneself. But in doing so, one is facing others in face of whom one is ashamed. How? By taking on their point of view in turning in shame toward oneself, as if one were taking on the face of the other and looking at oneself with another's face (the face of genuine contrition, of shame, and so on); but in the very same moment one is facing away from the others, not looking them in the face, and showing that one cannot face oneself as others do (perhaps the face of contrition is a mask). In the hang-dog gesture of shame, one acknowledges the other's position only by showing that one cannot coincide with it, that one faces shame only by not facing it. There is something tremendously complex going on here, and I suspect it indicates something deep about the phenomenology of facing: that facing can never entirely encompass what it faces, that we can never take on the face of the others we face. Facing is thus an index of responsibility and care in the deep grammar of our facing bodies.

This suggests that the topology of residing, and our *sens* of orientation, via our bodies, open into an ethical dimension, and so too does our sense of space. Plato already knew this. In *Timaeus*, he writes:

In the face of these disturbances they scrupled to stain the divine soul only to the extent that this was absolutely necessary, and so they provided a home for the mortal soul in another place in the body, away from the other, once they had built an isthmus as boundary between the head and the chest by situating a neck between them to keep them apart.

. . .

Now we ought to think of the most sovereign part of our soul as god's gift to us, given to be our guiding spirit. This, of course, is the type of soul that, as we maintain, resides in the top part of our bodies. It raises us up away from the earth and toward what is akin to us in heaven, as though we are plants grown not from the earth but from heaven. In saying this, we speak absolutely correctly. For it is from heaven, the place from which our souls were originally born, that the divine part suspends our head, that is, our root, and so keeps our whole body upright. (Plato, *Timaeus*, 69e and 90a)

Plato draws out something phenomenologically significant, namely the role of the head in the body (although on face reading, he divides head and body altogether too much), and its relation to our sense of being upright, with our head rooted in the heavens, as the root of Aristotle's plant is rooted in the soil. Plato embeds the topo-logic of body, neck, and head in a cosmological topology—although given that it is Plato who is in question here I would not trust my initial reading of *Timaeus* for a minute. There is a Yiddish curse, sometimes deployed by my Zaidie Buntsche: "*Vakst vi a tzibele mit dein kop in der erd un di fees in di luften*"—Grow like an onion with your head in the ground and your feet in the air.[8] What makes the curse compelling, apart from its humor, is its Aristotelian image of us as inverted and rooted in place, passively sucking up nutrients from the stomach of the Earth, rather than scrabbling about; Pascal's "thinking reed" becomes a sedentary onion; the tables are turned on Lucifer, who is revealed not as the upright lord of Inferno, but a hairy reed stuck headfirst in the ground. In truth we are not root-heads but move about on earth and face it and others, and our very sense of 'up' and 'down' stems from this moving concern. My study does not topple Plato's topological linkage of morals, mortal bodies, orientation, and the gods, but brings it down to Earth.

All of the above turns us to the role of care (a theme broached at the end of the last chapter) and the ethical (a theme anticipated in the introduction) within the topo-logic of the body, within the deep grammar of our *sens* of orientation. It is worth dwelling on this conception a bit more.

Posture is constrained by biologically fixed relations between the head, upper torso, arms, trunk and legs. This simple constraint unfolds as a series of further constraints: we can see the fronts of our bodies if we choose to, but for the most part we cannot see our backs. Overall, this distinguishes a vanishing back from a front whose visibility is under our control, and a visible 'ahead' from an invisible 'behind.' This is the basis of a corporeal *sens* that can become explicit as we develop, that is contracted into our body as we learn to move around. Return for a moment to my thought experiment with the sphere-creature. Such a creature's bodily engagement with the world would not be constrained by the long axis of the human body, or by any axis at all, and it would not be constrained by a variable way of facing its own body; it could care for itself equally in any orientation. It would be hard to imagine such a creature having a sense of up and down that would much depend on bodily orientation in its environment, and it could not depend on gross posture. It is easier to imagine that up and down—if the creature had a sense of this at all—would simply depend on the creature's practical grasp of things.

For us, on the other hand, learning to move about is always also learning to care for our body via posture. Just as learning to drive is a matter of learning how *not* to be explicitly concerned with the car, learning to move is a matter of *not* being explicitly concerned with one's own body. But this unconcern, of course, depends on an implicit concern for our body moving in place. This becomes explicit when we have to look out: when I step out into the Canadian ice storm, I look down at my feet, I face my body. In the usual case I face in the direction I am going, yet this implicitly takes care of my body. Eleanor Gibson's famous experiment with the "visual cliff," in which the crawling infant will not venture out onto a glass surface suspended over a drop, shows that learning to move is learning to care for oneself in place (E. Gibson 1995; Adolph, Eppler, and E. Gibson 1994; also see Bushnell and Boudreau 1993; Kermoian and Kilbride 1975). But learning to move as learning to care is constrained by basic corporeal constraints. So (given the analysis of learning as expression in chapter 3) learning to move articulates, expresses, the *sens* inherent in the basic constraint we have been studying.

Of course, this constraint on its own, without culture, situation and language would not lead to a developed *sens*, or rather this constraint goes back into all sorts of processes (evolutionary, historical, cultural, developmental) that create *sens* in the first place. I am just suggesting that the constraint in question (of being able to face or not face oneself and others) will be an inherent issue in any human body, and will thus motivate some *sens* that couples with issues of care and emotion.

This leads to a question about individual variations. What of someone, for example, who cannot move his neck or bend his body? Of course the answer would lie in that person's report on his actual experience of up and down. But even if there are individual variations, we share a common bodily and cultural inheritance, a body and a body language, and this would have some importance. On the other hand, the *sens* in question here is just *con-*

strained by the articulation of the body at the neck, not determined by it; there will be variations.

In general, though, we can anticipate that the bodily constraint of having a visible front and a hidden back would contract some *sens* in any body. For example, if the history of one's body has been one of terror, the fact that the back intrinsically evades the body's own protective relation to itself can contract the *sens* of the back as an ill-defined region of vulnerability or terror. In thinking about this pattern of interpretation, in which a fact of the body contracts a *sens* through development, one can usefully recall Freud's discussion of sexuality and the way that parts of the body acquire meanings, although I am arguing for a much more social and cultural development of meaning than is apparent on certain readings of Freud.

The topology I have uncovered complements Edward S. Casey's minimal description of the body in place. Casey distinguishes three dimensions of the body: ahead-behind, left-right, and above-below, and shows that there are internal relations between the pairs in these dyads: ahead turns into behind, and so on; moreover, when we move about, left-right and ahead-behind entwine with one another. Casey closely allies the above-below dimension with the uprightness of the body (Casey 1993, chapter 4). My discussion gives a framework for making sense of this topology and its *sens* in terms of body-world movement, and complicates Casey's discussion by drawing a topological link between front-back (the ahead-behind of the body) and above-below, through the position of the head.

CONCLUSION

Our sense of orientation is not rooted in neural structures, a priori intuitions, and so on. It is rooted in a way of moving and grasping the world, and in a deep grammar of the body, a topo-logic of a body that can face or not face itself, and thereby (conversely) not face or face others and its place. The topology of residing constrains body-world movement, giving rise to movements that contract a *sens* of 'up' or 'down.' In this movement of residing, of facing and and not facing others and place, we detect an emotional *sens* and a concern for place.[9]

Emotion in this context must not be understood in the traditional sense of a secondary attitude to the world riding on top of a more basic sensory or cognitive relation. It must be understood in the manner of Heidegger, Merleau-Ponty, and Collingwood, who reverse the tradition.[10] Emotion is not glandular detritus coughed up on a rational substratum, rather, it is fundamental, the foundation of our orienting attitude toward the world. All three argue that language, reason, and so on, are elaborations and articulations of our emotional being, of our pre-objective care for our being in the world.

The previous chapter showed how the sense of depth is rooted in constrained body-world movement, how it involves a body moving in larger place and thus implies care in movement. In this chapter we come one step closer to care in movement, for our central topic is a body that not only moves in larger place, but faces itself. In depth we move carefully, but moving carefully is so much a part of being a body that we can hardly get a distance on it, we can hardly bring this care into view. (We can disintegrate orientation by hurling the body into space, but can we disintegrate depth without disintegrating the body?) Disintegrating orientation brings care in movement into view, in the form of phantom earth, in traces of an emotional relation of being up or down on earth. If our sense of depth is a matter of a care for our being, so fundamental that it vanishes into the background, in our sense of orientation we can detect a care for this care, a care not just for being in place, but a care for the place in which we move and for the way in which we carefully move in place, in our own eyes and the eyes of others.

This point, about depth as care, and orientation as care for care, I would argue, is mirrored in our language. The deep grammar of the body surfaces in our words. Metaphors of depth, solidity, volume, and expansiveness are used to describe someone's being, whereas metaphors of orientation are used to describe their relation to their being in the world, their way of going about things; for example: she *is* deep, but she would be more on top of things if she did not reverse her position so often. And our basic concerns—sexual, political, ethical, and so on—are often put in terms of orientation. Depth is a matter of being, orientation reflects on being. (For more suggestions on these lines, see Casey 1993, Cataldi 1993, and Ströker 1987.)

Our *sens* of orientation thus involves a moving care for place in face of others, a nexus of themes that might be captured in the Greek word *ethos*, a word for custom that importantly encompasses one's own habit and the customs of one's tribe or people, and thence encompasses custom as one's habitat (habitat is the topic of ethology).

With this observation that our *sens* of space stems from a movement of being amid others we begin opening an ethical dimension of lived space, a dimension more closely approached in the next chapter. Lived space is not a container into which we are dropped, whose dimensions we reconstruct from sensory clues. Our *sens* of space refers to body-world movement, to a moving schema of perception. But the body moves by growing, grows by moving. Space grows. We grow into space. By turning to developmental psychology and studying how our *sens* of space develops through moving and growing, by showing how care in movement is integral to development and facing others, we will deepen this point about the ethical dimension of lived space.

CHAPTER 6

GROWING SPACE

THE DIFFERENCE BETWEEN living in a house with a very young infant and living in a house with a toddler is astounding. It calls for nothing less than a transformation of the household, of attitudes towards things in the house, of ways of caring and playing. Simply put, in moving about, the toddler becomes a different, more independent participant in the moving activity of the household.

The development of movement, from lying in place to turning over and squirming, to sitting up, crawling, and toddling, is correlative to the development of posture. In what follows I detect something crucial in the developmental shift from symmetrical to asymmetrical posture, which is also a shift from closed posture to open posture. As in the previous chapter, closed and open postures bear upon orientation and the individual's concern for herself or himself. In this chapter, though, the link appears in development: the development of the asymmetrical posture is crucial to the infant's ability to reach out from her or his own place into the social place of the household, and is crucial in the development of the infant's orientation toward things and other people. Crucially, these developments are inflected by social relations, and by issues of concern, emotion, and anxiety. The *sens* contracted in our sense of space reflects social and emotional development, and thus takes us into the ethical.

I arrive at this conclusion by studying recent results in developmental psychology, to gain an insight into what I call the topology of concern, a link between posture, concern, and emotion, over the course of development.

METHODOLOGICAL AND CONCEPTUAL REMARKS

(1) I use the term *infant* very generally to designate the very young child from birth to toddlerhood.

(2) I use the term *family* very generally to designate the adults taking care of the infant. Infants develop socially and learn to move by interacting with others. Developmental psychologists highlight this when they take the *dyad,* that is, an infant and adult couple, as their unit of study. When I speak of 'family,' I am not necessarily speaking of a traditional unit. The traditional unit of course varies across traditions, but in all traditions, the infant depends on an entourage of 'familiars,' some-bodies who take care of the infant. I use *family* to designate this care-taking group, whatever it might be. We must keep in mind that the family as site of care-taking can also be the site of neglect, or even violence.

(3) Psychology depends on reports by subjects or interpretation of their behavior. This leads to deep and well-known problems about psychology as science—problems discussed by philosophers as diverse as Dennett and Sartre.[1] The deep problem surfaces directly in developmental psychology, since infants cannot speak. Claims about the infant's psychological states ultimately rely on the psychologist's ingenuity in discovering and interpreting behavior that gives insight into the infant's experience; for example, psychologists take startled behavior or preferential attention as signs of interest in something unusual, which leads to inferences about the infant's usual conception of the world (see Fogel 1984).

When it comes to the experience of basic spatial phenomena, such as up and down, or depth, there are further problems. Ghent, Bernstein, and Goldweber (1960) conducted experiments that tested whether the uprightness of pictured items is "preserved" when children look at pictures when bent over, and Gazjago and Day (1972) tested whether uprightness is preserved when children observe pictures inverted relative to one another. These experiments require the subject's verbal ability to report on orientation; make assumptions about what counts as upright in a picture in the first place; and assume that the subject already knows the difference between the upright and the upside down. But infants cannot speak and do not follow instructions, and presumably we do not know whether infants know the difference between upright and upside down as we do, although some of them certainly find it quite funny to look at things upside down. An experiment can compensate for this by testing how infants smile at faces that are oriented at different angles (Watson, Hayes, Vietze, and Becker 1979). But this raises the following questions: (1) Do infants smile less at faces ninety degrees to their own because the faces are at ninety degrees, and therefore less familiar? Or (2) is the unfamiliarity of odd-looking faces the basis of one's experience of angles of orientation—that is, does the face appear angled away from normal because it looks funny? Consider Merleau-Ponty's vivid description of an upside-down face seen from behind the headboard of a hospital bed, the "hairless head with a red, teeth-filled orifice in the forehead and, where the mouth ought to be, two moving orbs edged with glistening hairs and underlined with stiff brushes" (PP 292/252); or the familiar Gestalt psychological observation that a square tilted at forty-five degrees looks like a different figure, an upright diamond, rather than a tilted square; or the like phenomenon with a picture hanging crooked on the wall. All of these suggest that (2) is the case. But we have no sure way of telling, if the infant cannot speak. Experiments about up-down orientation in infants will keep running into this sort of problem.

To avoid this problem I focus on a different sort of orientation, namely the directedness of the infant toward things and people, as manifest in ways of reaching and facing others. This directedness is also called orientation in the psychological literature. I call it other-orientation (where possible) to distinguish it from the up-down orientation studied in the previous chapter (even if the two senses of orientation turn out to be interrelated). The advantage of studying other-orientation is that reaching directly manifests the infant's own behavioral orientation toward things. Other-orientation, is so to speak, interpreted for us by the infant, insofar as it is an integral part of the infant's moving relation with the world.

THE TOPOLOGY OF CONCERN

Up-Down Orientation and Open and Closed Postures

Before taking up other-orientation, let us take a look at some literature that suggests a few things about up-down orientation in infancy, leading to some observations on the theme of concern.

In relation to orientation in weightlessness, it is interesting to note that the fetus floats in the womb and for the most part the head is directed toward the Earth (Maurer and Maurer 1988).[2] It is not clear that we should make anything of this, other than to observe that birth is, among other things, a transition from an existence in a medium that buoys one's body, to Neruda's "gray war of space."

McGraw (1940) conducted an interesting study in which she identified four phases in the infant's response to being inverted when held up by the feet. The study was longitudinal, that is she returned to the same infants year after year, studying how their responses changed from their first to fifth year. Her interest was in the relation between the development of neuromuscular capacities and responses to inversion, but given the discussion of up-down orientation and open and closed postures in the previous chapter, the phases she discovers are quite interesting: (1) When held upside down, newborns cry or struggle to move up and down; knees, hips, head, and arms are curled up into the front of the body away from the ground—a closed posture. (2) After the first four to six weeks, the inverted infant's posture opens: the spine and head are arched back away from the front, with the face parallel to the ground, the arms opened up and pulled back, with little flexion at the knees, curving the head back toward the body; there is little crying. (3) In a few more months posture closes again: the pelvis is flexed so that the shoulders are brought forward and up toward the knees, the head is held up toward the body, and the infant may seize its own thighs or reach out for the experimenter or support objects; there is considerable emotional arousal, muscles are tense, and crying is common. (4) In the final phase there is an absence of marked flexion or tension, and the body, head, and arms hang down toward the ground; even if the child "finds inversion distasteful, he apparently realizes that strenuous effort to right himself is futile"; crying is uncommon, and there are some infants who take this as an occasion for play. Given the previous chapter's results concerning up-down orientation, the connection between open and closed postures and different emotional relations to inversion is quite striking: closed postures correlate with distress at being upside down, open postures with lack of distress, indifference, or even play. The closed posture in weightlessness expresses a sense of being upside-down, emotionally at odds with the world (and vice versa with the open posture); the infant's closed posture when actually turned upside down in a gravitational field expresses emotional distress at the situation (and vice versa).

It would be tendentious to make anything of this if it were not for the issue of play in the relaxed phase. The posture of phase (4) is the one that infants assume when adults are playing 'upside down' with them. In the upside-down game, the infant's behavior seems to express that the infant knows there is something different about being upside down but at the moment this is not distressing, rather it is fun or interesting—and it is striking how interested some infants are in the game. We would have to ask, however, whether the infant is 'interested' or 'having fun' because the experience is in fact fun and interesting, or because the adult is making all the signs that this should be fun and interesting, and the infant catches on to that. Certainly there are points where it is no longer fun for the infant and adults perceive the game as inflicting violence on the infant. This emphasizes that the game (and play in general) is an intercorporeal/intersubjective phenomenon, indeed it is ethical in some sense.

MOVEMENT AND DEVELOPMENT AS SOCIAL AND ETHICAL

Even before birth the fetal body moves in response to itself and its surround (De Vries, Visser, and Prechtl 1984; Maurer and Maurer 1988). At birth, the infant is well equipped with a suite of 'reflexes' and 'reactions' that prepare it for the transition to a nonbuoyant environment and contribute to the development of bodily movement, locomotion, and exploration (Cratty 1986; Casaer 1979; Fogel 1984). But as Merleau-Ponty and Dewey argue, reflex behavior does not mark an independent neurophysiological circuit within the organism, provoked by a stimulus that exists in itself (*PP*, especially "'Attention' and 'Judgement'"; *SdC*; Dewey 1972). Instead, it marks an overall circular interdependence between the organism and the environment.

In the case of infancy, this circle is specified not by purely organic structures, but by joint social activity of infants and adults. Consider the 'righting reflex': if the head is turned by an adult, the infant's body follows, and vice versa; this is thought to contribute to the development of turning over (Cratty 1986; Casaer 1979). Outside the medical situation, though, adults are probably not explicitly aware of this reflex or do not conceive this behaviour as a reflex. Adults do not provide mere stimuli for the reflex; they solicit and aid the complete behaviour of the infant turning over, they gen-erate the stimulus *and* the response at once in the infant. The reflex does not operate autonomously and *subsequently* add up to the movement of turning over: adults are *already* trying to help the infant turn over. It is crucial to note that the adult can do this only with the cooperation of the infant: try encouraging an infant to roll over if she does not want to. So the circle between the infant and the world is shaped and constructed by the mutual behavior of the infant and the adult, a claim congruent with one made by Fogel, discussed below.[3]

The circular crossing of body and world does not merely go back and forth between the individual and the natural world, but goes back into the developmental folding of body-world movement—and this development is inherently social given that we learn to move in relation to others. Other research in developmental psychology supports this point. Casaer (1979) observed how adult and infant posture are interdependent during nursing and carrying and that the way adults place infants in different positions affects infant posture. Various researchers have shown how cultural play practices have an impact on the development of posture and movement (Kilbride and Kilbride 1975; Bril and Sabatier 1986; Hopkins 1976; Hopkins and Westra 1988; Zelazo 1984, 1983). As noted in previous chapters, Thelen and Smith suggest how the history of development and social factors shape patterns of reaching and walking (Thelen and Smith 1994). Fogel's recent theoretical work deepens this point, through his criticism of accounts that appeal to schemata specified in advance of the social (for example, Piaget) or to social structures specified prior to the infant-adult relation (for example Bruner and Vygotsky). He proposes a "dynamic interactionism" in which developmental change arises through the infant and adult's co-regulation of each other's behavior, in a self-organized dynamic process, rather than through prespecified schemata or structures (Fogel 1992). For example, Fogel argues that the development of reaching depends on "scaffolding" provided by the adult, but scaffolding arises in a frame mutually constructed by the infant and adult soliciting one another's activity (Fogel 1993, 109–114). Development is to be understood as a relational and cultural activity that establishes "invariant patterns of co-regulated action called *frames*" that situate development. Fogel argues that, within these consensual frames, the world already has a moral, esthetic and emotional meaning. (Fogel 1997, 423)

The point that the crossing of body and world is social resonates with Merleau-Ponty's argument that the body schema—what I call the moving schema of perception—is intersubjective and intercorporeal. In the *Phenomenology of Perception*, he argues that it would be impossible to account for intersubjective relations at all if we did not already have a pre-objective relation to one another through our bodies, and that such a relation is necessary if we are to account for disturbances of sexuality, expression, and imitation in adults and infants.[4] Merleau-Ponty's continual interest in child development—he was chair of psychology and pedagogy at the Sorbonne from 1949 to 1952 and lectured on developmental psychology—prompted a return to this point. In the lecture series "The Child's Relation with Others" he draws on the work of Guillaume, Wallon, and other contemporaries in child psychology to renew his claim about the intercorporeality of the body schema, arguing that infants first live in a syncretic relation with others, and that the body schema is originally one system with two terms, namely, one's own behavior and the behavior of others.[5] These points about the intercorporeality of the body and its schema are fundamental to the ethical orientation of Merleau-Ponty's phenomenology. Recent work by Gallagher and Meltzoff challenges aspects of Merleau-Ponty's account, but supports the basic point that the schema is intersubjective, and more recent work by Gallagher as well as Russon, about the embeddedness of movement in its context, supports the claim that this context is ultimately social and ethical.[6]

The social aspect of the developing, moving body becomes directly apparent when we see how care and anxiety matter in the development of reaching and other-orientation.

ASYMMETRY AND SYMMETRY: REACHING, UNCONCERN, AND THE OPEN POSTURE

A number of results show that visual involvement with things—visual other-orientation—correlates with an asymmetrical posture, whereas a symmetrical posture is a constraint on the infant's involvement with things.

Rochat and Bullinger (1994) studied the relation between posture and reaching. They noted that infants privilege a sort of "fencer's position" that looks much like an *en-garde*. In this asymmetrical posture, one hand and leg are extended outward, while the opposite hand and leg close in. The hand in front of the infant serves as a privileged target and anchor for visual exploration, but the infant's head is stable and in this position infants can follow targets across the visual field. This posture opens the body and, given the way the developing body works, lets the infant have a stable visual involvement with things beyond the body. In contrast, an infant seated in a symmetrical posture with head aligned at center has reduced head control, and tends to grab for things by closing the hands together toward the midline, closing the posture. When fixing on targets at an edge of the visual field, the infant in this posture slumps away from the target; and infants in this posture have difficulty attending to the middle of the visual field, where posture and gaze are destabilized. The symmetrical posture that closes toward the midline affords the infant little stability. The infant may compensate by activities such as sucking and rapid breathing that provide a temporary "pneumatic" tonic state, a way of holding the body steady.

This suggests a link between asymmetry, opening, and other involvement, on the one hand, and symmetry, closure, and self-involvement, on the other hand, a link that becomes more explicit when we shift from vision to reaching. Rochat and Bullinger discovered a marked difference in the reaching behaviors of infants who are capable of sitting up (sitters) and those who cannot situp (non-sitters): non-sitters tend to reach for things symmetrically, with both hands clasping the object at midline and the hands coming together as a pair, "in what was tentatively typified as a 'crabbing' motion of the upper limbs"; sitters tend to reach asymmetrically, with one hand extending toward the object. The exception is when non-sitters are put in a seat; in this situation non-sitters fall forward into their own laps if they try to reach with both hands, so instead they tend to reach with one hand, using the other to prevent falling. In general, in the asymmetrical reaching of sitters, there is an active coordination of leaning and reaching outward, whereas in the symmetrical reaching of non-sitters reaching takes place mostly in the hand and upper limbs.[7] In sum, sitters reach in an asymmetrical manner that opens and extends the trunk and upper limbs away from the infant's position, toward things. In contrast, non-sitters reach in a symmetrical manner that brings the limbs toward each other and toward the body, in a posture that closes the infant body and involves the infant with its midline; this posture can render the infant unstable in relation to the world.

As in Lackner's experiment, McGraw's results, and the upside-down game, the open posture correlates with the possibility of the infant being unconcerned for her own body's rootedness in the world, whereas the closed posture correlates with a behavioral concern for this rootedness. Where the open posture of the sitter gives her a stable, unconcerned background for reaching and other-involvement, the non-sitter ends up being more self-involved because of concerns about falling over, or by inducing a "pneumatic" tonic state to hold the body in place—perhaps something like this is at play in panic breathing.

The link between symmetry, the closed posture, and self-involvement gibes with the expressive repertoire of adulthood. Placing the hands together symmetrically is a gesture of prayer, contemplation, rest or removed observation, that encloses body in itself. We clasp things to us with both hands, or grab ourselves with both arms in pain and in reaction away from things. These are all gestures of self-involvement, of self-concern, or concern for the world that stems from self-concern. In contrast, we reach out for things and others with one hand, in a gesture that turns the body out of itself and opens up its surfaces to the world and others in it; or we point at distant things with one hand rather than two, or berate others with one wagging finger, and so on. The latter are all gestures of other-involvement, and of unconcern for our own world-rootedness, since berating or reaching out implies that our concerns are already taken care of or have receded into the background. It is also worth recalling that in vision symmetrical, balanced things appear to be in repose whereas asymmetrical things are "off kilter," look unstable, and open into movement (Arnheim 1974).

This is not to say that in the adult expressive repertoire the correlation between open postures, asymmetry, other-directedness, and unconcern (and vice versa) is univocal or straightforward. But if there are reversals or complications of meaning, they play themselves out in terms of this initial correlation. Neither is this to say that the meaning of such adult expressions is *caused* by an associative process in infancy, or that the biokinetic constraints on the infant's postural involvement with things are the *cause* of such meaning. On the other hand, the postural constraints of development—that the developing infant body can reach in certain ways and not others—specify a topo-logic of the body, a constraint on the interrelation of different places across the body, and on the body's movement in place.

This topo-logic, though, does not cause *sens*, rather its *sens* is articulated through the social development of movement. This social dimension is revealed by the fact that adult support of the infant body can encourage the development of the open posture and world involvement, and lack of such support, or interventions, can discourage it. Rochat and Bullinger observed that placing inflatable supports around the infant's hips makes non-sitters behave more like sitters, and Amiel-Tison and Grenier observed that supporting the head of infants encourages precocious reaching activity (Rochat and Bullinger 1994). Fogel and his collaborators conducted a series of studies of infant activity and posture during face-to-face interaction with their mothers. Infants who can reach gaze more at their mothers than nonreachers (Fogel, Dedo, and McEwen 1992), although frequency of gaze at the mother may correlate better with the onset of upright posture than with the onset of reaching (Fogel, Messinger, Dickson, and Hsu 1999). But there is a social dimension in this phenomenon, since a mother tends to change her infant's position more frequently when (1) the infant is gazing away from the mother, compared to (2) when the infant is gazing at the mother. Behaviors in case (1) fall in two groups: some mothers put infants in a posture that faces the infant away from the mother, others position the infant as if trying to recapture the gaze. This whole dynamic shifts over time: "all but one of the dyads changed over time from a co-constructed pattern of interaction in which the joint focus of the interaction is on the partner's face to a pattern in which the shared focus of attention is elsewhere." More, the dynamics of this shift vary across dyads: in some mother-infant dyads, as soon as the infant started looking away most of the time, there was an immediate decline in frequency of use of "facing mother positions," and for infants in these dyads "most of their sessions consisted of jointly constructed interactions in which their posture was supported by the mother in ways that facilitated the infant's apparent gaze direction preference, either at the mother in early sessions, or away from mother in later sessions." But for other infants, this kind of match occurred only in sessions after they began to reach, so there was a period in which the mother's manipulation of the infant's posture was at odds with the infant's gaze direction. (Fogel, Nowkah, Hsu, Dedo, and Walker 1993)

The development of upright posture and reaching opens up possibilities of other-involvement that take the infant's gaze away from adult bodies. Reaching out and away from adults, which depends on an asymmetrical opening of body and upright postural control, expresses the infant's ability to break away from adult concern and be unconcerned for her own posture. But this development is supported by dynamic social relations, and can be disrupted by the adult, with the infant's attempts to open posture away from the adult turned back into a closure with the adult's posture. The adult's concernful involvement with the infant, which can go well or badly, supports or intervenes in the infant's own concern for her body and for the world, and in the infant's development of the ability to be unconcerned with her body.

As Fogel (1992) notes, "How mothers hold their infants in relation to the infant's intended focus may have a marked effect on the infant's resultant emotion expression and later communicative action." The emotional impact of such interventions would give a different *sens* to the relation between the infant's open posture, unconcern with the body, and other-involvement. In other words, the topo-logical constraint specified by the postural abilities of the infant is specified not by the organic possibilities of an isolate, moving body, but by the "jointly constructed interactions" (Fogel) of adult and infant that are vital to the development of posture and movement. As Fogel notes, "Because relationships create frames that serve as the basis for future action and innovation while preserving the history of the relationship, very small early differences in environmental opportunities, individual propensities or social processes may become amplified into emergent frames that regulate the system for an indefinite period" (Fogel 1997, 436). This topo-logical constraint crosses the body and the social world, and the *sens* contracted in articulating it has a social and historical dimension.

The issue of children and parents looking or not looking at one another, their postural bearing toward one another, their regulating of one another's visual/postural involvement, does not go away. Rather it becomes the site of intense struggles and the matter of intersubjective violence, or, if felicitous, a matter of support. If children and parents do not literally engage in the Hegelian struggle to the death, the issue at stake in this struggle—the mutual recognition of one another as having opposing points of view—is often played out in scenes of looking and not looking, listening and not listening.[8] This observation highlights the social and ethical issues at stake in early developments and interventions.

This section begins tracing what I call a topology of concern: a linkage between constraints on development, concernful and unconcernful postures, and other-involvement. Significantly, this topology is one in which *sens* is contracted through social development. Since the topology of concern informs our involvement with others, the results so far would suggest that the topo-logic of facing and not facing one another (discussed in the previous chapter in relation to the topology of residing and the *sens* of up-down orientation) has a social-ethical dimension. The next section more directly shows how a social-ethical dimension colors the *sens* of other-orientation, by tracing a developmental link between the topology of concern and the infant's sense of other-orientation.

UNCONCERN, OTHER-ORIENTATION AND ANXIETY

In the literature, questions about the infant's sense of other-orientation stem from Piaget's pioneering investigations of the child's conception of things and of space. Piaget's account is in part based on observation of the ways that infants reach and search for things in the "wrong" place—"search errors." These errors suggest to Piaget that stage three (four- to eight-month-old) infants conceive things and space as not being present in their own right, and that stage-four (eight- to twelve-month-old) infants conceive things and their place as being dependent on the child's searching activity. As Bremner reports, Piaget's interpretation is hotly contested, and our previous discussion of development puts Piaget's notion of "stages" into question. There is little dispute, though, that the infant searches in different ways over the course of development, and that these changes shed light on a changing sense of what I call other-orientation. Piaget's observations have inspired many studies of how infants orient themselves toward things.[9]

The studies of interest here are those that focus on the "stage four search error," in which infants reach for hidden things, but persist in searching for the thing in its initial hiding place, even if the thing has been moved by someone else, in full view of the infant, to another hiding place, or if the hiding place (a container, for instance) has been moved. The infant's search seems oriented by a relation between the thing (or its initial hiding place) and the infant's body, as if things and hiding places appear in a space defined by the infant's moving body. Studies by Bremner (1978, 1993) and Acredolo (1985; Acredolo, Adams, and Goodwyn 1984) refine this point by attending to the relation between the search error and the infant's movement. For example, Bremner conducted an experiment in which things were hidden in one of two wells on a table. Hiding places (wells) were moved relative to the infant by either (a) turning the table 180 degrees, or (b) having the infant move to the other side of the table. Remarkably, infants were better at locating the hidden object in case (b), even though the two rearrangements are the same geometrically. We would have to conclude that the infant's moving relation to things and places makes a difference. Overall Bremner and Acredolo's results suggest that: (1) When a stationary infant is allowed an active reaching involvement with a thing and its hiding place, it is likely that the infant will subsequently search for it in a location that stays the same relative to the infant's body (egocentrically). (2) The infant is more likely to search for the thing in its observed hiding place (allocentrically), or to not confine her search to a location specified relative to her body: (i) if she has not had an active reaching involvement with the thing and its hiding place; or (ii) if the place of hiding is distinctively marked; or (iii) if the infant moves relative to the hiding place in a way that maintains an active involvement with the hiding place. (Allocentric searching is less likely if the hiding place is hidden (by a screen) from the moving infant's view, or if the infant is moved by a parent, rather than moving herself.) The station-ary infant's reaching seems to generate an egocentric search space; the mov-ing infant's active engagement with places seems to generate an allocentric search space.

The infant's sense of other-orientation depends on her moving engage-ment with things and places, and thence on the postural possibilities that support such movement. Other observations and results from Bremner (1993) help deepen the latter point. Bremner notes that in the course of develop-ment sitters gain control over head movements before they gain control over rotational movements of the trunk. In the studies cited above, infants can control their head movements, and changes in head direction do not change the direction of egocentric searches. What would happen if the experimenter intervened and rotated the infant's trunk? Bremner conjectured that in the case of infants who cannot control their own trunk rotations, the search direction would rotate with the trunk, but the search direction would be unchanged for infants who can control trunk rotation. There is evidence to support this conjecture.

This leads to the speculation that the scope of bodily control grounds the infant's other-orientation. When the infant can control her head direction, the body, which supports head turning, grounds her orientation to things; when the infant can control trunk rotation, the seated torso, which supports that rotation, grounds orientation to things; when the infant can move about, the place that supports that movement grounds orientation to things.

In experiential terms, what the psychologist calls "control" should be interpreted as a domain of pre-objective unconcern that is background to the infant's concernful relations to things. The same sort of background uncon-cern is implicit in adult activity: in searching for a snack in the fridge during the day, my concern is choosing the snack, and the spatial route and move-ments that take to me to the snack figure as an unconcernful background; not so in the night, when I have to be concerned with my route and movements, until I turn on a light. The difference between infant and adult is that, for the adult, background unconcern is sedimented with habitual meanings, whereas that of the infant would seem to arise in a more original manner. But anxiety and disturbances, as Heidegger (1977) argues in "What is Metaphysics?," can slide the adult back to this more original state.

This speculative-theoretical point allows a reinterpretation of Bremner's and Acredolo's experiments. The infant's developing postural and moving possibilities open ever more expansive grounds of unconcern: first the trunk supporting concernful head movements, then the seated torso supporting concernful trunk movements; then, when the infant moves about, larger place serves as a background of unconcern that supports concernful explorations; larger place is further differentiated by landmarked places and hiding spots that ground new concerns for individuated places.

This reinterpretation draws a link between posture, unconcern, other-orientation, and thence emotion, since concern and unconcern in face of others is a site of emotion and anxiety. The link may seem *too* speculative, but I am prompted by Acredolo's (1985) insightful and remarkable discovery that anxiety and being at home (or not) have a bearing on the infant's performance in the stage four search task. Bremner conducted his experiments in the infant's home, and Acredolo's results fit with Bremner's when she replicated his experiment in the home. But when she replicated the experiment in the laboratory, the frequency of egocentric search behavior rose dramatically. In a previous experiment, designed to see if emotional dependence on things was a factor in retrieving them from hiding, Lingle and Lingle instead found that results depended on *who* conducted the experiment, and eventually concluded that it depended on the level of anxiety raised by the individual experimenter. So Acredolo designed a test for this anxiety factor, and found that in the lab environment egocentric searching dropped dramatically (76 percent of subjects to 3 percent) in sessions where, prior to the experiment, the infant, mother, and experimenter played with toys for fifteen minutes. Acredolo concluded that "Since familiarity in this case did not involve increased knowledge of landmarks, the results demonstrated the need to expand the concept of familiarity to include the impact of emotional factors like increased feelings of security." (Acredolo 1985, 126)[10]

The background that makes things be familiar or unfamiliar, that orients the infant, is not a mere matter of things, places, and landmarks, or simply control over the body, but of anxiety and emotion. Anxiety motivates an egocentric sense of other-orientation. In the extreme version, we could imagine that anxiety undermines all concerns except the infant's most primordial pre-objective concern for the crossing of body and world, leaving no place of unconcern to ground other-orientation. Heidegger writes of anxiety, which is not to be confused with an objective fear of a given object:

Anxiety is indeed anxiety in the face of . . . , but not in the face of
this or that thing. Anxiety in the face of . . . is always anxiety for . . . ,
but not for this or that. The indeterminateness of that in the face
of which and for which we become anxious is no mere lack of
determinations but rather the essential impossibility of determining
it. [. . .]

[In anxiety, all] things and we ourselves sink into indifference. This,
however, not in the sense of mere disappearance. Rather in this very
receding things turn toward us. The receding of beings as a whole
that closes in on us in anxiety oppresses us. We can get no hold on
things. (Heidegger, 1977, 102–103, ellipses outside brackets
Heidegger's)

The anxiety mentioned by Acredolo is not to be confused with Heidegger's
anxiety, and we have no way of knowing whether the infant's experience of
anxiety is like that described by Heidegger, or that his description of the
recession of things, and so on, applies to infants. But the point of Heidegger's
discussion is to show that our sense of the identity of things, world, and self
is always skating on thin ice that hovers over what Lingis (1976) calls the
void of anxiety, and that without this void that comes to the fore in explicit
experience of anxiety, there would be no meaning at all. We have no reason
to think that this tension between anxiety and the lucidity of everyday
concerns is not fermenting in the infant. Indeed, David Wood has suggested
that the experience of anxiety described in "What Is Metaphysics?" has
affinities with separation anxiety in the infant.[11] Heidegger's description is
likely relevant to an empathic reconstruction of the experience of the anxious infant in an unfamiliar place. It would be easy to think that the infant's
concern with others slips away in anxiety, and the infant is returned to the
moving body as the central question and locus of pre-objective concern. So
it would make sense that in less extreme versions of anxiety, as in Acredolo's
experiment, the infant would retain a relation to things, but one in which
things turn back toward the body-self, as in Heidegger's description of things
receding in relation to us.

Here we can also recall the relation between emotion and up-down
orientation detected in the previous chapter. Feeling upside down in outer
space correlates with a posture of being emotionally down and closed on
oneself, self-absorbed; and when the astronaut Kerwin closes his eyes and
loses anchorage in Skylab, he is quite anxious and needs to "grab hold of
whatever was nearest and just hang on, lest I fall" (Kerwin 1977, 27). Emotional being in the world and orientation seem to be counterpart to one
another: emotional security and unconcern enable other-orientation, and
emotional postures give a *sens* of up-down orientation in weightlessness.

CONCLUSION

The infant's ability to move about, adopt postures, and reach for things—
to constitute a background of unconcerned being in the world—informs
the infant's other-orientation. Altogether, other-orientation arises in a development that moves from a symmetrical closed posture to an asymmetrical open posture, from postural-movement possibilities that constrain the
infant to concernful relations with herself, to postural-movement possibilities that enable unconcernful movement in larger place. This development
articulates the infant's background of unconcern—translates this background
through new sorts of movement—thus contracting different senses of other-
orientation. There is a social-ethical dimension to this development, since
it emerges in and is shaped by social-intercorporeal interaction. Further,
concern and anxiety are an issue in other-orientation, and anxiety in this
case clearly has to do with the relation between the infant and other
individuals (and also the infant's relation to social places, the home versus
the laboratory). The infant's developing sense of other-orientation is entwined with social and other concerns. This social-ethical dimension would
also seem to haunt the up-down orientation studied in the previous chapter, so far as the *sens* of up-down orientation points us back to postures of
facing and not facing others, and these postures develop in the social
processes discussed in this chapter.

Previous chapters argued that our *sens* of space does not refer to any
sort of ready-made space, but to patterns in body-world movement, patterns that contract their *sens*, over the course of development, from constraints in the expressive topo-logic of the body. This chapter detects
something deeper in these patterns, namely concern, emotion, and a relation to the social and ethical. The topo-logical constraints that generate
the *sens* of space are not merely to be located in the individual body, or
even in the crossing of the body and the earth, but in the developmental
crossing of the body and the social world, which is not simply kinetic, but
involves emotional care in movement. The *sens* of space does not merely
contract the *sens* of a natural bodily topology, it contracts the sense of a
social-ethical development and the issues of emotion and concern that
figure in such development.

The ethical side of these results will be explored in the conclusion.
Here we can conclude that the infant's *sens* of lived space grows through the
social development and articulation of the infant's moving relation to the
world. The growth in question involves the development of a background of
unconcern. But as the ground of unconcern is eroded by anxiety and loss of
postural and movement possibilities, lived space contracts. This description
is not too far from the familiar experience of things intruding on us, or
looming at us, or failing to stay in place when we are tired to the point of

crankiness or hallucination, and it secures a crucial insight into the labile phenomena of depth perception discussed in the introduction. Our sense of space is buoyed by and refers to a moving, emotional being in the world, by an ability to posture ourselves and concern ourselves with our social world and our place in it. It is not surprising, then, that our sense of space sways with changes in our emotional, social, moving, and postural relation to the world. We can better understand our labile *sens* of space by tracing it back into the development that informs it, by grasping shifts in the *sens* of space as slippages of developed habits, postures, and attitudes in emotional and social situations.

CONCLUSION

SPACE, PLACE, AND ETHICS

OUR BODIES CROSS with the world, cross the earth, cross with our development and with our social world. Our sense of space refers to and makes sense of this crossing, it is not the reconstruction of an already constituted spatial order or container into which we have been dropped. Against our conceptual tendency to root experience in a subjectivity or consciousness closed on itself, or in a closed and solidified body, our sense of space testifies to the fact that experience is a movement open to the world. What are the implications for ethics, space, and place?

Jean-Paul Sartre is sitting on his bench in the park. An other walks by. What does this mean? Cartesian philosophy closes consciousness and thereby runs aground on what Sartre calls the reef of solipsism. Sartre tacks around this reef by miring consciousness (nothingness) in being. In our relation to others this miring is manifest in the look and lived space: as we saw in the introduction, according to Sartre, the other appears as a hole in being who makes her or his space with my space. Merleau-Ponty agrees that consciousness is bogged down in the world (see, for example, *PP* 275/238), but is critical of Sartre's tactics. In the look, the relation between being and nothingness unfolds as an alternation between being a subject who objectifies the other, and an object objectified by the other. In contrast, Merleau-Ponty detects something metaphysically significant in our sexual being: to be sexual is to be a mix of subjectivity and objectivity, and the other's look would never affect one if one's body and the body of the other did not already appear as such a mix. (*PP*, part 1, chapter five)

Nonetheless, Sartre and Merleau-Ponty agree that if the other were constituted on the terms of one's own consciousness or subjectivity, then the other would not be an other. One's relation to the other is thus an openness to something that exceeds oneself. In this respect Sartre and Merleau-Ponty belong to a stream of philosophy (I return to it below) that argues that ethics cannot be rooted in the transcendental subject (as in Kantianism) or in the calculations of self-enclosed individuals (as in liberal or utilitarian philosophy). Ethics is rooted in a responsibility to something that exceeds us, a responsibility already implied in our being before we even reflect on it. Far from an ethics derived from the transcendental or practical imperatives of a closed subjectivity, what we call subjectivity instead arises in face of imperatives, imperatives that we inherently face because we are open to something that exceeds us. Sartre thinks such openness is a complex wrench in freedom; Merleau-Ponty thinks it is the very condition of freedom. But they agree that the ethical would be founded on such an openness and their dispute is about its precise texture.

Sartre's and Merleau-Ponty's accounts of ethics open us to our situation in the world, and thus presuppose spatial perception. To face or not face others, one already has to be oriented in depth. But as we have seen, other-orientation and depth perception go back into a developing body that is already socially and ethically involved with others. The ethical and the spatial cannot be pried apart: our sense of space develops in a social relation that will have ethical implications; our sense of others and thence of the ethical presupposes our sense of space, for this gives us our initial sense of a responsibility to something beyond us. The ethical and the spatial encircle one another, and if we trace the workings of this circle we find ourselves going back into development, the social, social history, and nature, at each point finding movements that exceed us by crossing us with larger places and developments that we cannot subsume into ourselves. So the ethical relation is textured as a doubled openness: it is an openness to the other through an openness to movement, place, the social, nature.

This theoretical result can be put in terms of a larger debate. Sartre's and Merleau-Ponty's point about openness echoes in philosophers as various as Nietzsche, Heidegger, Levinas, de Beauvoir, Derrida, Irigaray, Cornell, Butler. Within their highly complex disagreements, these philosophers share the conviction that our experience of otherness—and thence our ethical relation to others—cannot be constituted within the isolated individual but always already presupposes an opening to something that exceeds us (for example genealogy, being, God, historical struggle, *différance*, twoness, the symbolic and the imaginary, performativity). Drucilla Cornell's analysis of law and ethics in *The Philosophy of the Limit* traces this sort of ethical position as a response to Hegel (she focuses on Levinas and Derrida). Briefly, the position takes seriously Hegel's argument that identity depends on difference, that one's identity depends on others whom one faces and who face one as others, and that the ethical emerges from this. The problem of the ethical is preserving difference, otherness, in face of what is viewed as the totalizing effect of Hegel's system. Cornell shows how Derrida is especially sensitive to this problem, realizing that responses to Hegel often neglect problems that Hegel himself identified. Derrida thus develops a philosophy of the limit— Cornell's name for deconstruction—a philosophy attuned to the difficulties of having philosophy be open to what is beyond its limit without yet encompassing that beyond. The philosophy of the limit faces the problem that what is beyond the limit cannot quite be said without subsuming it beneath the limit, that the beyond must rather be pointed to within language in an effort to say what can be detected only in limit experiences such as the death of the other, in death as that which is beyond philosophy. Another way to put this point is in terms of Levinas's "*il y a*": Levinas wants to be thinking of ethics in terms of a responsibility that ultimately points to a "there is" that cannot be subsumed to thinking or consciousness; Derrida points out that such a "there is," if positioned beyond the limit of what can be said, is in fact constituted in relation to our projection of it beyond ourselves. The problem is detecting a "there is," a limit, that opens *within* our relation to otherness, not entirely beyond it.

This is what we have detected hovering in our sense of space—not in our sense of an already constituted objective space but in the sense of lived space studied above. In making sense of living movement that crosses us with the world, with place, with the social, we abbreviate, articulate, 'sum up in different form,' movements that exceed our present moment and cannot really be abbreviated. In one and the same moment, our movement opens us into something excessive that we cannot encompass, yet claims to encompass it in articulating a sense of space. Our *sens* of space makes sense of living movement—and thus abbreviates, disowns, and articulates the excessiveness, indeed, death, that hovers within movement as *non-sens*. In Sartre's story "The Wall," the protagonist feels his death in his hand touching the bench: in touching inanimate things, we are touched as beings who could become inanimate; the movement of touch crosses an animate body with inanimate things and is thus a "chronicle of a death foretold." We have seen how our sense of depth expresses care for our moving being in place, and how our sense of orientation expresses care for this care. Our articulation of a sense of space is thus a movement away from death, a movement that at once faces death as a limit and turns that limit into something else, turns *non-sens* into *sens*. Consider the experience of space collapsing inward when one faints, or changing as one becomes ill; space verges into *non-sens* as we lose ways of engaging living movement in the world. Or consider the way that we feel up or down about our lives through postures that change our way of making *sens* of our living movement.

Death is not just an issue for the philosopher tracing the limits of philosophy, it hovers pre-philosophically in our sense of space. Hegel draws a connection between self-consciousness and death in his analysis of the struggle to the death: self-consciousness crucially depends on the ability to interpret the world in terms of the self, and a self-conscious being would at first rather give up life than give up on her or his interpretation of the world. Of course this staking of life is contradictory if it ends in death, but what Hegel's analysis shows is that interpretation that does not give up on life is nonetheless always open to something more, to others who recognize oneself as interpreting, but ultimately to an otherness that points back to death as the limit of interpretation. But sensing things in space is already an interpretation, an articulation, of our living movement, an interpretation that similarly opens us to a crossing with the world that ultimately points back to death, to our bodily being as spilling over its own boundaries and as open to a world that can spill into us. We thus detect an echo or prelude of the Hegelian logic of recognition, of Derrida's philosophy of the limit, in our sense of space as an articulatory movement that already crosses us with otherness. And we thus take this logic back into a movement that exceeds us in a different way: in time, in development, in nature.

The liberal tradition founds ethics on the premise of an individual who is self-contained, or gets to contain herself or himself in property, as if the life of the individual could be sealed within certain limits, or as if the individual could be sealed from the vagaries of life, protected by limits.[1] Our analysis questions this premise by showing how our experience of lived space belies such limits. The sense of space does not belong to a being who can be bounded or protected by limits, but belongs to a moving being who crosses limits and in doing so has a sense of space that always implicitly signals the limit of death, signals something that is there before us that can be neither encompassed nor sealed off.

If we encounter one another as other only in space—we do—and if the ethical is unthinkable absent our relation to one another as moving bodily beings in place—it is—then our sense of space opens us, within our ethical relation to one another, to something that exceeds us, a movement in place, development, and the social sphere that ultimately signals death as our limit, signals *non-sens* as the other of spatial *sens*. By detecting this point about space we add a new dimension to the effort to think the ethical as rooted in our existence, to think of our ethical relation to others as driven by an imperative phenomenally manifest within our existence, in this case an imperative not to die, not to be transgressed—but also an imperative not to transgress others. If we feel death in our hand touching the bench, we also feel life in the hand of the other, feel our life in their touch upon our hand, and feel the possibility of the other's death in the touch of their hand or in our touch of their hand. Merleau-Ponty detects a circuit of care in the phenomenon of double touch, of one hand touching another within one's own body; but in the analysis of the sense of depth we detected this sort of care spilling over the bounds of the body through place and back. This care in our sense of depth opens a responsibility to others: our hands touch, and move together in a caring or uncaring way. Far from an ethics of seeing, remoteness, and the face, when we become attuned to our sense of space as a sense of living movement that crosses us with the world and other bodies, we find an ethics of being in touch, of movement, that goes back into the prior movement of development, place, and the social, a movement limited by death in the here and now, rather than the infinite of God, as in Levinas's ethics of the face.

On a finer-grained level, if our sense of space contracts *sens* through social development, then we should be able to read the ethical/social and the spatial off one another, at the level of individuals and cultures. The insights of previous chapters, into the relation between spatial perception, movement, place, emotion, posture, and development, would suggest specific approaches to this relation that would add to existing investigations.[2] One very important dimension that would have to be added is a study of the sexed body, both at the level of sexual differences in bodies, and differences that appear in virtue of social/ethical attitudes to sexed bodies and their movement, a topic not addressed here but explored by feminist scholars, for example, Sue Cataldi (1993), Iris Marion Young (1990), Elizabeth Grosz (1995), and Lorraine Code (1995). How do differences in attitudes of caring, socialized differences in movement, differences in the experience of the body, especially pregnancy and birth, change the points studied above?

These points about ethics connect with a point about place, since our openness is an openness to place. Our results about movement and space let us respond and add to Casey's study of place, which shows that place is of utmost importance.

Our movement crosses into place. If movement in every moment ultimately indexes a possibility of death and thus indexes our finitude, our movement in place indexes a different sort of finitude. Place, as Casey argues, is radically irreducible, unique. We can detect this radical uniqueness by observing a connection between mortality and place. Only a god could be no-place. A mortal is born in one place and no other, and from the start mortal finitude and the finitude of place are reciprocally entwined. We could rewrite Joseph Conrad's matchbook-cover novel—"He was born, he suffered, he died"—in the following way: "He was born one place, he moved, he died and was buried in another place." But everywhere he moved, he was in space, the 'same' space. Space, as Casey argues, does not have the irreducible uniqueness that place does, and for Casey this marks a deep problem: the way we have given space priority over place, to the detriment of place. We can make new sense of the relation between space and place if we take it up in terms of movement.

Our sense of space is the living sense that we take away from our movement in place, a living sense that inherently turns away from the sort of limit that it crosses, ultimately death but also place. Place is not a limit that threatens *non-sens*, as death does. But place is a limit since it is irreducible, it is an irreducible "*il y a*" in the most basic sense of that term. As Casey shows, place is irreducible since it cannot be encompassed, surrounded, absorbed. Place instead encompasses, surrounds, absorbs us—a phenomenon most palpable in wild places. Place exceeds us, but not in the way that death does. Place is not ultimate *non-sens*, rather place is where spatial *sens* runs to ground in *non-sens*, place is a ferment of *sens-non-sens*.

To explain this in terms of movement: The above account points to an ontology and nature in which *sens* inheres in movement (chapter three). In the discussion of depth perception (chapter four), I argued that perception of things is dependent on the places they are in. There I suggested that place is movement moved, movement spread out and traced in the texture of things. This texture is lacking in Turrell's rectangle of light, which is no-place, and does not move when we move around it. Place, on the other hand, shines in the texture of land roughed up by geological plications and by growing and moving things, in the texture of things built and lived in. Place is the *sens* of movement spread out and traced in things. In place the moving *sens* of living, building, growing, verges toward *non-sens* by being sedimented, traced, and spread out in unmoving things. Lived space is the *sens* we make of our movement in place, lived space is the *sens* of place reanimated in our movement. Here it is tempting to say our *sens* of lived space is a *sens* re-moved from place: it is at once a reanimation, a re-moving, of a *sens* of place that would otherwise remain *non-sens*; and something that we take away, remove, from place. Imagine coming across a path in the landscape, a path made by the movement of other moving beings, animals and people, who converge on one way of moving through a unique landscape. In following this path we organize our spatial *sens* of the landscape, we reanimate a *sens* traced by moving beings who have preceded us, and we, together with these predecessors, reanimate a *sens* that had been *non-sens*, in the background, of this landscape qua worked out in natural movement. But as we move through this landscape, reanimating its *sens*, we leave it, we take that *sens* away from it, we do not quite get to that *sens* that would be there if we were to hunker down and dwell in this spot.

Our sense of space, in other words, is our articulation of a *sens-non-sens* that goes back to place; it is an abstraction that nonetheless goes back to the place in which we move. On this conception, geometrical space, the objective space of the scientist, would be place over and done with, dried up, place with all movement removed from it, a space whose sense we gain not by moving through it, but by defining in advance our way of moving through it. Or rather, we define what amounts to this advance movement by instituting a *measure*, a metric, that instantaneously (without even moving) encompasses everything by claiming to apply everywhere in the same way. Whereas our sense of lived space is attuned to the specifics of moving through a place and dealing with things in place, objective space abstracts from all places and things by claiming space as something present all at once without movement in it. No doubt the physicist's effort to think of space and time as insuperable and emerging in one moving big bang complicates the matter, but still the thought of universal laws that apply through all space-time would conceive space as over and done with.

What we detect in lived space is a deeper complicity between space and the moving body. Lived space is what appears to us when we move in place, the sense we take away from place in moving through it. But this suggests that there is perhaps a different sense of space. When we move through place, we encounter a space sensed by our movement, that is, given sense by our articulating movement. When we do not merely move through place, but move *in* it, *dwell* in it, perhaps *place* senses our movement, that is, place gives our movement a sense, direction, in the way that a partially completed puzzle gives pieces a sense that helps us fit them into place. When we dwell in a place we connect with it in a different way, and that connection makes us re-sense our sense of space. I call space of this sort dwelling space, to contrast it with lived space. We could probably also speak of habitual spaces, spaces whose sense depends on habitual movement patterns that we carry with us, habitual patterns insensitive to places we are in. And we might also distinguish growing space, a sense of space that arises when we are learning to navigate new sorts of places, or to first learn how to move in place.

Our sense of geometrical space abstracts from place, whereas our senses of lived, dwelling, habitual, and growing space all involve movement in place and thus go back to place. But still our sense of space is something we take away from place, even in careful dwelling—and here is where I perhaps diverge from Casey. We cannot quite fully get back into place, because at its limit place exceeds us, it is a sheer "*il y a*": we move; but place, although it gives rise to life, approaches what is not living, it approaches movement over and done with; or rather place gives rise to movement only in relation to living beings; place is not place on its own, but is place in relation to those moving beings that animate place. We cannot fully get back into place because place stands as place in relation to life and moving bodies; even a buried body is *in* place only through those who mourn it. So always there will remain a tension between space and place, a tension that directs us back to that opening in which our bodies cross with the world, others, and place, an opening in which we in turn cross places with life and our social world. There will always be, as Neruda suggests, "manufactured products" or "simply infinite air"—the gap between living movement and death, between space and place—

something tenaciously involved between my life and the earth
something openly unconquerable and unfriendly.

NOTES

INTRODUCTION

1. Casey 1991a. On the ways in which we should not interchange depth with height and width, see Casey 1993 and Casey 1997.

2. Casey 1991a distinguishes between depth and distance: distance objectifies depth, whereas depth is the proper dimension of what Casey calls volume. To simplify discussion, I use the term *distance* to speak of the spread between oneself and things, but distance in this sense is not to be taken as an already objectified and measured dimension.

3. See Casey 1993, part 2, for a detailed study of these elements of space in relation to the body.

4. Someone adopting the point of view of scientific reductionism might argue that the difference between ordinary and extra-ordinary depth is nominal, a difference in name only. Thus our omission of 'here-there' orderings, etc., when speaking of bodily experience is simply an expedient shorthand. The underlying referent remains something ordered in space like any other thing, but the simplification confers an evolutionary advantage, say. But evolutionary adaptations must do something if they are to be an advantage. So we would have to ask: Why is it an evolutionary advantage to perceive one's body as a unified thing without an internal depth ordering? Presumably it is because the body stands in its environment as a thing that is to have its own unity. From this beginning we could argue, against the reductionist, that the distinction between extra-ordinary and ordinary depth is not merely nominal, but has an ecological reality, in J. J. Gibson's sense, because a being that feels itself and acts as an indivisible whole is better able to live in its environment.

5. Various philosophers remark on the error of thinking that fixed divisions entrenched in our language and concepts apply to phenomena themselves. Cf., e.g., Dewey 1929, chap. 1; Bergson 1991, 1998; Merleau-Ponty 1942, 1945; and Hegel 1969.

6. On this point, cf. Heidegger's (1977) analysis of the bridge in "Building, Dwelling, Thinking." Note that architectural and other conventions reverse this relation: once conventional markers such as doorsills and borders are established, placing them demarcates regions to be crossed.

7. See Merleau-Ponty 1968, but also OE. Evans and Lawlor 2000 is a help-ful collection on the issue; the editor's introduction, Renaud Barbaras's "Perception and Movement," and Bernhard Waldenfels's "The Paradox of Expression" are espe-cially helpful at contextualizing these concepts across Merleau-Ponty's work. Also see Dillon 1988.

8. See PP, esp. introduction, chap. 1; James 1950, esp. 1: chap. 5–7; Dewey 1929, esp. chap. 1.

9. Kant 1929, A22/B37–A30/B45; James 1950, 2: chap. 20, esp. 134–144.

10. On this presumption about sensations, see PP, esp. the introduction, and Dillon 1988.

11. The point will be made in the case of depth perception, but it is worth putting it in more general terms, which will also help clarify the claim being made. Consider the experience of looking at an abandoned mirror lying on the grass. Cru-cially, a single array of sensations gives perceptual experience of two different things: the mirror with its silvery surface, and what it reflects, say the blue of the sky. Is it the case (a) that the mirror together with the sky, etc., specifies an underlying order that causes an array of sensations that we subsequently decode as being caused by two things, mirror and sky? Or is it the case (b) that the internal web of sensation has tensions within it that first of all drive us to notice that there are two things at play in our perceptual experience, silvery mirror and sky? In other words, (a) are two different causes producing one array of sensations in us, or (b) is a tension within an already cohesive web of perception prompting a meaningful order in which we first of all notice two different things, mirror and sky? The latter (b) is suggested by the fact that prereflective experience knows so little about the actual component causes of arrays of sensations. (In this case, is it a mirror, water in a clean-cut hole, some artist's installation with a painting of the sky or a mirror-pond installed in a field?) Eleanor Gibson's famous experiments with infants on the 'visual cliff' (infants refuse to venture onto a solid sheet of glass suspended over a staircase that can be seen through the glass) suggest that our perception is not hung up on actual causes but environmental meanings. Again, this supports (b), and so does the argument that the perceptual meaning of sensory arrays depends on the organism (on the latter, see the works by J. J. Gibson, and Thompson, Palacios, and Varela 1992). It is also worth noting that seeing takes some looking: in the mirror-sky scenario you might find yourself stopping to take a closer look because there is something funny about that patch of blue stuff in the field; you might have to move and look around a bit before you can see that it is a mirror, not blue paper, etc. In other words, it is your looking that constitutes the meaningful order in which you see what is given as manifesting the interaction of two different things, mirror and sky. Likewise with depth perception.

Finally, the traditional position (a) leaves a difficult problem: specifying a mechanism for sorting out the difference between light shining at us and light reflecting off something, or the difference between the color of a thing and color reflected by something. This difference is key to reconstructing multiple causes from unified arrays of neutral sensations; but by hypothesis the difference cannot be contained in sen-sation itself, since sensations are uniform in being sensations; so the ability to recon-struct causes from sensations always depends on something further, which begs the question of how one learns to perceive in the first place. Position (b) claims that such differences are relative to perceptual activity.

12. Morris 1997a gives a more detailed discussion of the problems in Descartes's and Berkeley's accounts, and is the basis for what follows. Also see Atherton 1997; Schwartz 1994.

13. *An Essay Toward a New Theory of Vision*, §II, in Berkeley 1963. Also see Berkeley 1982.

14. See Descartes's *Optics*, in Descartes 1965.

15. This is the "inverse projection approach"; see Epstein and Rogers 1995, chap. 1, for a helpful statement of this problem and its metatheoretical implications. Note that the inferences in question here need not be explicit. Descartes is thinking of the mind making more or less explicit inferences from sensory input, without being self-conscious of them, but in more recent accounts the "inference" is carried out by subconscious or nonconscious brain processes, etc. The important point is that in inferential accounts the philosopher or scientist conceives such processes as amounting to inferences.

16. Morris 1997a charts this issue.

17. Churchland, Ramachandran, and Sejnowski 1994 summarizes this sort of problem, with nice examples.

18. For more on the ready-made world, see Dillon 1988; Madison 1981; Mallin 1979.

19. The examples are from the *Optics*, and from *Discourse on Method*, in Descartes 1965.

20. See *An Essay Toward a New Theory of Vision* in Berkeley 1963, and the discussion in Morris 1997a.

21. Descartes also compares vision and language, but his concepts of language and correlatively of vision are very different from Berkeley's. See Morris 1997a.

22. The point that a synthesizing mind would not be subject to the variations we find in experience is central to Merleau-Ponty's criticism of intellectualist accounts of perception, especially spatial perception. See *PP*, esp. the chapter "Space."

23. See Al-Haytham 1989 for a striking anticipation of some of Gibson's points in Islamic neo-Aristotelian philosophy.

24. Gibson's focus is what he calls direct perception. Just what is meant by the term *direct*, and what concepts follow from it, are quite controversial. See, e.g., Ullman 1980, Costall 1989, Costall and Leudar 1998, Sharrock and Coulter 1998, Costall and Still 1989. The term *intrinsic* is meant to be neutral to these problems. Gibson's account and ecological accounts share features with Merleau-Ponty's phenomenology. On Gibson and Merleau-Ponty, see Rojcewicz 1984, Sanders 1993, Casey 1991a, and Costall 2000, which mentions in passing that, according to Robert Shaw and Harry Heft, Gibson was "aware of [Merleau-Ponty's] work, and enthusiastically recommended him to students." In particular, both Gibson and Merleau-Ponty criticize the doctrine that perception is assembled from atomic sensations.

25. Gibson's own comments about Berkeley are quite disparaging, and he would almost certainly object to being classed with Berkeley. Gibson's comments, though, suggest that he is oriented more by what people say about Berkeley than by an attempt to engage Berkeley from within.

26. Cf. Bergson's point that in Cartesian dualism ideas are a useless duplicate of matter, MM, "Summary and Conclusion," §§I–II.

27. On affordances, see the works cited in notes 24 and 28.

28. For some of the controversy, see Heft 1989; the works by Costall, and Sharrock and Coulter; Kadar and Effken 1994, in response to Turvey 1992a; Turvey 1979, 1992b; Turvey and Shaw 1995.

29. For this point about the individual, the historical and the social in developmental psychology, see the works by Fogel, Thelen, and Costall. Also see Juarrero 1999 and Morris 1997b, 1999 for a critical discussion.

30. The works by Turvey and Shaw all pertain to dynamic systems theory. For a lucid introduction see Thelen and Smith 1994. Also see Varela 1991 for a study of life as self-organizing.

31. The conflict is noted in the literature of ecological psychology. See the works cited in note 28, esp. Turvey and Shaw's attempts to secure an "ontology."

32. Heidegger 1962, p 62 in the standard pagination. On this issue, see Olafson 1987.

33. Levin 1999 and Levin 1985, esp. chap. 1. A postscript is required here on behalf of ecological psychology. When Turvey and Shaw (1995) seek a physics that would enable a physical psychology, they admit that information would be a primitive of this physics. They have something like the insight that meaning is crucial; they want to specify meaning in terms of information, and thence physics. It is not quite clear if they can do this and at the same time avoid a dualism of subject and object. In any case, there is a tension between making information an explanatory term in their psychological physics and having information be something that intrinsically is for an interpreter.

34. Cf. Leder's discussion of illness and the body (Leder 1990, 79–83); Goldstein's (1995) observations on how to interpret sickness; and Merleau-Ponty's expansion of these points throughout SdC and PP.

35. Cf. Heidegger's reflection on mood (Stimmung) in Being and Time (1962); on indifference and boredom in "What is Metaphysics?" (1977); and Sartre (1993) on the emotions.

36. Cf. Sartre on the look in Being and Nothingness. Also see Mirvish's (1996) discussion of Sartre on embodiment and childhood. Mirvish's article makes some interesting suggestions about spatiality and human being, through Lewin's concept of hodological space.

37. Hamlet, in Hamlet, Prince of Denmark, II, ii, 254–5.

38. See Cataldi 1993 and Heaton 1968, part III, esp. chapter 7. Also see the extraordinary cases documented by Hoff and Pötzl 1988.

39. This discussion raises problems about truth, problems too difficult to pursue here. The claim that illusions are not errors is not the claim that we do not make perceptual mistakes or errors. The claim is that the criterion of error is in the first instance in our perceptual relation to things. Things are not illusory because they fail to match up with our own transcendental standards of truth, things are illusory because they are at odds with themselves; the Müller-Lyer's figure itself is odd, since it invites further explorations that reveal that if you look at it one way the arrows do not match, if you look at it another way, they do. Internal tensions of this sort prompt augmentation of perception, by constructing instruments like rulers and balances that let us return to perception and transform it. This transformation amounts to discovery of new standards immanent in the phenomena, and against these standards phenomena like the Müller-Lyer's figure can be interpreted as involving errors—but not of perception, of measurement. Truth itself is in movement.

40. Carello and Turvey 2000, discussed further in Morris 2002b.

41. Aristotle is already attuned to this point in *On the Soul*.

42. For this usage of imperatives, see the work of Alphonso Lingis.

43. Cf. Russon 1997 and 1995 for discussions of Hegel that emphasize this interpretative aspect of recognition. Also see Russon 2003.

CHAPTER 1: THE MOVING SCHEMA OF PERCEPTION

1. Merleau-Ponty's concept of the body schema is well treated in the literature, as is its role in perception and its origin in studies by Head (1920), Holmes, and Schilder (1935). It is important to note with Shaun Gallagher that the role of the body schema in the *Phenomenology of Perception* is obscured in the English translation, in which "*schéma corporel*" is rather indifferently translated as "body *image*" and "body *schema*." Gallagher argues that there is a tremendous difference between the body image and the body schema. Roughly, the former has to do with the implicit image I have of my body and the latter has to do with my posture and movement. My concern is with the body schema.

On the issue of the translation of "*schéma corporel*" and the distinction between body image and body schema, see Gallagher 1995, Gallagher 1986a, Gallagher and Meltzoff 1996, which are also helpful on the body schema in general and connect Merleau-Ponty with more recent discussions. Gallagher 1986b, 1986c, and Gallagher and Cole 1995 should also be consulted, as should Casey 1984, Gans 1982, Lingis 1996, and Tiemersma 1982, who reviews the history of the concept of the body schema and its appearance in Merleau-Ponty's philosophy. Madison 1981 also has some helpful remarks about the body schema. In Morris 1999 and Morris 2001b I investigate the body schema and its role in perception. Also see the various essays in *The Body and the Self* (Bermúdez, Marcel, and Eilan 1995), which includes Gallagher 1995, and the articles in Eilan, McCarthy, and Brewer 1993. Stein 1991 includes (among some dubious claims about philosophers) a brief history of scientific discussion of the body schema. Gail Weiss (1998, 1999a, 1999b) has a number of studies of the related topic of the body image.

2. I draw the term *placial* from the work of Casey, and also the connection between habit and inhabiting.

3. The OED's entry on *schema* is quite interesting and instructive on this issue, and seems to home in on the philosophical and psychological issues that are my concern here. Its first entry concerns the Kantian usage of *schema*, and one of the examples is from Edward Casey's translation of Dufrenne's *The Notion of the A Priori*. The entry also includes the quote from Head that I cite below, and materials on Piaget.

4. See Morris 1999 and Dillon 1987. One place to track this issue in *PP* is in Merleau-Ponty's discussion, in "Sense Experience," of phenomenology as radical reflection which criticizes Kantian reflection, *PP* 252–56/218–22; the chapter culminates in Merleau-Ponty's claim that reflection grasps its significance only through "an original past, a past which has never been a present," what Levinas and Derrida might call a "*trait*." Also see Merleau-Ponty's discussion of the breakdown of the a priori-a posteriori distinction in the opening pages of the discussion of the human order in *SdC*.

5. See *PP*, "The Spatiality of One's Own Body and Motility," esp. *PP* 116/100 and 166–72/142–147.

6. For a line of thinking that points out the problem of reifying the body schema, and takes Merleau-Ponty as doing this, see Sheets-Johnstone 1999a, esp. 260–262. Sheets-Johnstone challenges Meltzoff and Gallagher's elaboration of the concept of the body schema, arguing that the relevant primitive structure is not "an abstract image, or a neurological-network . . . or a representational schema, or any other kind of hypothetical entity," but belongs to the order of primal animation. Behind this is the criticism that Merleau-Ponty's phenomenology does not pay enough attention to movement in and of itself; I want to suggest how Merleau-Ponty's concept of the body schema demands a turn to movement, even if his own concepts and writing sometimes obscure this.

7. See PP 237–239/205–206 for Merleau-Ponty's discussion of the illusion. Merleau-Ponty cites results by Tastevin, Czermak, and Schilder, quoted by Lhermitte in L'Image de notre corps; the reference to Tastevin is to Tastevin 1937. Merleau-Ponty refers to the illusion as Aristotle's illusion, as does the psychological literature. (Aristotle discusses it in Metaphysics IV·6 and On Dreams 2.) Benedetti coins the terms tactile diplopia (diplopia is the term used to describe double vision) and diplesthesia to describe the illusion. See Benedetti 1985, 1986a, 1986b, 1988a, 1988b for overviews and extensive studies.

8. E.g., Benedetti notes that doubling occurs when the middle and index fingers are immobilized and squeezed so that areas of the finger pads that are not normally adjacent are pushed together, but goes away when the same fingers are allowed to explore things.

9. See the works of Sheets-Johnstone, and Morris 2002a.

10. Intentionality is a current topic in ecological psychology and dynamic systems theory, although it is important to distinguish the phenomenological and psychological concepts. On prospectivity, see Turvey 1992a; on intentionality see Juarrero 1999 and Heft 1989.

11. All the quotes are from PP 268–269/232–233. See Rojcewicz 1984 for further discussion, as well as Mallin 1979.

12. The metaphor of sculpting is suggested by an anecdote in Duden 1993 about an expert dissector who views himself as a sculptor, i.e., his view is that he is drawing out clean divisions between organs that are not manifest as such in the living body. Perception fills in things, see Pessoa, Thompson, and Noë 1998.

13. For points (1) and (2), see Howard 1982 (note that in Stratton's own experiment with inverting lenses, the apparatus was monocular, so we should not make conclusions about binocular vision from his description; see Stratton 1896 and 1897); for (3) see Fisher and Ciuffreda 1990; for (4) see Ichikawa and Egusa 1993; for (5) see Kinney 1985.

14. Both Craske and Lackner and Taublieb report great variety across subjects's gross responses to the tests; as well Craske (1977, 72) reports a high between-subject variability in the error in hand localization, but a much lower within-subject variability. Cf. Thelen and Smith's (1994) argument that the individual should be the unit of analysis (97–99) and their application of this principle studying reaching (247–77).

15. On habit, cf. Russon 1994, 2003; Morris 2001a.

CHAPTER 2: DEVELOPING THE MOVING BODY

1. Bergson 1998; "Introduction to Metaphysics" in Bergson 2002.

2. Cf., e.g., Sheets-Johnstone 1999a, 1999b, Thelen and Smith 1994, Kelso 1999, Juarrero 1999; also see Clark 1997 and Hurley 1998.

3. For more on the relation between science and phenomenology, see Gallagher 1997.

4. Geison and Laublicher 2001. Also see Laublicher 2000, which studies such issues in relation to the history of Gestalt psychology and the history of German science, giving helpful background to studying SdC and Goldstein (1995) on the organism.

5. There are other grounds for arguing that it is mistaken to install organisms and the body in an entirely closed system. As Bergson points out, it is conceptually difficult to distinguish a universe driven by teleology from a closed universe driven by efficient causes—in both cases everything is determined and so the universe could equally be considered as ordered to an end or ordered by a beginning (Bergson 1998, 2002). If evolution is not a predetermined process, if it actually depends on contingencies, if nature itself is some sort of experiment that could turn out this way or that—if, in short, time and movement matter—then we must consider organisms as being part of this experiment, as having a certain openness, a certain dynamism that is not to be reduced to a larger closed system.

6. For more on Bergson's method see Deleuze 1988; also see Mullarkey 2000 for a helpful survey.

7. Even if Bergson's central conceptual results remain on the periphery of the Phenomenology (Barbaras 1998, chap. 2) or remain oddly mistreated (Lawlor 1998), it is impossible to read the Phenomenology without seeing the influence of Bergson in Merleau-Ponty's choice and deployment of scientific results, and in his manner of engaging in a dialogue with the tradition and opposing poles of rationalism and empiricism in order to identify common underlying assumptions and misstated problems. Merleau-Ponty is a thinker and writer infected with Bergson's style and orientation to the world of problems. For more on Merleau-Ponty and Bergson, see Mullarkey 1994 and Geraets 1971, who, as Barbaras remarks, cites Bergson as an even deeper influence than Husserl.

8. For a full study of this point about the motor schema and a comparison of it with Merleau-Ponty's body schema, see Morris 2001b. I have since revised my thoughts on the issue of expression.

9. There we start running into problems, for we would have to locate this restricted causality in relation to mere possibility, and combining the two leads to problems.

10. A question that arises at this point is whether the empirical and theoretical sides of science are compatible. The answer would be that you can very well adopt the theoretical attitude, abstracting from the reality of phenomena in time in order to give a general account—indeed the utility of adopting this attitude is what motivates the usual scientific practice, according to Bergson. But the account given from this attitude will never actually capture or substitute for the reality of things unfolding in time. We could give an analogy here: you might be able to give a perfect chemical analysis of the ingredients and formation of a souflée, but if you want to actually bake one you are going to have to wait for a chicken to lay eggs, for the ingredients to be assembled and beaten, and for the souflée to bake, etc.; or, if you appeal to some sort of Star Trek-like matter replicator as a souflée maker, you are either (1) going to have to have it exactly replicate an existing souflée, in which case you have not eliminated the temporality of making the master souflée, or you are (2) going to have build a simulation of the time of these processes into your souflée-making program, and your program is going to have to run in real time to simulate the time

of souflée making. Without the theoretical side you would not be able to simulate or explain the souflée, but without the empirical side there would be nothing to explain; the mistake, according to Bergson, is to think that the side of explanation, the side of abstract theory, can be severed from the temporal-empirical side that gives rise to it.

11. For a study of this theme in geology as it matters to Deleuze, see DeLanda 1997.

12. This observation is due to Todd May. See note 15.

13. For the importance of metaphors to scientific thinking, cf. Merleau-Ponty's remarks in the beginning of *OE* on the way that "gradients" took over as a central organizing concept and metaphor at a certain point in history. Also see Canguilheim's (1994) remarks on the history of the concept of the "cell" in biology, and the interaction of the metaphor with different concepts of the cell. Finally, see Johnson 1987 and Lakoff and Johnson 1999 for a study of metaphors in language, from a perspective interested in the relation between body, mind, and language.

14. Dynamic systems theorists think through metaphors too. A preferred metaphor (see Thelen and Smith) is that of a riverbed: the movement of the water through the bed carves out channels that constrain the water's movement, and the formation of channels that split the flow leads to formation of new splits and constraints farther downstream. The advantage of our metaphor, our 'vehicle' for thinking, is that the process, the thing processed, and the temporal record of the process are all implied in one another in the origami figure, whereas they tend to be separated in the water and riverbed metaphor.

15. The concept of folding discussed here is prompted by Deleuze's (1993) book *The Fold*, and the discussion of origami (also mentioned by Deleuze, p 6) in Todd May's "Gilles Deleuze, Difference and Science," presented at "Science and Continental Philosophy: An International Conference," University of Notre Dame, September 2002. But the fold is of course an important metaphor for Merleau-Ponty, not only in *The Visible and the Invisible*, but in the earlier philosophy of *SdC*, where the metaphor is drawn from Hegel by way of Hyppolite: nature folds back on itself to form structures, and structures of this sort will later fill the role of the body schema. See Morris 1999. The connection to Hyppolite via the fold is of interest here, given Hyppolite's influence on Deleuze. (See Lawlor 1998, and Hyppolite 1997, which includes Deleuze's review of Hyppolite's work.)

16. Cf. Descartes's derisory remarks about scholastic species in the beginning of the *Optics*.

17. The discussion of walking is based on Thelen 1984, 1995, Thelen and Fisher 1982, Thelen and Smith 1994.

18. See the preface to Dillon 1988. Merleau-Ponty explicitly mentions the seeker's paradox at *PP* 425/371.

19. Merleau-Ponty's statement of the problem of learning to see red and blue is woven into his discussion of the problem of learning and the theories of attention and judgment, *PP* 34–39/26–30. His resolution of the problem appears in the chapter "The Synthesis of One's Own Body."

CHAPTER 3: THE TOPOLOGY OF EXPRESSION

1. *PP* 171–172/146–147, trans. modified. The reference to the unreflective fund of experience is to *PP* 280/242, discussed in the previous chapter. In the sentence following the last one cited, Merleau-Ponty says that "My body is that meaningful core" which serves the general function that the rationalists had located in the

pure "I," thus suggesting that the content to which meaning clings is the body. But that seems imprecise, for the body is not a solid, but crosses into the world, is a perceiving body in virtue of its moving schema, and it is the study of the moving body that has led to the new *sens* of *sens*. Merleau-Ponty's suggestion seems another instance in which his conceptual inheritance is at odds with his discoveries; it is analogous to the problem, discussed in the previous chapter, of turning the body schema into a possession of the body, into a new kind of a priori.

2. For a discussion that supports this general claim, through analysis of the importance of movement in relation to Merleau-Ponty's early and late philosophy, see Barbaras 2000.

3. The points made in this section are made possible by Lawlor's (1998) analysis of expressionism in Deleuze and Merleau-Ponty.

4. For these points, see "The Body as Expression, and Speech," in *PP*. McNeill 1992 is a recent study of sign language and gesture by a linguist who shows a similar link between gesture, speech, and thinking. Also see Lakoff and Johnson (1999), who, inspired by Sheets-Johnstone's analyses of the body and its movement as a template for concepts, argue that bodily gesture and the like inform language. (See Sheets-Johnstone 1990.)

5. On this paradox of expression, and on this sense of translation, see Waldenfels 2000.

6. For example, it would be absurd to say that the imprint of my foot in the sand represents my foot simply because it duplicates my foot's shape in different material. It represents my foot *for me*, but is the imprint a representation *for the sand*? (The problem here goes back to the problem with impressions in the wax in Plato's *Theaetetus*.) Something more is needed for a representational relation, something that finds a radical difference between the imprint and the imprinter, such that the imprint is not merely a causal duplicate of the shape of the imprinter but is on a different register altogether. Otherwise we should eventually have to say that everything represents everything, that the tide represents the moon, the foundation the pressure of the building. The question being begged is that of the difference in virtue of which a representation is a representation proper. Bits in silicon processors (or activation levels in a neural network) are not much better than sands or tides if we cannot say how they come to be representations, and if we answer by appeal to a material process that represents by virtue of mere duplication (imprinting, recording, etc.), then won't we also have to say that the state of a bit represents the state of other bits in the circuit, that it represents the state of the power supply, that it represents the state of the hydroelectric network and the water in the river that runs the generator? How are we to locate the difference in virtue of which the bits in the silicon represent *all and only* those things that we have designed the machine and software to represent? We beg the question once again if we answer by reference to our designs or our representations, to what counts as different for us. An appeal to Claude Shannon's information theory, which interprets information in terms of uncertainty about the states of physical systems, and might thereby suggest a physical criterion for representation, will not help, for it would just turn our question about the difference between representation and the represented into a question about the difference between certainty and uncertainty.

7. This is the relation of the expression and the expressed in Deleuze's concept of expression; Lawlor 1998 shows the convergence between Merleau-Ponty and Deleuze on this point.

8. No doubt we would have to say this sort of movement involves the virtual becoming actual, thus drawing a link between our position and current Deleuzian discussion of Bergson. Cf. Boundas 1996.

9. *PP* 448/391. Cf. also Merleau-Ponty's point on *PP* 208/178–179 that grasping new meanings in speech is a process in which the indeterminate is brought to light retrospectively, yet nonetheless there is a meaning immanent within speech that has not yet been grasped.

10. Cf. the discussion of expression and emotion in Collingwood 1938, esp. chap. 11, which is startlingly convergent with Merleau-Ponty's discussion of expression.

11. It should be noted that this is nothing less than an account, in terms of movement, of what Merleau-Ponty calls motivating relations, relations in which "an antecedent" "acts only through its *sens*" (*PP* 299–300/258–9). It is only through movement that the motive of movement is clarified—and this clarification is expression.

12. See Bergson 2002, chap. 2. Also see Morris 2001b. Cf. Bergson's point that affect is perception that reflects not on a point outside the body, but on a point within the body.

13. Cf., e.g., *PP* 239/206, where Merleau-Ponty writes that the body schema is an expressive unity that communicates its structure to the sensible world; and *PP* 207/177: "The denomination of objects does not follow upon recognition, it is itself recognition." If linguistic expression accomplished recognition, perceptual recognition is also an expressive accomplishment.

14. Cf. Merleau-Ponty's point that the "body is the third term, always tacitly understood, in the figure background structure" (*PP* 117/101). The body in question is habitual. Although the figure-ground structure that is Merleau-Ponty's immediate concern in this passage is not quite the one I have just indicated, Merleau-Ponty's point and my point are related.

15. Cf. Deleuze 1988, esp. "One or Many Durations?"

16. Cf. Boundas 2002, Morris 2002a.

17. Cf., e.g., Young 1990, Irigaray 1984, Allen 1993, Butler 1990; but also see feminist reception and criticism of de Beauvoir's (1989) concept of the body in *The Second Sex*, which incorporates more of Merleau-Ponty than Sartre. (Simons 1995 contains a very good selection.)

18. See MM, chap. 2, esp. 109–116. My locution "synthesis by repeating an analysis" is the reverse of Bergson's concept of perceptual recognition as an "analysis" "effected by a series of attempts at synthesis" (102). For more on analysis, synthesis, and repetition, see Morris 2001b.

19. On Merleau-Ponty's relation to Schelling cf. Burke 1999 and Casey 1999. On the narcissism of the other, see Levin 1991.

20. The work is Hyppolite 1938. See Hyppolite 1997, which contains a review of Hyppolite by Deleuze, and comments by the editors on the relation between Deleuze and Hyppolite; also see Lawlor 1998.

21. For further suggestions about this reconception of nature implied by the later Merleau-Ponty, see the works by Barbaras 1999, 2000; Bernet 1993.

CHAPTER 4: ENVELOPING THE BODY IN DEPTH

1. Cf. Merleau-Ponty's discussion of perception of a cube in depth in his chapter on "Space" in *PP*.

2. See Ebenholz 1992, DiZio and Lackner 1992, and the other articles in *Presence* (not a philosophy journal, but one focused on virtual computer environments) vol. 1, no. 3.

3. Cf. Levy's (1993) discussion of the anthropologist's report of the BaMbuti tribesperson who, when looking at buffalo on the plain from the top of the hill, asks, "What insects are those?" If the report is to be trusted, it strongly suggests that seeing on the plain requires a sort of looking different from seeing in the dense forest that is the usual environment of the BaMbuti. It is worth noting that in the unfamiliar situation the buffalo are seen as living beings.

4. *PP* 256/221. This claim arises in the context of Merleau-Ponty's discussion of why he has adopted the thesis that every sensation is spatial: sensation as a form of primordial contact with being is constitutive of a spatial setting of co-existence because it is achieved through the body.

5. I was led to the concept of zones in trying to make sense of Bergson's motor schemas without reducing the body to an assemblage of parts; see Morris 2001b.

6. Casey calls such a "larger place" "region" in Casey 1991a, and Casey 1993 makes a distinction between various sorts of place. Here I will just talk about larger place.

7. On the latter, see Elder 1989.

8. Bushnell and Boudreau 1993; also see the works by Klatzky.

9. See Geraets 1981, Mallin 1979, Casey 1991a for more on maxima.

10. In the case of habits, this price becomes permanent: our movement becomes fixed and we become insensitive to things. My thanks to Michael Bruder for pointing this out.

CHAPTER 5: RESIDING UP AND DOWN ON EARTH

1. My thanks to Eric Sanday for his observations on the role of Earth in Aristotle.

2. *Parts of Animals*, II·3·650a21–23. I am indebted to John Russon for drawing my attention to this quote and its significance. One might complain that Aristotle has been proved wrong on this count, since we now know of plants that digest things, e.g., Venus flytraps and pitcher plants. But these are plants that live in watery marsh regions where the earth cannot serve as stomach.

3. See the chapter on "Space" in *PP* (the quote is from *PP* 282/244), and Kockelmans 1976 for commentary. Stratton 1896 and 1897 should be consulted since Stratton's experiment with the inverting lens system, which is now a classic, is reported in the first person (Stratton was his own subject) and gives experiential data not available in recent experiments. Howard 1982 is a recent handbook on the issue. Also see Epstein and Rogers 1995 and Schöne 1984.

4. The aircraft was a Boeing KC-135. Microgravity lasted for twenty-five to thirty seconds during each parabola, and forty parabolas were flown during each flight.

The subjects in the experiment were sixty-eight male college students between 18 and 31 years of age. The research was conducted for NASA, and, as far as I can tell, all literature in the area involves male subjects. This leads to the question whether orientation may be experienced differently by women vs. men. If the phenomenon is rooted in an expressive body, then gender may be a shaping factor in the meaningfulness of body that appears in such phenomena. This would be implied by the studies of Irigaray, Young, Code, Cataldi, and others. Then again, perhaps the sort of training that allows one to get onboard in the first place already habituates a body to the technical-political machinery of the space program.

5. For other examples of causal accounts of orientation and a discussion of the role of sensory organs such as the inner ear and neural systems that are at the heart of such accounts, see Howard 1982 and Schöne 1984.

6. My thanks to Michael Neumann for raising this objection.

7. For a recent phenomenological-scientific discussion that shows the centrality of face to the bodily sense of self, see Cole 1999.

8. Thanks to Henzel Jupiter and Pearl Elman with the transliteration and details of the Yiddish.

9. I would like to thank John Russon for discussions of what I would now call the concernful aspects of spatial dimensions, and Kym Maclaren for her ongoing thoughts about the emotional in Merleau-Ponty and in Collingwood, particularly in her paper "Emotion, Expression and the Coming to Be of a Full-fledged Symbol," at the 23rd Annual Meeting of the Semiotics Society of America, Victoria College, 1998. Both of their reflections have helped and inspired the development and refining of this and previous sections.

10. For Merleau-Ponty, see PP, esp. the chapters on the body as expression and the sexual being of the body; also see works such as Cataldi 1993 and Weiss 1998, 1999a, 1999b. For Heidegger, see "What is Metaphysics?" and Being and Time. For Collingwood, see Principles of Art. Sartre's (1993) work on the emotions gives a related account.

CHAPTER 6: GROWING SPACE

1. Cf., e.g., "The Body as Being-For-Itself: Facticity" in Sartre 1956, or the discussion of heterophenomenology in Dennett 1991.

2. For an important feminist study of the conceptual-historical impact of techniques of visualizing the fetus, see Duden 1993. Also see Irigaray 1984 for a critical discussion of Merleau-Ponty that raises the issue of the womb.

3. Cf. Fogel's point, following Bruner, Rogoff, and Vygotsky, that "In the development of play routines involving complex movement patterns, parents start off by playing both roles in the game or by asking and answering their own questions" (Fogel 1992, 397). Gradually children take over both sides. In supporting the roll-over behavior, parents are provoking both sides of a motor-perceptual dialogue within the infant-world-adult system.

4. PP "The Spatiality of the Body Itself, and Motility," "The Body in its Sexual Being," "The Body as Expression, and Speech," and "Other Selves and the Human World"; for the points about body schema, intercorporeality and disturbances of imitation, see PP 164–166/140–142.

5. Merleau-Ponty 1964b, esp. pp 117–119; also see Merleau-Ponty 1993.

6. Gallagher and Meltzoff 1996 presents a study of infant imitation and the experience of phantom limbs in children born without a limb. Their discussion supports the claim that the body schema is intercorporeal, but challenges Merleau-Ponty's claim that it is syncretic. On the intercorporeality of the body schema in Merleau-Ponty, also see O'Neill 1989. On the ethical aspect of the moving body, see Gallagher and Marcel 1999, Russon 1994, Russon 2003.

7. Rochat and Bullinger 1994, 23–27 and Rochat 1992. For the relation between gravity and reaching see Savelsbergh and van der Kamp 1994; for the importance of posture and reaching's dependence on it, see section three of Fogel 1992, Thelen and Spencer 1998, Bertenthal and von Hofsten 1998, and Out, Soest, Savelsbergh, and Hopkins 1998; for the development of reaching see von Hofsten 1986 and von Hofsten and Rönnqvist 1988.

8. On this connection between Hegel and the family, cf. Harris (1997), who claims that a study of the family and development is relevant to Hegel's analysis of desire and recognition in the *Phenomenology of Spirit*. Also see Russon 2003 and Sartre (1956) on the look.

9. Bremner 1994, chap. 4 gives a helpful survey of the issue. Also see Piaget 1955, 1973; Piaget and Inhelder 1963; Piaget, Inhelder, and Szeminska 1960; Bremner 1989, 1993; Acredolo 1985.

10. Acredolo's claim would need to be reconciled with the fact that Piaget's initial observations of egocentric search behavior were made on his own children in his own household.

11. In "Things at the Edge of the World: Part One, The Mouth," presented at the *Collegium Phaenomenologicum*, 1999, Città di Castello, Italy.

CONCLUSION

1. Cf. Lampert 1997.

2. See, e.g., Ardener 1993; Bachelard 1964; Casey 1993; Damisch 1995; de Certeau, Giard and Mayol 1998; Deleuze and Guattari 1987; Duncan 1996; Hillier 1989; Lefebvre 1991; Panofsky 1991; but the idea behind this is pervasive in literature, plastic art, and the human sciences.

REFERENCES

Acredolo, Linda P. 1985. "Coordinating Perspectives on Infant Spatial Orientation." In *The Development of Spatial Cognition*, ed. R. Cohen. Hillsdale, N.J.: Lawrence Erlbaum.

Acredolo, Linda P., Anne Adams, and Susan W. Goodwyn. 1984. "The Role of Self-Produced Movement and Visual Tracking in Infant Spatial Orientation." *Journal of Experimental Child Psychology* 38: 312–327.

Adolph, Karen E., Marion A. Eppler, and Eleanor J. Gibson. 1994. "Development of Perception of Affordances." *Advances in Infancy Research* 8: 51–98.

Allen, Jeffner. 1993. "Through the Wild Region: An Essay in Phenomenological Feminism." In *Merleau-Ponty and Psychology*, ed. Keith Hoeller. Atlantic Highlands, N.J.: Humanities Press.

Ardener, Shirley, ed. 1993. *Women and Space: Ground Rules and Social Maps*. Oxford: Berg.

Aristotle. 1936. *On the Soul; Parva Naturalia; On Breath*. Trans. W. S. Hett. Cambridge: Harvard University Press.

———. 1978. *De Motu Animalium*. Trans. Martha Craven Nussbaum. Princeton: Princeton University Press.

———. 1984. *Parts of Animals*. Trans. W. Ogle. In *The Complete Works of Aristotle*, ed. Jonathon Barnes, Vol. 1. Princeton: Princeton University Press.

Arnheim, Rudolf. 1974. *Art and Visual Perception: A Psychology of the Creative Eye; The New Version*. Berkeley: University of California Press.

Atherton, Margaret. 1997. "How to Write the History of Vision: Understanding the Relationship Between Berkeley and Descartes." In *Sites of Vision: The Discursive Construction of Sight in the History of Philosophy*, ed. David Michael Levin. Cambridge: MIT Press.

Bachelard, Gaston. 1964. *The Poetics of Space*. Trans. Maria Jolas. New York: Orion Press.

Barbaras, Renaud. 1998. *Le tournant de l'expérience: recherches sur la philosophie de Merleau-Ponty.* Paris: J. Vrin.

————. 1999. "The Movement of the Living as the Originary Foundation of Perceptual Intentionality." In *Naturalizing Phenomenology: Issues in Contemporary Phenomenology and Cognitive Science,* ed. Jean Petitot, Francisco J. Varela, Bernard Pachoud, and Jean-Michel Roy. Stanford: Stanford University Press.

————. 2000. "Perception and Movement: The End of the Metaphysical Approach." In *Chiasms: Merleau-Ponty's Notion of Flesh,* ed. Fred Evans and Leonard Lawlor. Albany: State University of New York Press.

Benedetti, Fabrizio. 1985. "Processing of Tactile Spatial Information with Crossed Fingers." *Journal of Experimental Psychology: Human Perception and Performance* 11 (4): 517–525.

————. 1986a. "Spatial Organization of the Diplesthetic and Nondiplesthetic Areas of the Fingers." *Perception* 15: 285–301.

————. 1986b. "Tactile Diplopia (Diplesthesia) on the Human Fingers." *Perception* 15: 83–91.

————. 1988a. "Exploration of a Rod with Crossed Fingers." *Perception & Psychophysics* 44 (3): 281–284.

————. 1988b. "Localization of Tactile Stimuli and Body Parts in Space: Two Dissociated Perceptual Experiences Revealed by a Lack of Constancy in the Presence of Position Sense and Motor Activity." *Journal of Experimental Psychology: Human Perception and Performance* 14: 69–76.

Bergson, Henri. 1991. *Matter and Memory.* Trans. N. M. Paul and W. S. Palmer. New York: Zone Books.

————. 1998. *Creative Evolution.* Trans. Arthur Mitchell. Mineola, N.Y.: Dover.

————. 2002. *The Creative Mind: An Introduction to Metaphysics.* Trans. Mabelle L. Andison. New York: Citadel Press.

Berkeley, George. 1963. *Works on Vision.* Ed. Colin Murray Turbayne. Westport, Conn.: Greenwood Press.

————. 1982. *A Treatise Concerning the Principles of Human Knowledge.* Ed. Kenneth Winkler. Indianapolis: Hackett.

Bermúdez, José Luis, Anthony Marcel, and Naomi Eilan, eds. 1995. *The Body and the Self.* Cambridge: MIT Press.

Bernet, Rudolf. 1993. "The Subject in Nature: Reflections on Merleau-Ponty's *Phenomenology of Perception.*" In *Merleau-Ponty in Contemporary Perspective,* ed. Patrick Burke and Jan van der Venken. Dordrecht: Kluwer.

Bernstein, Nikolai. 1967. *The Co-Ordination and Regulations of Movements.* Trans. A. R. Luria. Oxford: Pergammon Press.

Bertenthal, Bennett, and Claes von Hofsten. 1998. "Eye, Head and Trunk Control: The Foundation for Manual Development." *Neuroscience and Biobehavioral Reviews* 22 (4): 515–520.

Boundas, Constantin V. 1996. "Deleuze-Bergson: An Ontology of the Virtual." In *Deleuze: A Critical Reader*, ed. Paul Patton. Oxford: Blackwell.

———. 2002. "An Ontology of Intensities." *Epoché* 7 (1): 15–37.

Bremner, J. Gavin. 1978. "Egocentric Versus Allocentric Spatial Coding in Nine-Month-Old Infants: Factors Influencing the Choice of Code." *Developmental Psychology* 14 (4): 346–355.

———. 1989. "Development of Spatial Awareness in Infancy." In *Infant Development*, ed. A. Slater and G. Bremner. Hove: Erlbaum.

———. 1993. "Motor Abilities as Causal Agents in Infant Cognitive Development." In *The Development of Coordination in Infancy*, ed. G. J. P. Savelsbergh. Amsterdam: Elsevier.

———. 1994. *Infancy*. Second ed. Oxford: Blackwell.

Bril, Blandine, and Colette Sabatier. 1986. "The Cultural Context of Motor Development: Postural Manipulations in the Daily Life of Bambara Babies (Mali)." *International Journal of Behavioural Development* 9: 439–453.

Brooks, R. 1991. "Intelligence without Representation." *Artificial Intelligence*: 139–159.

Burke, Patrick. 1999. "Creativity and the Unconscious in Merleau-Ponty and Schelling." In *Framing a Vision of the World: Essays in Philosophy, Science and Religion*, ed. André Cloots and Santiago Sia. Louvain: Leuven University Press.

Bushnell, Emily W., and J. Paul Boudreau. 1993. "Motor Development and the Mind: The Potential Role of Motor Abilities as a Determinant of Aspects of Perceptual Development." *Child Development* 64: 1005–1021.

Buss, L. W. 1987. *The Evolution of Individuality*. Princeton: Princeton University Press.

Butler, Judith. 1990. "Sexual Ideology and Phenomenological Description: A Feminist Critique of Merleau-Ponty's *Phenomenology of Perception*." In *The Thinking Muse: Feminism and Modern French Philosophy*, ed. J. Allen and I. Young. Bloomington: Indiana University Press.

Canguilhem, Georges. 1994. *A Vital Rationalist: Selected Writings*. Ed. François Delaporte. Trans. Arthur Goldhammer. New York: Zone Books.

Carello, Claudia, and Michael T. Turvey. 2000. "Rotational Invariants and Dynamic Touch." In *Touch, Representation and Blindness*, ed. Morton A. Heller. Oxford: Oxford University Press.

Casaer, Paul. 1979. *Postual Behaviour in Newborn Infants*. London: William Heinemann Medical Books.

Casey, Edward S. 1984. "Habitual Body and Memory In Merleau-Ponty." *Man and World* 17: 279–297.

————. 1991a. " 'The Element of Voluminousness': Depth and Place Re-examined." In *Merleau-Ponty Vivant*, ed. M. C. Dillon. Albany: State University of New York Press.

————. 1991b. "Getting Placed: Soul in Space." In *Spirit and Soul*. Dallas: Spring Publications.

————. 1993. *Getting Back into Place: Toward a Renewed Understanding of the Place-World*. Bloomington: Indiana University Press.

————. 1997. *The Fate of Place: A Philosophical History*. Berkeley: University of California Press.

————. 1999. "The Unconscious Mind and the Prereflective Body." In *Merleau-Ponty, Interiority and Exteriority, Psychic Life and the World*, ed. Dorothea Olkowski and James Morley. Albany: State University of New York Press.

Cassirer, Ernst. 1955. *The Philosophy of Symbolic Forms*. New Haven: Yale University Press.

Cataldi, Sue L. 1993. *Emotion, Depth, and Flesh: A Study of Sensitive Space—Reflections on Merleau-Ponty's Philosophy of Embodiment*. Albany: State University of New York Press.

Churchland, Patricia S., Vilayanur S. Ramachandran, and Terrence J. Sejnowski. 1994. "A Critique of Pure Vision." In *Large Scale Neuronal Theories of the Brain: Computational Neuroscience*, ed. Christof Koch and Joel L. Davis. Cambridge: MIT Press.

Clark, Andy. 1997. *Being There: Putting Brain, Body, and World Together Again*. Cambridge: Bradford Books/MIT Press.

Code, Lorraine. 1995. *Rhetorical Spaces: Essays on Gendered Locations*. New York: Routledge.

Cole, Jonathon. 1999. "On Being 'Faceless': Selfhood and Facial Embodiment." In *Models of the Self*, ed. S. Gallagher and J. Shear. Thorverton, UK: Imprint Academic.

Cole, Jonathon, and Jaques Paillard. 1995. "Living without Touch and Peripheral Information about Body Position and Movement: Studies with Deafferented Subjects." In *The Body and the Self*, ed. José Luis Bermúdez, Anthony Marcel, and Naomi Eilan. Cambridge: MIT Press.

Collingwood, R. G. 1933. *An Essay in Philosophical Method*. London: Oxford University Press.

————. 1938. *Principles of Art*. New York: Oxford University Press.

Costall, Alan. 1989. "A Closer Look at 'Direct Perception'." In *Cognition and Social Worlds*, ed. Angus Gellatly and Don Rogers. Oxford: Clarendon Press.

————. "Getting Seriously Vague: Comments on Donald Borrett, Sean Kelly and Hon Kwan's Modelling of the Primordial." *Philosophical Psychology* 13: 229–232.

Costall, Alan, and Arthur Still. 1989. "Gibson's Theory of Direct Perception and the Problem of Cultural Relativism." *Journal for the Theory of Social Behaviour* 19: 433–441.

Costall, Alan, and Ivan Leudar. 1998. "On How We Can Act." *Theory and Psychology* 8: 165–171.

Craske, Brian. 1977. "Perception of Impossible Limb Positions Induced by Tendon Vibration." *Science* 196: 71–73.

Cratty, Bryant J. 1986. *Perceptual and Motor Development in Infants and Children.* Third ed. Englewood Cliffs, N.J.: Prentice-Hall.

Daganzo, C. F., M. J. Cassidy, and R. L. Bertini. 1999. "Possible Explanations of Phase Transitions in Highway Traffic." *Transportation Research Part A* 33: 365.

Damisch, Hubert. 1995. *The Origin of Perspective.* Trans. John Goodman. Cambridge: MIT Press.

Dante. 1994. *Inferno.* Trans. Robert Pinsky. New York: Farrar, Straus and Giroux.

de Beauvoir, Simone. 1989. *The Second Sex.* New York: Vintage Books.

de Certeau, Michel, Luce Giard, and Pierre Mayol. 1998. *The Practice of Everyday Life.* Trans. Timothy J. Tomasik. Minneapolis: University of Minnesota Press.

DeLanda, Manuel. 1997. "Immanence and Transcendence in the Genesis of Form." *South Atlantic Quarterly* 96: 499–514.

Deleuze, Gilles. 1988. *Bergsonism.* Trans. Hugh Tomlinson and Barbara Habberjam. New York: Zone Books.

———. 1993. *The Fold: Leibniz and the Baroque.* Trans. Tom Conley. Minneapolis: University of Minnesota Press.

Deleuze, Gilles, and Félix Guattari. 1983. *Anti-Oedipus: Capitalism and Schizophrenia.* Trans. Robert Huxley, Mark Seem, and Helen R. Lane. Minneapolis: University of Minnesota Press.

———. 1987. *A Thousand Plateaus: Capitalism and Schizophrenia.* Trans. Brian Massumi. Minneapolis: University of Minnesota Press.

Dennett, Daniel C. 1991. *Consciousness Explained.* Boston: Back Bay Books/Little, Brown.

Dennett, Daniel, and Marcel Kinsbourne. 1992. "Time and the Observer: The Where and When of Consciousness in the Brain." *Behavioral and Brain Sciences* 15: 183–247.

Descartes, René. 1965. *Discourse on Method, Optics, Geometry.* Trans. Paul J. Olscamp. Indianapolis: Bobbs-Merril.

de Vries, J. I. P, G. H. A. Visser, and H. F. R. Prechtl. 1984. "Fetal Motility in the First Half of Pregnancy." In *Continuity of Neural Function from Prenatal to Postnatal Life*, ed. H. F. R. Prechtl. London: Spastics International Medical Publications.

de Waal, Frans. 2001. *The Ape and the Sushi Master: Cultural Reflections of a Prima-tologist.* New York: Basic Books.

Dewey, John. 1929. *Experience and Nature.* New York: W.W. Norton.

———. 1972. "The Reflex Arc Concept in Psychology." In *The Early Works, 1882–1898,* Vol. 5, ed. Jo Ann Boydston. Carbondale: Southern Illinois University Press.

Dillon, M. C. 1971. "Gestalt Theory and Merleau-Ponty's Concept of Intentionality." *Man and World* 4: 436–459.

———. 1987. "Apriority In Kant and Merleau-Ponty." *Kant-Studien* 78: 403–423.

———. 1988. *Merleau-Ponty's Ontology.* Bloomington: Indiana University Press.

DiZio, Paul, and James R. Lackner. 1992. "Spatial Orientation, Adaptation, and Motion Sickness in Real and Virtual Environments." *Presence* 1: 319–328.

Duden, Barbara. 1993. *Disembodying Women: Perspectives on Pregnancy and the Un-born.* Cambridge: Harvard University Press.

Duncan, Nancy, ed. 1996. *Body Space: Destabilising Geographies of Gender and Sexu-ality.* New York: Routledge.

Ebenholtz, Sheldon M. 1992. "Motion Sickness and Occulomotor Systems in Virtual Environments." *Presence* 1: 302–305.

Eilan, Naomi, Rosaleen McCarthy, and Bill Brewer, eds. 1993. *Spatial Representation: Problems in Philosophy and Psychology.* Oxford: Basil Blackwell.

Elder, R. Bruce. 1989. *Image and Identity: Reflections on Canadian Film and Culture.* Waterloo, Ontario: Wilfred Laurier University Press.

Elkins, James. 1996. *The Object Stares Back: On the Nature of Seeing.* New York: Simon and Schuster.

Embree, Lester. 1981. "Merleau-Ponty and the Examination of Gestalt Psychology." In *Merleau-Ponty: Perception, Structure, Language: A Collection of Essays,* ed. John Sallis. Atlantic Highlands, N.J.: Humanities Press.

Epstein, William, and Sheena Rogers, eds. 1995. *Perception of Space and Motion.* San Diego: Academic Press.

Evans, Fred, and Leonard Lawlor, eds. 2000. *Chiasms: Merleau-Ponty's Notion of Flesh.* Albany: State University of New York Press.

Fielding, Helen. 1996. "Grounding Agency in Depth: The Implications of Merleau-Ponty's Thought for the Politics of Feminism." *Human Studies* 19: 175–184.

Fisher, S. Kay, and Kenneth J. Ciuffreda. 1990. "Adaptation to Optically-increased Interocular Separation Under Naturalistic Viewing Conditions." *Perception* 19: 171–180.

Fogel, Alan. 1984. *Infancy: Infant, Family, and Society.* Saint Paul: West Publishing Company.

———. 1992. "Movement and Communication in Human Infancy: The Social Dynamics of Development." *Human Movement Science* 11: 387–423.

———. 1993. *Developing through Relationships: Origins of Communication, Self, and Culture*. New York: Harvester Press.

———. 1997. "Information, Creativity, and Culture." In *Evolving Explanations of Development: Ecological Approaches to Organism-Environment Systems*, ed. C. Dent-Read and P. Zukow-Goldring. Washington, D.C.: American Psychological Association.

Fogel, Alan, Daniel S. Messinger, K. Laurie Dickson, and Hui-Chin Hsu. 1999. "Posture and Gaze in Early Mother-Infant Communication: Synchronization of Developmental Trajectories." *Developmental Science* 2: 325–332.

Fogel, Alan, Eva Nwokah, Hui-Chin Hsu, Jae Young Dedo, and Heather Walker. 1993. "Posture and Communication in Mother-Infant Interaction." In *The Development of Coordination in Infancy*, ed. G. J. P. Savelsbergh. Amsterdam: Elsevier.

Fogel, Alan, Jae Young Dedo, and Irene McEwen. 1992. "Effect of Postural Position and Reaching on Gaze During Mother-Infant Face-to-Face Interaction." *Infant Behaviour and Development* 15: 231–244.

Full, Robert J., and Claire T. Farley. 2000. "Musculoskeletal Dynamics in Rhythmic Systems: A Comparative Approach to Legged Locomotion." In *Biomechanics and Neural Control of Posture and Movement*, ed. Jack M. Winters and Patrick E. Crago. New York: Springer Verlag.

Gallagher, Shaun. 1986a. "Body Image and Body Schema: A Conceptual Clarification." *Journal of Mind and Behaviour* 7: 541–554.

———. 1986b. "Hyletic Experience and the Lived Body." *Husserl Studies* 3: 131–166.

———. 1986c. "Lived Body and Environment." *Research in Phenomenology* 16: 139–170.

———. 1995. "Body Schema and Intentionality." In *The Body and the Self*, ed. José Luis Bermúdez, Anthony Marcel, and Naomi Eilan. Cambridge: MIT Press.

———. 1997. "Mutual Enlightenment: Recent Phenomenology in Cognitive Science." *Journal of Consciousness Studies* 4: 195–214.

Gallagher, Shaun, and Andrew Meltzoff. 1996. "The Earliest Sense of Self and Others: Merleau-Ponty and Recent Developmental Studies." *Philosophical Psychology* 9: 211–233.

Gallagher, Shaun, and Anthony J. Marcel. 1999. "The Self in Contextualized Action." In *Models of the Self*, ed. S. Gallagher and J. Shear. Thorverton, UK: Imprint Academic.

Gallagher, Shaun, and Jonathan Cole. 1995. "Body Image and Body Schema in a Deafferented Subject." *Journal of Mind and Behavior* 16: 369–390.

Gajzago, Christine, and R. H. Day. 1972. "Uprightness Constancy with Head Inversion in Young Children and Adults." *Journal of Experimental Child Psychology* 14: 43–52.

Gans, Steven. 1982. "Schematism and Embodiment." *Journal of the British Society for Phenomenology* 13: 237–245.

Geison, Gerald L., and Manfred D. Laubichler. 2001. "The Varied Lives of Organisms: Variation in the Historiography of the Biological Sciences." *Studies in History and Philosophy of Biological and Biomedical Sciences* 32: 1–29.

Geraets, Theodore F. 1971. *Vers un nouvelle philosophie transcendetale: la genèse de la philosophie de M. Merleau-Ponty jusqu'à la phénoménologie de la perception*. The Hague: Martinus Nijhoff.

———. 1981. "Sens perçu, profondeur et réalité dans la *Phénoménologie de la perception*." In *Studi filosofici*, ed. Leo S. Olschki, Vol. IV. Napoli: Istituto Universitario Orientale.

Ghent, Lila, Lilly Bernstein, and Arthur M. Goldweber. 1960. "Preferences for Orientation of Form Under Varying Conditions." *Perceptual and Motor Skills* 11: 46.

Gibson, Edward G. 1977. "Skylab 4 Crew Observations." In *Biomedical Results from Skylab*, ed. Richard S. Johnston and Lawrence F. Dietlin: 22–26. Washington, D.C.: National Aeronautics and Space Administration.

Gibson, Eleanor J. 1995. "Exploratory Behavior in the Development of Perceiving, Acting and the Acquiring of Knowledge." *Advances in Infancy Research* 9: xxi–lxi.

Gibson, J. J. 1950. *The Perception of the Visual World*. Cambridge: Houghton Mifflin.

———. 1966. *The Senses Considered as Perceptual Systems*. Boston: Houghton Mifflin.

———. 1979. *The Ecological Approach to Visual Perception*. Boston: Houghton Mifflin.

Goldstein, Kurt. 1995. *The Organism*. New York: Zone Books.

Grosz, E. A. 1995. *Space, Time, and Perversion: Essays on the Politics of Bodies*. New York: Routledge.

Gurfinkel, V. S., F. Lestienne, Yu. S. Levik, K. E. Popov, and L. Lefort. 1993. "Egocentric References and Human Spatial Orientation in Microgravity: II. Body-centred Coordinates in the Task of Drawing Ellipses with Prescribed Orientation." *Experimental Brain Research* 95: 343–348.

Gurfinkel, V. S., and Yu. Levick. 1991. "Perceptual and Automatic Aspects of the Postural Body Scheme." In *Brain and Space*, ed. Jacques Paillard. New York: Oxford University Press.

Harris, H. S. 1997. *Hegel's Ladder I: The Pilgrimage of Reason*. Indianapolis: Hackett Publishing.

Hatfield, Gary. 1990. *The Natural and the Normative: Theories of Spatial Perception from Kant to Helmholtz*. Cambridge: MIT Press.

Head, Henry. 1920. *Studies in Neurology*, Vol. 2. London: Oxford University Press.

Heaton, J. M. 1968. *The Eye: Phenomenology and Psychology of Function and Disorder.* London: Tavistock Publications.

Heelan, Patrick A. 1983. *Space-Perception and the Philosophy of Science.* Berkeley: University of California Press.

Heft, Harry. 1989. "Affordances and the Body: An Intentional Analysis of Gibson's Ecological Approach to Visual Perception." *Journal for the Theory of Social Behavior* 19: 1–30.

Hegel, G. W. F. 1969. *Science of Logic.* Trans. A. V. Miller. Atlantic Highlands, N.J.: Humanities Press International.

———. 1977. *Phenomenology of Spirit.* Trans. A. V. Miller. New York: Oxford University Press.

Heidegger, Martin. 1962. *Being and Time.* Trans. John Macquarrie and Edward Robinson. New York: Harper and Row.

———. 1977. *Basic Writings.* New York: Harper and Row.

Held, Richard, and Alan Hein. 1963. "Movement Produced Stimulation in the Development of Visually Guided Behaviour." *Journal of Comparative and Physiological Psychology* 56: 872–876.

Hillier, Bill. 1989. *The Social Logic of Space.* Cambridge: Cambridge University Press.

Hoff, H., and O. Pötzl. 1988. "Disorders of Depth Perception in Cerebral Metamorphosia." Trans. George Dean, Ellen Perecman, Emil Franzen, and Joachim Luwisch. In *Agnosia and Apraxia: Selected Papers of Liepmann, Lange and Pötzl*, ed. Jason W. Brown. Hillsdale, N.J.: Lawrence Erlbaum.

Hopkins, Brian. 1976. "Culturally Determined Patterns of Handling the Human Infant." *Journal of Human Movement Studies* 2: 1–27.

Hopkins, Brian, and Tamme Westra. 1988. "Maternal Handling and Motor Development: An Intracultural Study." *Genetic, Social, General Psychology Monographs* 114: 379–407.

Howard, Ian P. 1982. *Human Visual Orientation.* Chichester: John Wiley.

Hurley, S. L. 1998. *Consciousness in Action.* Cambridge: Harvard University Press.

Husserl, Edmund. 1970. *The Crisis of the European Sciences and Transcendental Phenomenology.* Trans. David Carr. Evanston: Northwestern University Press.

———. 1981. "Foundational Investigations of the Phenomenological Origin of the Spatiality of Nature." In *Husserl: Shorter Works*, ed. P. McCormick and F. A. Elliston. Notre Dame: University of Notre Dame Press.

———. 1991. *Cartesian Meditations.* Trans. Dorion Cairns. Dordrecht: Kluwer.

Hyppolite, Jean. 1938. "Vie et prise de conscience de la vie dans la philosophie hégélienne d'Iena." *Revue de métaphysique et de morale.*

———. 1997. *Logic and Existence*. Trans. Leonard Lawlor and Amit Sen. Albany: State University of New York Press.

Ibn Al-Haytham. 1989. *The Optics*. Trans. A. I. Sabra. London: The Warburg Institute, University of London.

Ichikawa, Makoto, and Hiroyuki Egusa. 1993. "How is Depth Perception Affected by Long-term Wearing of Left-right Reversing Spectacles?" *Perception* 22: 971–984.

Irigaray, Luce. 1984. *An Ethics of Sexual Difference*. Trans. Carolyn Burke and Gillian C. Gill. Ithaca: Cornell University Press.

James, William. 1950. *The Principles of Psychology*. Two volumes. New York: Dover Publications.

Johnson, Mark. 1987. *The Body in the Mind: The Bodily Basis of Meaning, Imagination, and Reason*. Chicago: University of Chicago Press.

Juarrero, Alicia. 1999. *Dynamics in Action: Intentional Behavior as a Complex System*. Cambridge: MIT Press.

Kadar, Endre, and Judith Effken. 1994. "Heideggerian Meditations on an Alternative Ontology for Ecological Psychology: A Response to Turvey's (1992) Proposal." *Ecological Psychology* 6: 297–341.

Kant, Immanuel. 1929. *Critique of Pure Reason*. Trans. Norman Kemp Smith. London: Macmillan Education.

Katz, David. 1989. *The World of Touch*. Hillsdale, N.J.: Lawrence Erlbaum.

Kelso, J. A. Scott. 1999. *Dynamic Patterns: The Self-Organization of Brain and Behaviour*. Cambridge: MIT Press.

Kermoian, Rosanne, and Joseph J. Campos. 1988. "Locomotor Experience: A Facilitator of Spatial and Cognitive Development." *Child Development* 59: 908–917.

Kerner, B. S. 1998. "Experimental Features of Self-Organization in Traffic Flow." *Physical Review Letters* 81: 3797.

Kerner, B. S., and H. Rehborn. 1997. "Experimental Properties of Phase Transitions in Traffic Flow." *Physical Review Letters* 79: 4030.

Kerwin, Joseph P. 1977. "Skylab 2 Crew Observations and Summary." In *Biomedical Results from Skylab*, ed. Richard S. Johnston and Lawrence F. Dietlin. Washington, DC: National Aeronautics and Space Administration.

Kilbride, Janet E., and Philip L. Kilbride. 1975. "Sitting and Smiling Behavior of Baganda Infants: The Influence of Culturally Constituted Experience." *Journal of Cross Cultural Psychology* 6: 88–107.

Kinney, Jo Ann S. 1985. *Human Underwater Vision: Physiology and Physics*. Bethesda, Maryland: Undersea Medical Society.

Klatzky, Roberta L., and Susan J. Lederman. 1999. "The Haptic Glance: A Route to Rapid Object Identification and Manipulation." In *Attention and Performance*

XVII: Cognitive Regulation of Performance: Interaction of Theory and Application, ed. Daniel Gopher. Cambridge: MIT Press.

Klatztky, Roberta L., Susan J. Lederman, and C. Reed. 1987. "There's More to Touch Than Meets the Eye: The Salience of Object Characteristics with and without Vision." *Journal of Experimental Psychology: General* 116: 299–302.

Klatzky, Roberta L., Susan J. Lederman, and V. A. Metzger. 1985. "Identifying Objects by Touch." *Perception and Psychophysics* 37: 299–302.

Kockelmans, Joseph J. 1976. "Merleau-Ponty on Space Perception and Space." In *Phenomenology and the Natural Sciences: Essays and Translations*, ed. Joseph J. Kockelmans and Theodore J. Kisiel. Evanston: Northwestern University Press.

Kosman, L.A. 1973. "Understanding, Explanation and Insight in Aristotle's *Posterior Analytics*." In *Exegesis and Argument: Studies in Greek Philosophy Presented to Gregory Vlastos*, ed. E. N. Lee, A. P. D. Moralatos and R. M. Rorty. Assen: Van Gorcum.

Lackner, James R. 1992. "Spatial Orientation in Weightless Environments." *Perception* 21: 803–812.

Lackner, James R., and Amy Beth Taublieb. 1984. "Influence of Vision on Vibration-Induced Illusions of Limb Movement." *Experimental Neurology* 85: 97–106.

Lackner, James R., and Ashton Graybiel. 1979. "Parabolic Flight: Loss of Sense of Orientation." *Science* 206: 1105–1108.

———. 1983. "Perceived Orientation in Free-Fall Depends on Visual, Postural, and Architectural Factors." *Aviation, Space and Environmental Medicine* 54: 47–51.

Lakoff, George, and Mark Johnson. 1999. *Philosophy in the Flesh: The Embodied Mind and its Challenge to Western Thought*. New York: Basic Books.

Lampert, Jay. 1997. "Locke, Fichte and Hegel on the Right to Property." In *Hegel and the Tradition: Essays in Honour of H. S. Harris*, ed. M. Baur and J. Russon. Toronto: University of Toronto Press.

Laubichler, Manfred D. 2000. "The Organism Is Dead. Long Live the Organism." *Perspectives on Science* 8: 286–315.

Lawlor, Leonard. 1998. "The End of Phenomenology: Expressionism in Deleuze and Merleau-Ponty." *Continental Philosophy Review* 31: 15–34.

Leder, Drew. 1990. *The Absent Body*. Chicago: University of Chicago Press.

Lederman, Susan J., and Roberta L. Klatzky. 1987. "Hand Movements: A Window into Haptic Object Recognition." *Cognitive Psychology*: 54–64.

Lefebvre, Henri. 1991. *The Production of Space*. Trans. Donald Nicholson-Smith. Oxford: Blackwell.

Levin, David Michael. 1985. *The Body's Recollection of Being*. London: Routledge and Kegan Paul.

———. 1991. "Visions of Narcissism: Intersubjectivity and the Reversals of Reflection." In *Merleau-Ponty Vivant*, ed. M. C. Dillon. Albany: State University of New York Press.

———. 1999. "The Ontological Dimension of Embodiment: Heidegger's Thinking of Being." In *The Body: Classic and Contemporary Readings*, ed. Donn Welton. Malden, Mass.: Blackwell.

Levy, David M. 1993. " 'Magic Buffalo' and Berkeley's *Theory of Vision*: Learning in Society." *Hume Studies* 19: 223–226.

Lingis, Alphonso. 1996. *Sensation: Intelligibility in Sensibility*. Atlantic Highlands, N.J.: Humanities Press International.

———. 1976. "The Void that Awaits the Force of Anxiety." *Journal of Phenomenological Pyschology* 6: 153–163.

Madison, Gary Brent. 1981. *The Phenomenology of Merleau-Ponty: A Search for the Limits of Consciousness*. Athens: Ohio University Press.

Mallin, Samuel B. 1979. *Merleau-Ponty's Philosophy*. New Haven: Yale University Press.

Margulis, Lynn. 1981. *Symbiosis in Cell Evolution: Life and Its Environment on the Early Earth*. San Francisco: W. H. Freeman.

Maurer, Daphne, and Charles Maurer. 1988. *The World of the Newborn*. New York: Basic Books.

McGraw, Myrtle B. 1940. "Neuromuscular Mechanism of the Infant: Development Reflected by Postural Adjustments to an Inverted Position." *American Journal of Diseases of Children* 60: 1031–1043.

McNeill, David. 1992. *Hand and Mind: What Gestures Reveal About Thought*. Chicago: University of Chicago Press.

Melville, Herman. 1988. *Moby-Dick: or The Whale*. New York: Penguin Books.

Merleau-Ponty, Maurice. 1942. *La structure du comportement*. Paris: Quadrige/Presses Universitaires de France.

———. 1945. *Phénoménologie de la perception*. Paris: Gallimard.

———. 1962. *Phenomenology of Perception*. Trans. Colin Smith. Atlantic Highlands, N.J.: The Humanities Press.

———. 1964a. "Cézanne's Doubt." Trans. Hubert L. Dreyfus and Patricia Allen Dreyfus. In *Sense and Non-Sense*. Evanston: Northwestern University Press.

———. 1964b. "The Child's Relation with Others." Trans. William Cobb. In *The Primacy of Perception*, ed. James M. Edie. Evanston: Northwestern University Press.

———. 1964c. "Eye and Mind." Trans. Carleton Dallery. In *The Primacy of Perception*. Evanston: Northwestern University Press.

———. 1964d. *L'Oeil et l'esprit*. Paris: Gallimard.

———. 1965. *The Structure of Behaviour*. Trans. Alden L. Fisher. London: Methuen.

———. 1968. *The Visible and the Invisible*. Trans. Alphonso Lingis. Evanston: Northwestern University Press.

——. 1993. "The Experience of Others." Trans. Fred Evans and Hugh J. Silverman. In *Merleau-Ponty and Psychology*, ed. Keith Hoeller. Atlantic Highlands, N.J.: Humanities Press.

Mirvish, Adrian. 1996. "Sartre on Embodied Minds, Authenticity and Childhood." *Man and World* 29: 19–41.

Mittelstaedt, H., and S. Glasauer. 1993. "Illusions of Verticality in Weightlessness." *Clinical Investigator* 71: 732–739.

Morris, David. 1997a. "Optical Idealism and the Languages of Depth in Descartes and Berkeley." *The Southern Journal of Philosophy* 35: 363–392.

——. 1997b. Review of *A Dynamic Systems Approach to the Development of Cognition and Action*, by Esther Thelen and Linda B. Smith. *International Studies in the Philosophy of Science* 11: 210–213.

——. 1999. "The Fold and The Body Schema in Merleau-Ponty and Dynamic Systems Theory." *Chiasmi International* 1: 275–286.

——. 2001a. "Lived Time and Absolute Knowing: Habit and Addiction from *Infinite Jest* to the *Phenomenology of Spirit*." *Clio* 30: 375–415.

——. 2001b. "The Logic of the Body in Bergson's Motor Schemes and Merleau-Ponty's Body Schema." *Philosophy Today*, SPEP Supplement.

——. 2002a. "Thinking the Body, from Hegel's Speculative Logic of Measure to Dynamic Systems Theory." *The Journal of Speculative Philosophy*.

——. 2002b. "Touching Intelligence." *Journal of the Philosophy of Sport* 29: 149–162.

Mullarkey, John. 1994. "Duplicity in the Flesh: Bergson and Current Philosophy of the Body." *Philosophy Today* 38: 339–355.

——. 2000. *Bergson and Philosophy*. Notre Dame: University of Notre Dame Press.

Neruda, Pablo. 1973. *Residence on Earth*. Trans. Donald D. Walsh. New York: New Directions.

Olafson, Frederick A. 1987. *Heidegger and the Philosophy of Mind*. New Haven: Yale University Press.

O'Neill, John. 1989. *The Communicative Body: Studies in Communicative Philosophy, Politics, and Sociology*. Evanston: Northwestern University Press.

Out, L., A. J. van Soest, G. J. P. Savelsbergh, and B. Hopkins. 1998. "The Effect of Posture on Early Reaching Movements." *Journal of Motor Behavior* 30: 260–272.

Panofsky, Erwin. 1991. *Perspective as Symbolic Form*. Trans. Christopher S. Wood. New York: Zone Books.

Pessoa, Luiz, Evan Thompson, and Alva Noë. 1998. "Finding Out About Filling In: A Guide to Perceptual Completion for Visual Science and the Philosophy of Perception." *Behavioral and Brain Sciences* 21: 723–748.

Piaget, Jean. 1955. *The Contruction of Reality in the Child*. Trans. Margaret Cook. New York: Basic Books.

———. 1973. *The Child's Conception of the World*. Trans. Joan Tomlinson and Andrew Tomlinson. Frogmore, UK: Paladin.

Piaget, Jean, and Bärbel Inhelder. 1963. *The Child's Conception of Space*. Trans. F. J. Langdon and J. L. Lunzer. London: Routledge and Kegan Paul.

Piaget, Jean, Bärbel Inhelder, and Alina Szeminska. 1960. *The Child's Conception of Geometry*. Trans. E. A. Lunzer. London: Routledge and Kegan Paul.

Plato. 1997. *Timaeus*. Trans. Donald J. Zeyl. In *Plato: Complete Works*, ed. John M. Cooper. Indianapolis: Hackett.

Plomer, Aurora. 1991. *Phenomenology, Geometry and Vision: Merleau-Ponty's Critique of Classical Theories of Vision*. Aldershot, UK: Avebury.

Portmann, Adolf. 1961. *Animals as Social Beings*. Trans. Oliver Coburn. London: Hutchinson.

———. 1967. *Animal Forms and Patterns: A Study of the Appearance of Animals*. New York: Schocken Books.

Rilke, Rainer Maria. 1978. *Duino Elegies*. Trans. David Young. New York: W.W. Norton.

Rochat, Philippe. 1992. "Self-Sitting and Reaching in 5- to 8-Month-Old Infants: The Impact of Posture and Its Development on Early Eye-Hand Coordination." *Journal of Motor Behavior* 24: 210–220.

Rochat, Philippe, and André Bullinger. 1994. "Posture and Functional Action in Infancy." In *Early Child Development in the French Tradition: Contributions from Current Research*, ed. A. Vyt, H. Bloch and M. H. Bornstein. Hillsdale, N.J.: Lawrence Erlbaum.

Rojcewicz, Richard. 1984. "Depth perception in Merleau-Ponty: A motivated phenomenon." *Journal of Phenomenological Psychology* 15: 33–44.

Roll, J. P., R. Roll, and J. P. Velay. 1991. "Proprioception and Space Perception." In *Brain and Space*, ed. Jacques Paillard. New York: Oxford University Press.

Russon, John. 1994. "Embodiment and Responsibility: Merleau-Ponty and the Ontology of Nature." *Man and World* 27: 291–308.

———. 1995. "Hegel's Phenomenology of Reason and Dualism." *Southern Journal of Philosophy* 31: 71–96.

———. 1997. *The Self and its Body in Hegel's Phenomenology*. Toronto: University of Toronto Press.

———. 2003. *Human Experience: Philosophy, Neurosis and the Elements of Everyday Life*. Albany: State University of New York Press.

Sanders, John T. 1993. "Merleau-Ponty, Gibson and the Materiality of Meaning." *Man and World* 26: 287–302.

Sartre, Jean-Paul. 1956. *Being and Nothingness*. Trans. Hazel E. Barnes. New York: Washington Square Press.

———. 1993. *The Emotions: Outline of a Theory*. Trans. Bernard Frechtman. New York: Citadel.

Savelsbergh, Geert J. P., and John van der Kamp. 1994. "The Effect of Body Orientation to Gravity on Early Infant Reaching." *Journal of Experimental Child Psychology* 58: 510–528.

Schilder, Paul. 1935. *The Image and Appearance of the Human Body*. London: Kegan Paul, Trench, Trubner.

Schöne, Hermann. 1984. *Spatial Orientation: The Spatial Control of Behaviours in Animals and Man*. Trans. Camilla Strausfield. Princeton: Princeton University Press.

Schwartz, Robert. 1994. *Vision: Variations on Some Berkeleian Themes*. Cambridge: Blackwell.

Shakespeare, William. 1969. *Hamlet Prince of Denmark*. In *The Complete Pelican Shakespeare*, ed. Alfred Harbage, vol. The Tragedies. Middlesex, UK: Penguin.

Sharrock, Wes, and Jeff Coulter. 1998. "On What We Can See." *Theory and Psychology* 8: 147–164.

Sheets-Johnstone, Maxine. 1990. *The Roots of Thinking*. Philadelphia: Temple University Press.

———. 1999a. *The Primacy of Movement*. Amsterdam: John Benjamins.

———. 1999b. "Phenomenology and Agency: Methodological and Theoretical Issues in Strawson's 'The Self'." In *Models of the Self*, ed. S. Gallagher and J. Shear. Thorverton, UK: Imprint Academic.

Simons, Margaret A. 1995. *Feminist Interpretations of Simone De Beauvoir*. University Park: Pennsylvania State University Press.

Stein, J. F. 1991. "Space and the Parietal Association Areas." In *Brain and Space*, ed. Jacques Paillard. New York: Oxford University Press.

Stratton, George M. 1896. "Some Preliminary Experiments on Vision without Inversion of the Retinal Image." *Psychological Review* 3: 611–615.

———. 1897. "Vision without Inversion of the Retinal Image." *Psychological Review* 4: 341–360, 463–481.

Straus, Erwin. 1966. "The Upright Posture." In *Phenomenological Psychology: The Selected Papers of Erwin W. Straus*. New York: Basic Books.

Ströker, Elisabeth. 1987. *Investigations in the Philosophy of Space*. Trans. Algis Mickunas. Athens: Ohio University Press.

Tastevin, J. 1937. "En partant de l'expérience d'Aristote." *Encéphale* 32: 57–84, 140–158.

Thelen, Esther. 1983. "Learning to Walk is Still an 'Old' Problem: A Reply to Zelazo (1983)." *Journal of Motor Behavior* 15: 139–161.

———. 1984. "Learning to Walk: Ecological Demands and Phylogenetic Constraints." *Advances in Infancy Research* 3: 213–250.

———. 1995. "Motor Development: A New Synthesis." *American Psychologist* 50: 79–95.

Thelen, Esther, and D. Fisher. 1982. "Newborn Stepping: An Explanation for a 'Disappearing' Reflex." *Developmental Psychology* 18: 760–775.

Thelen, Esther, and John P. Spencer. 1998. "Postural Control During Reaching in Young Infants: A Dynamic Systems Approach." *Neuroscience and Biobehavioral Reviews* 22: 507–514.

Thelen, Esther, and L. B. Smith. 1994. *A Dynamic Systems Approach to the Development of Cognition and Action.* Cambridge: MIT Press.

Thompson, Evan. 1995. *Colour Vision: A Study in Cognitive Science and the Philosophy of Perception.* London: Routledge.

Thompson, Evan, Adrian Palacios, and Francisco J. Varela. 1992. "Ways of Coloring: Comparative Color Vision as a Case Study for Cognitive Science." *Behavioral and Brain Sciences* 15: 1–74.

Tiemersma, D. 1982. "'Body-Image' and 'Body-Schema' in the Existential Phenomenology of Merleau-Ponty." *Journal of the British Society of Phenomenology* 13: 246–255.

Turvey, M. T. 1992a. "Affordances and Prospective Control: An Outline of the Ontology." *Ecological Psychology* 4: 173–187.

———. 1992b. "Ecological Foundations of Cognition: Invariants of Perception and Action." In *Cognition: Conceptual and Methodological Issues,* ed. Herbert L. Pick, Paulus van den Broek, and David C. Krill. Washington DC: American Psychological Association.

Turvey, M. T., and C. Carello. 1995. "Dynamic Touch." In *Perception of Space and Motion,* ed. William Epstein and Sheena Rogers. San Diego: Academic Press.

Turvey, M. T., and Robert Shaw. 1979. "The Primacy of Perceiving: An Ecological Reformulation of Perception for Understanding Memory." In *Perspectives on Memory Research: Essays in Honor of Uppsala University's 500th Anniversary,* ed. Lars-Göran Nilsson. Hillsdale, N.J.: Lawrence Erlbaum.

———. 1995. "Toward an Ecological Physics and a Physical Psychology." In *The Science of the Mind: 2001 and Beyond,* ed. Robert L. Solso and Dominic W. Massaro. New York: Oxford University Press.

Ullman, S. 1980. "Against Direct Perception." *Behavioural and Brain Sciences* 3: 373–415.

Varela, Francisco J. 1991. "Organism: A Meshwork of Selfless Selves." In *Organism and the Origins of Self,* ed. Alfred I. Tauber. Dordrecht, NL: Kluwer.

von Hofsten, Claes. 1986. "Early Spatial Perception Taken in Reference to Manual Action." *Acta Psychologica* 63: 323–335.

von Hofsten, Claes and Louise Rönnqvist. 1988. "Preparation for Grasping an Object: A Developmental Study." *Journal of Experimental Psychology: Human Perception and Performance* 14: 610–621.

Waldenfels, Bernhard. 1981. "Perception and Structure in Merleau-Ponty." In *Merleau-Ponty: Perception, Structure, Language: A Collection of Essays*, ed. John Sallis. Atlantic Highlands, N.J.: Humanities Press.

———. 2000. "The Paradox of Expression." In *Chiasms: Merleau-Ponty's Notion of Flesh*, ed. Fred Evans and Leonard Lawlor. Albany: State University of New York Press.

Wallace, David Foster. 1996. *Infinite Jest*. Boston: Back Bay Books.

———. 1997. *A Supposedly Fun Thing I'll Never Do Again*. Boston: Back Bay Books.

Watson, John S., Louise A. Hayes, Peter Vietze, and Jacqueline Becker. 1979. "Discriminative Smiling to Orientations of Talking Faces of Mother and Stranger." *Journal of Experimental Child Psychology* 28: 92–99.

Weiss, Gail. 1998. "Body Image Intercourse: A Corporeal Dialogue between Merleau-Ponty and Schilder." In *Merleau-Ponty, Interiority and Exteriority, Psychic Life and the World*, ed. Dorothea Olkowski and James Morley. Albany: State University of New York Press.

———. 1999a. "The Abject Borders of the Body Image." In *Perspectives on Embodiment: The Intersections of Nature and Culture*, ed. Gaill Weiss and Honi Fern Haber. New York: Routledge.

———. 1999b. *Body Images: Embodiment as Intercorporeality*. New York: Routledge.

Young, Iris Marion. 1990. *Throwing Like a Girl and Other Essays in Feminist Philosophy and Social Theory*. Bloomington: Indiana University Press.

Zelazo, P. R. 1983. "The Development of Walking: New Findings and Old Assumptions." *Journal of Motor Behavior* 15: 99–137.

———. 1984. "Learning to Walk: Recognition of Higher Order Influences." *Advances in Infancy Research* 3: 251–260.

INDEX

Printed in Great Britain
by Amazon.co.uk, Ltd.,
Marston Gate.